Collaborative Worldbuilding for Video Games

This book is a theoretical and practical deep dive into the craft of world-building for video games, with an explicit focus on how different job disciplines contribute to worldbuilding. In addition to providing lenses for recognizing the various components in creating fictional and digital worlds, the author positions worldbuilding as a reciprocal and dynamic process, a process which acknowledges that worldbuilding is both created by and instrumental in the design of narrative, gameplay, art, audio, and more. **Collaborative Worldbuilding for Video Games** encourages mutual respect and collaboration among teams and provides game writers and narrative designers tools for effectively incorporating other job roles into their own worldbuilding practice and vice versa.

Features:

- Provides in-depth exploration of worldbuilding via respective job disciplines

- Deep dives and case studies into a variety of games, both AAA and indie

- Includes boxed articles for deeper interrogation and exploration of key ideas

- Contains templates and checklists for practical tips on worldbuilding

Collaborative Worldbuilding for Video Games

Kaitlin Tremblay

CRC Press
Taylor & Francis Group
Boca Raton London New York

CRC Press is an imprint of the
Taylor & Francis Group, an **informa** business

Cover image credit: Shutterstock.com

First edition published 2023
by CRC Press
6000 Broken Sound Parkway NW, Suite 300, Boca Raton, FL 33487-2742

and by CRC Press
4 Park Square, Milton Park, Abingdon, Oxon, OX14 4RN

CRC Press is an imprint of Taylor & Francis Group, LLC

ISBN: 978-1-032-38558-7 (hbk)
ISBN: 978-1-032-38554-9 (pbk)
ISBN: 978-1-003-34561-9 (ebk)

DOI: 10.1201/9781003345619

Typeset in Minion
by codeMantra

To my brothers, Brian and Eric, my original co-conspirators.

Contents

Author

Kaitlin Tremblay (they/she) is a writer and narrative designer, as well as a former book editor and media critic. Over the past ten years, Tremblay has worked across the video game industry, including on titles such as *Watch Dogs: Legion* (Ubisoft), *Grindstone* (Capybara Games), and *A Mortician's Tale* (Laundry Bear Games). Tremblay's personal game development work has focused on making horror games about difficult subject matter, and they are a public speaker and community organizer, serving on the board of advisors for GDC's Independent Games Summit. Tremblay is also a speculative fiction writer, with a focus on horror, and was the co-editor of the award-nominated anthology *Those Who Make Us: Canadian Creature, Myth, and Monster Stories* (Exile Editions). They are also the author of the deep dive into the *Borderlands* franchise and its storytelling, *Ain't No Place for a Hero: Borderlands* (ECW Press). Their full work can be found on their website: www.thatmonstergames.com

Acknowledgments

I just wanted to take a quick moment to thank everyone who helped me in the creation of this book, be it research, offering insights, reading chapters and providing feedback, editing, and emotional support. This book is about collaboration, and this book wouldn't be possible without a village full of supportive, brilliant people in both my personal and professional life.

To CRC Press, for their support in the writing and publishing of this book. To everyone who let me ask them questions or who lent insight, thoughts, references, support, and their experiences to me: Noreen Rana, Nate Purkeypile, Michelle Hwu, Priscilla Snow, Jurie Horneman, Braydon Beaulieu, Jen Costa, Michelle Burgess, and all of the rad folks in various Discords and Slacks who helped with resources and examples.

Many thanks to Gabby DaRienzo for their insight, feedback, and encouragement. To Liz England for her detailed feedback and brilliance (and for offering the perfect examples I was struggling to find). And to Joel Burgess for always being willing to be a sounding board, for his thoughts, and for letting me talk through this book often and at length.

To my family for being tireless supporters and my biggest fans. And finally, to Jon for letting me spend our dog walks thinking through ideas, for helping me find examples, for reading chapters, and for all of the love, support, and coffees (and for being on dog duty in the morning so I could write).

Introduction

Being in Awe

I USED TO BE REALLY intimidated by worldbuilding. I fall in love with worlds easily and effortlessly. The way certain authors identify and build on compelling aspects of how different worlds tick, and how the characters in these worlds respond to these political, geographical, and cultural differences has always had me in awe. Becky Chambers's ability to create bountiful sci-fi worlds built on optimism and kindness versus expansion and fear or the way Jeff VanderMeer can crack open cosmos to create beautiful, unnerving, and unforgettable vistas is nothing short of magic to me.

And it is magic. It's also craft, one you can (and will!) get better at with practice and experience.

I always used to be so envious of people who could seemingly conjure distant and wildly distinct planets and fantasy landscapes in their mind, and for a long time, thought that maybe I just wasn't cut out for that type of writing. Maybe I just wasn't that imaginative. But as I started out writing more professionally, working as an editor with authors and developing my own stories and games, I understood that worldbuilding was a muscle just like writing dialogue, creating compelling character arcs, and developing satisfying pacing. At one point or another, all creativity feels like magic. But that spark is the product of hard work and experience born out of practice. That magic is the way that we see craft in action.

As a writer and game developer, my first real crack at worldbuilding was in the horror genre. Horror's this amazingly malleable genre that may

DOI: 10.1201/9781003345619-1

feel slight on worldbuilding, but it's actually highly specific and focused in how it tackles new worlds and rules for those worlds. Horror takes our understanding of the world and pries open tiny pockets to let monsters in. And it's the way in which we stretch our reality and undermine what makes us feel safe that is where worldbuilding really comes to play in horror. I cut my teeth writing horror, learning to worldbuild in the constraints of that genre. And I'm glad I did so.

Horror to me has always been about liminality, the in-between spaces where normal, mundane spaces are stretched thin and become transitory for the things that live in the shadows. This made my job of worldbuilding focused: find the friction points in our reality that I wanted to contest and pull them apart at the seams. The last horror game I made *Halfway, to the Lamppost* (2018) is about a young kid who is meeting her friend halfway between their houses. This setting is utterly mundane: it's a residential street in a quiet town, with only six houses separating the playable character from her friend. But because I wanted *Halfway* to be about interrogating the way fear feels differently as an adult versus a child, it was important for me to layer in worldbuilding that defamiliarized this street. Shadows become the monster stalking the player because the worldbuilding was based upon the concept of what if shadows in our world were monsters? It's not a new concept, but it was effective for what I was trying to achieve with *Halfway*.

So because horror is about liminality (to me), whenever I approach writing a horror short story or a horror game, I think about the worldbuilding that lets me capitalize on this, rather than fully inventing a whole new world. It helps me generate stories, characters, and, importantly, mechanics. Worldbuilding is an avenue toward both story and gameplay, and worldbuilding is at its best when it's treated as this space for generating coherent, tangible effects and interactions in our games. But this isn't a book *just* about worldbuilding (and it certainly isn't a book about worldbuilding in horror). This is a book specifically about worldbuilding for video games.

Video games are, inherently, a collaborative medium. They are more than the sum of their parts, and each job role and discipline contributes something integral and specific to video games. Worldbuilding with teams (when I'm not just making my own, personal games) is always the most effective when it's treated as something that everyone can participate in (with a clear owner or vision holder), and when it's malleable enough to allow it to affect more than just the story of a game. Worldbuilding does affect story, yes, but it also affects mechanics, gameplay, environment art, audio, and so forth. Worldbuilding informs the identity of the game, across all aspects. It's a connector. So that ethos, of cross-discipline collaboration, is the throughline in this book, connecting the examples, the explorations of craft, and the discussion of worldbuilding theory and practice. Let's look at this more by discussing how I've structured this book and what you can expect from it.

HOW THIS BOOK IS STRUCTURED

First off, a note on examples. This book intentionally blends the theoretical and the practical together, offering concrete examples in conjunction with the theoretical approach to worldbuilding. As much as I can, I pair theoretical concepts or practical explanations with an example or two from video games specifically, melding my development experience with media analysis. For the most part, the examples used will be from a variety of digital games, ranging from AAA to indie to mobile as necessary. This is partly a reflection of who I am and my work experience: I've worked in mobile, ARGs, escape rooms, indie, and AAA, and each element of that experience absolutely informs the examples I think of and where I see effective worldbuilding. It's also a deliberate attempt to not hyperfocus on only one aspect of the industry–video games are a wide, eclectic medium, and I like my examples to reflect that when possible. Additionally, the examples I pull are often ones that I personally find motivating, inspiring, or particularly resonant. There are of course a lot more examples that exist out there, but the ones I pull are because they've made a mark on me in some capacity, and that's where I'm drawing my inspiration from.

Importantly, also, this book is written from my perspective. I am a writer, a former book and short story editor, and I am a narrative designer (which includes both story work and game design work). And since worldbuilding is a practice that often begins with or is heavily lifted up by narrative departments (and because of my experience and perspective), this book is written as a way to provide tools for games writers and narrative designers to learn how to approach worldbuilding as a collaborative effort with other job disciplines, in addition to growing their own craft. This book isn't exclusively for narrative folks, though, that is just my framing of it because of who I am. In fact, I hope this book is useful for any game developer interested in worldbuilding and finding avenues toward supporting a holistic and collaborative worldbuilding approach.

This book is a lens. It is not definitive nor is it exhaustive. Because of this perspective I am bringing to this book, there may be times when you disagree with something or a suggestion isn't practical in your studio's development cycle and culture. And that's okay! This book is a perspective, an additional lens to add to your repertoire. It is meant to chewed on, thought over, and disagreed with as is necessary. There is a lot in this book that is particular to both my varied experience in different production environments and also to my upbringing and life. So this book is best used as a jumping-off point, one lens to view video game worldbuilding from and through so that you can take what is productive and useful to you and integrate that into your own craft. Disagreement is beneficial to growing your own craft.

Okay, so now for how the book is structured in detail and not in concept. Chapter 1 is an introduction to what worldbuilding is and why it is important for video games. Chapter 1 establishes the two major arguments of this book up front. First, that worldbuilding is a collaborative, cross-discipline feat in video games, with each job discipline contributing specific elements to worldbuilding that players feel and experience. Second, that worldbuilding is important for video game development as it provides the foundation to grow both stories and mechanics from. Worldbuilding is a generator for stories (a story engine), but it is also the soil from which compelling and unique mechanics and interactions can be born, from which systems can be gleaned, and so forth. Chapter 1 argues that worldbuilding is not static, nor is it only background work, but rather is fundamental work to developing resonant and coherent video games in deeper ways than just lore and story.

Chapter 2 is meaty and the longest chapter of the book. In Chapter 2, worldbuilding is explored in relation to specific job disciplines. Chapter 2 is where each job discipline (art, programming, audio, game design, level design, narrative, and so forth) gets explored in depth, with a whole host of examples and craft thoughts from experts in those fields. This chapter is the meat of this book, as it navigates the specific elements each job discipline contributes to some aspect of digital worlds, either implicitly or explicitly. Chapter 2 is also where I explore what I refer to as "practical worldbuilding", aka the ways in which we express or surface worldbuilding through the act of creation. This chapter explores a lot of ways worldbuilding gets communicated to players, and in turn, how the decisions different job departments make enrich the worldbuilding, possibly extending it or growing it.

To offer a concrete way for narrative designers and game writers to grapple with everything established in Chapter 2, Chapter 3 then provides the practical elements of this book, including how to establish goals for your worldbuilding, as well as a world bible template and a checklist of tips to consider when beginning worldbuilding for your video game. Chapter 3 follows the extensive overview in Chapter 2 as a way to provide a concrete synthesis of the information provided in the overview, as well as a moment to breathe and to incorporate the ways in which worldbuilding is a cross-discipline effort and how this collaborative nature of worldbuilding can be applied to a writing and narrative design practice. Chapter 3 provides the roadmap for getting started and prepared to do the type of worldbuilding explored in Chapter 2. This may be counterintuitively laid out, but I wanted to provide the practical tips after forefronting the cross-discipline nature of worldbuilding.

Then Chapter 4 builds on this solid foundation by providing a series of deep dives into the specificity of worldbuilding for video games—to show the overlap between components and job disciplines—and using a more holistic lens to view how worldbuilding works as a foundation for many aspects of video games and how worldbuilding can be surfaced in organic ways in a video game. Chapter 4 deliberately counters the siloed nature of Chapter 2 by showing the need for collaboration and approaching worldbuilding via features rather than as job descriptions. Perhaps counterintuitively, this chapter doesn't immediately follow Chapter 2, but that is by design: Chapter 3 is a necessary break in between the theoretical and analytical in order to provide tools for practically grappling with the examples and concepts that exist in Chapters 2 and 4.

The final chapter of this book, Chapter 5, then shifts focus from the practical and theoretical lens of worldbuilding to discuss the importance for us as worldbuilders to understand what assumptions and biases we are drawing on from our real world. Chapter 5 asserts that worldbuilding does not occur in a vacuum and that it is in fact a political practice by exploring the different systems of bias and harm we should be aware of as worldbuilders. This chapter asks us to approach our craft with intentionality in order to build more creative worlds responsibly. Chapter 5 combines cultural thought and social impact with interdisciplinary craft. This section will tackle how we can avoid replicating some existing systems of harm into our imagined worlds and how to approach identity-based conflict with compassion for players. It is not exhaustive by any means (nor is it even close to being exhaustive), but it is rather an introduction to grappling with the biases we may hold and how to approach worldbuilding with intention.

And finally, case studies are sprinkled throughout these chapters. These case studies are hyper-specific explorations of games and their worldbuilding, with a particular angle toward exploring how different games use worldbuilding in different ways. These case studies are meant to illustrate the interdisciplinary nature of worldbuilding in a holistic, rather than compartmentalized, view.

WHAT TO EXPECT WITH THIS BOOK

So while I've hinted at it but not said it directly: this book is not just a practice guide or theoretical journey into the craft of worldbuilding. It is to a certain degree, but above and beyond that, this book is more concerned with highlighting the interdisciplinary nature of worldbuilding for video games specifically by focusing on the ways different job disciplines and team members contribute to creating new worlds. This book examines the specific ways video games express worldbuilding. While that includes narrative and writing, this book's focus is broader than just writing and, by necessity, is not exhaustive when it comes to all the tips and tricks for worldbuilding from a story perspective. For an incredibly thorough and insightful practice for worldbuilding from a purely writer's perspective, I recommend Stant Litore's *Write Worlds Your Readers Will Never Forget* (a book that was recommended by the incomparable Emily Short, who also has a great blog post dedicated to her thoughts on worldbuilding books that is worth reading).

Working with other game developers (including writers, game designers, level designers, artists, programmers, sound designers, QA, etc.) has made me a better developer, a better writer, and a better worldbuilder. And while I have seen first-hand the way writers and narrative designers often get treated as a job where anybody can do it (most folks experience stories on a daily basis, which can translate to a misappropriated experience with telling stories as effectively as trained and professional writers), I'm also a big proponent of collaboration. And I believe good collaboration is built on respect. So my aim with writing this book is, yes, to provide a look into the craft of worldbuilding for video games, but also to highlight the interdisciplinary nature of it so that each job discipline (including and especially narrative!) can be given the appropriate voice and respect they deserve in the process.

This is what made me want to write this book specifically. There exists such good thought on worldbuilding as is (it's a rich topic with a lot of useful theory and craft already offered by a wide range of writers, designers, and artists). But there's something so wonderful about the way video games specifically involve a cross-disciplinary approach to worldbuilding that has been really inspiring to me. I'm interested in worldbuilding, yes, but I'm way more engaged and energized when I get to do it with other talented individuals on my team. And more often than not, in my experience working with teams of a variety of different sizes, I've found the best designs and smoothest production experiences come when I get to work with other talented writers and narrative designers, but also with artists and level designers and programmers and anyone else on the team who has a hand on creating the world along with me.

Which is why it was important to me to include perspectives from others, as well. While this book is primarily aimed at game writers and narrative designers who want to collaborate cross-discipline in their worldbuilding (or those who want to intentionally nurture the collaboration that already exists therewithin), it was crucial for me to talk to people who occupy the job roles and disciplines that I don't. When possible, I've tried to include insight from domain experts to provide a lens and experience from other job disciplines that I lack (and I am eternally grateful for everyone who has shared their experience, either with me specifically, or by offering talks and books on their own approaches and craft). I am not an expert in these domains, so I hope I did the crucial work they do justice.

Even still, please bear in mind that this book is not definitive, nor is it exhaustive. It's an approach, and I hope it includes insights and perspectives that others find useful. The needs and approaches for each project are so tailored by the project's budget, timeline, team, and perspectives (among many other factors), so consider this book just a snapshot into one framework and perspective, a jumping-off point to determine what your worldbuilding needs and how to best execute on that vision with a full arsenal of cross-discipline tools. So, yes, there will be plenty of discussion of craft in here, but the primary purpose is to provide a deeper understanding of the many ways worldbuilding happens in a video game, so there will also be plenty of media analysis, as well.

To engage with this book, you do not need to be working in video games already, or a writer or narrative designer. This book (I hope!) can be a great introduction to worldbuilding for people who are just beginning to explore what that means in a video game context. Or perhaps it's a great way to provide additional lenses to your already robust worldbuilding chops, as either a narrative person or in any other job discipline. Or maybe even it'll help give language and common ground to collaborations with other job disciplines. Either way, I hope you find the perspectives detailed in here helpful in building your craft and your approach to worldbuilding collaboratively with your team.

Enjoy.

CHAPTER 1

Overview of Worldbuilding

WHAT IS WORLDBUILDING?

To start—what is worldbuilding? Simply put, worldbuilding is the process of creating a world. In addition to being the most obvious way I could've defined worldbuilding, that definition is also broad, and it can be applied in different ways depending on the type of medium you are creating in. For video games, even that definition can mean different things depending on context and job discipline. Worldbuilding can be the literal act of visualizing and building the world, from level design to level art to programming. But worldbuilding also refers to the work writers do to establish the rules and logic of a fictional setting, as well as setting the groundwork for characters and stories to emerge out of the world's structure.

In *An Architectural Approach to Level Design*, Christopher W. Totten defines worldbuilding as "the connections between narrative development, the embodiment of cultural ideas, and expressions of usable gamespace".[1] What I find particularly useful about Totten's definition of worldbuilding is the way it explicitly invokes the role of worldbuilding not just as narrative detail, but as an important part of communicating mechanics and gameplay—it is an expression of gamespace, particularly ones with rules and logic. Worldbuilding is not just the creation of the literal world players find themselves in, nor is it only story work geared toward cultivating

DOI: 10.1201/9781003345619-2

an expressive and compelling place—it is both and it is more than that. In video games, worldbuilding is a driver of story and an identity marker for games, but when applied to things like level design, worldbuilding is also a way to create coherent and learnable modes of play.

Worldbuilding is often treated as something you do before you start development, a task in concept and pre-production that then becomes static. To some, worldbuilding is the prologue to writing, developing, and production. But for me, worldbuilding is more than just the work that gets done before the writing and creation happen. Worldbuilding is a continual process throughout game development, a confluence of decisions that are made early on and that inform the work writers, designers, artists, composers, and so forth do, as well as decisions that get made in the course of development. Technical constraints can cause us to have to go back and revisit the worldbuilding. Distinct ways of surfacing details about the world can also provide the space to flesh out a specific aspect of the worldbuilding. Worldbuilding isn't static, and it doesn't begin and end in concept or pre-production. It is constantly being done at all stages of development, in both big and small ways. It is a dynamic backdrop to our stories and our mechanics.

I am a big proponent of how everyone on a team contributes to story in a video game (provided there is domain respect and trust for expertise within those domains). And the same is true for worldbuilding for me. But even beyond that, I'm also a believer that worldbuilding isn't something that happens exclusively in concept or pre-production. Worldbuilding is often thought of as a writer filling out a giant world bible with minute details of a place, its geography, and its civilization. That is true, yes, and a necessary practice to define the necessary conditions for creation. But, in my experience, worldbuilding also emerges in practice and implementation, in how aspects of the conceptual details get surfaced and expressed, and in the solutions that need to be implemented for technical and budgetary reasons.

Of course, major narrative and world decisions need to be made in concept and pre-production so that each team can begin their work without having major elements from the world change. But this doesn't mean that the worldbuilding can't be fleshed out, given specificity and life, by smaller decisions made in the course of development and implementation. A lot of worldbuilding is the expression thereof, and this expression can be composed of micro instances in a variety of places. Specificity and tangibility come from implementation, built up from the conceptual worldbuilding done early on and informing the practical worldbuilding that players then experience directly.[2] Respect the crucial work in concept and pre-production, but be aware of how production and implementation can build out and enliven those decisions.

So when I talk about worldbuilding, I mean all of this, the conceptual and the practical. I mean the work that gets done before any in-engine work begins, the work that is contained in a world bible and informs production. But I also mean the work done during production, the decisions and elements we as game developers make and emphasize as we begin building the game. This latter is what I mean when I say "surfacing" elements of worldbuilding in this book (which I will say a lot). How we surface, or express, elements of worldbuilding is just as important a process in constructing new worlds as a world bible is—and it creates a more organic, collaborative process for creating resonant and coherent worlds across all elements of game development, such as mechanics, art, and sound.

Worldbuilding is context and it is identity, even when it is at its most minimal, and worldbuilding can be a driver for a lot of creative decisions within game development, above and beyond story. So what is worldbuilding composed of?

To start, let's consider: what is a world? Before even getting into the details on this, we need to know: Is it our world, or is it a secondary world (a world that is not ours and different from it in key elements), or is it a combination, a stretching of the rules and boundaries of our existing world to contain new spaces and rules? A world is a geographical place, with a range of specific and unique landmarks and geographical conditions. Is your world made entirely of ice? Is it a desert world? Or does it contain a multitude of biomes, some with real-world analogs or not?

But a world is more than just the physical space of it—it's the people that live there. So who lives in your world? What is their relationship to geography? What infrastructure have they built to contend with the environment (if it's hostile) or to maximize use of it (if it's resource abundant)? What social systems do they have in place, and how do their politics and religions reflect or obstruct these social systems? What creatures exist here? What is the ecosystem like, between creatures and people and the geography? Similarly, what of the flora? Where does it grow and why? What technology was created as a natural result of these aspects of your world? Or, if not technology, how does magic work in your world?

Worldbuilding is all of this (plus much more) or only some of this. Worldbuilding is composed of all the physical parts of a place, but all the intangible aspects as well, such as culture, belief, interpersonal relationships, and so forth. And knowing which levers to pull and which aren't needed for a specific project is all a part of the craft of worldbuilding. Because worldbuilding is a craft, like writing or illustrating or designing, and as this book demonstrates, worldbuilding for video games is an inherently cross-discipline craft, which is composed of a multitude of elements, including plot, character, environment, mechanics, soundscapes, UI, and so forth.

A DETOUR THROUGH MYTHOPOEIA

Mythopoeia, a term used to describe the act of making artificial myths or writing that takes on the quality of myth, is a term popularized by J.R.R. Tolkien's poem of the same name. Mythopoeia is a highly specific and wonderfully useful approach to a specific type of worldbuilding that aims to take on the qualities of a mythology (that is, a self-referential collection of stories loosely concerned with some sort of phenomena in our everyday lives). Mythopoeia is a compelling element of worldbuilding because it creates a lived-in texture to the world, as myths involve the process of people engaging with and rationalizing aspects of their lived experiences that exceed their immediate comprehension.

Let's take a quick look at *Where the Water Tastes like Wine* (Dimbulb Games, 2018), which is set in America, but takes on mythic proportions as players roam the country collecting stories. Players collect a variety of stories and these, while based on real tales embedded deep in Americana, begin to take on a mythic quality. *Where the Water Tastes like Wine* becomes mythopoeia in the ways in which the stories themselves are things that grow, reflecting the lived experiences of the people both sharing and listening to the story (the player).

Mythopoeia is a useful approach to worldbuilding because it bakes in a lot of concepts that help give worlds a sense of place and believability: it introduces pantheons, folklore, or superstitions, all of which stitch together a belief system; it provides fodder for how humans try to understand the rules of their world in tangible experiences versus purely academic writings; and it provides a throughline that lets references build and layer on each other to create a sense of natural evolution of thought and practice in the world. Games need not be based on myth to take on mythic qualities, as the *Where the Water Tastes like Wine* example proves.

WHY IS WORLDBUILDING IMPORTANT?

Whether you're building an entirely new secondary world, or expanding our existing world in speculative ways, worldbuilding is the foundation, it is the bones of your story and the space your story occurs in, so the qualities of your worldbuilding can and will influence the overall tone and experience of your game, in both explicit and implicit ways. And this effect is why intentionality and care in your worldbuilding matters. Worldbuilding exists as a practice for reasons far beyond simply[3] creating the world in which your players are going to spend hours engaging in gameplay, doing missions, interacting with systems, building emotional bonds with NPCs, etc. Worldbuilding serves to create coherence across all aspects of your game, from the visual identity to the narrative tone to the gameplay experience. It is, essentially, a set of guiding principles and rules for what makes your world tick and how your world creates fodder for gameplay and story.

Stant Litore, in his excellent book *Write Worlds Your Readers Won't Forget*, describes worldbuilding "as a process for identifying opportunities for conflict and exerting pressures on your characters".[4] What I find particularly useful about Litore's definition is the way in which it necessitates an interaction with characters to generate drama or scenarios. And viewing worldbuilding in this way inherently establishes worldbuilding as a story engine. A story engine is a useful term that describes how elements inherent to your story/setting can propel characters and plot forward. Story engines are the internally beating mechanisms where plotlines, conflict, and change naturally occur because there is a framework that allows for them.[5] Worldbuilding as a story engine opens up both the game and the world for potential new stories and gameplay modes, based entirely on self-governing and self-generating possibilities that are inherent to the conflicts, pressures, and systems established in your worldbuilding.

Worldbuilding can be a story engine, and it's often most effective and practical when it is treated this way, rather than as a static place that your characters are simply existing in. Think of our world—our political systems, our cultural norms, our societal standards, our religious pantheons, our geographical landmarks, and how all of these exert different types of pressures on different people. How we live, how we survive, and how we function all interconnect with the systems of our world. A world isn't static, and, furthermore, people feel a certain way about the world, and that all creates pressure, conflict, and drama.

But even beyond this—and this is a concept we'll dig more into in Chapter 2—worldbuilding is also an engine that can propel new mechanics, new gameplay modes, specific methods of interactions, and coherent modes of play for your game. In their chapter "Making Worlds into Games—A Methodology" in *World-Builders on World-Building: An Exploration of Subcreation*, Clara Fernández-Vara and Matthew Weise explain that "The creative act of story and game crafting are more similar than they appear, specifically when we look at them through the lens of world-building as foundation for both".[6] Treating your world as something that can contain within it new stories, new systems, and new connections opens the door for this to create new gameplay and mechanics, as well. Worldbuilding isn't just a story engine—it's also the beating heart that can drive gameplay iteration in the same way that it can drive new stories and characters.

Since narrative design is game design practice, just with a focus on how gameplay is supporting storytelling, it makes sense then that worldbuilding as a story engine would create the possibilities for new gameplay experiences. In her book *Narrative Tactics for Mobile Games*, Toiya K. Finley references the fact that game modes can be an effective manner for showcasing worldbuilding outside of the traditional boundaries of storytelling.[7] And, conversely, when your worldbuilding is set up as a story engine, it also makes it easier to add in new game modes because the world is already set up in such a way as to be dynamic and open. Worldbuilding provides fodder, it provides the soil for resonant ideas to grow from, and these ideas span far beyond the realm of story and character, but into gameplay.

Treating worldbuilding as more than a setting, but as a story engine provides a treasure chest of inherent and coherent missions, puzzles, and other types of gameplay for us to draw on, in addition to compelling characters and engaging scenarios to put those characters in, it opens up the spaces for gameplay (and sound design and environment art and creature design, and so forth) that is deeply resonant—by which I mean, in which all components of the game are working toward the same goal, with the same themes, toward the same purpose.

KEY PRINCIPLES OF WORLDBUILDING

Cool. So now that we've established generally what worldbuilding is and why it's important, let's talk about craft next. Worldbuilding is a craft, it's a muscle that gets stronger the more you exercise it, and there are certain principles I've focused on as ways that help me solidify and evolve my practice of worldbuilding. These are not goals but are tangible practices I can work on and work into a world I am building in order to achieve a variety of worldbuilding outcomes.

I keep these key principles fairly loose because I don't want them to be overbearing—instead, I want these key principles to work for me and my team, and that involves a certain level of flexibility. Not every game is going to need the same level of worldbuilding, even if you are making a brand-new secondary world. Some secondary worlds need less detail than others, and this is dependent upon the game you are making, in terms of its genre, its audience's expectations, and your budget (both technical and financial). But regardless of how robust your worldbuilding needs to be, these are the few concepts that I always strive to emulate in my worldbuilding.

These key principles are as follows:

- Prioritize believability

- Be expansive/open

- Focus on tangibility

- Find inherent pressures

Let's dig a bit more into these separately.

Prioritize Believability

This principle comes from the premise that the game's world should strive to be believable rather than realistic. This is a concept Joel Burgess spoke about often when discussing the world direction for *Watch Dogs: Legion* (Ubisoft Toronto, 2020). Burgess, the world director on *Watch Dogs: Legion* and with a long legacy leading level-design practices at Bethesda on games such as *Fallout 4* and *Skyrim*, explained that when he was providing direction for the team to recreate our near-future version of London, the goal was to make our London believably feel like the real-world London versus being a faithful replication of it. Similarly, in a workshop about crafting secondary worlds, award-winning speculative fiction writer N.K. Jemisin points to the difference between science and plausibility, and the importance of striving for plausibility in our worldbuilding.[8]

Plausibility and believability[9] as terms both get at the core of the same idea: namely that your world should function, and it should tick, and it should do so in a way that makes sense with all its parts working together. You can have a believable sci-fi world set centuries in the future because what makes it believable isn't necessarily the setting, but the rules, the culture, the politics, and the way the characters interact with both the elements of the world and each other.[10] Believable doesn't mean it needs to obey all of the rules we understand for our world (that would be realistic)—it just means that the rules of this new world need to work together in a way that is coherent and consistent. Believability builds coherence and a seamless experience for players, rather than creating potential friction that can be cumbersome to explain and integrate seamlessly, because believability is about picking and choosing the right details to convey your world, rather than delineating every detail.

In addition to not overburdening an experience with too many details in the name of realism, believability strives for erasing narrative friction when your world is very, very weird. *Bugsnax* (Young Horses, 2020) is a game about a furry humanoid creature (a Grumpus) going to an island where eating a half-bug half-food creature transforms part of your body into that food. *Bugsnax* is a world rife with cute, body horror weirdness, but because the rules of *Bugsnax* are internally consistent, it's believable that eating a Pinkle (whose torso is a jar with pickle legs) would turn part of a character's body into a pickle. Or that a Ribblepede can turn an arm into a barbequed rib. Eating a bugsnax changes Grumpsus's bodies, and it changes them every time.

An engaging world isn't strictly realistic nor is it so off-the-wall and inconsistent in its rules that it is difficult to have your audience buy into it. And if your audience doesn't buy into the rules of your world, then it's harder to build tension and expectations. Too much focus on making your world 100% realistic becomes cumbersome and heavy under its own weight. Too little realism means it's impossible to set your expectations and build connections with the world and the characters because anything can happen without any internal consistency.

There's only a certain level of suspension of disbelief that audiences are able to accommodate for, and believable worlds provide the baseline for weirdness to radiate out from. One avenue for making *Bugsnax*'s world believable is the internal consistency of this (feed any character a bug and Frankenstein their body into a half-sentient, half-food monstrosity).

But it's also in the character dynamics. The characters and their relationships are a grounding force for the body horror aspects of its worldbuilding. Characters are deeply human in their wants and needs, and it provides the perfect foundation for the game's world. For example, Chandlo is a buff body builder who is overly preoccupied with being able to physically meet any challenge that comes his way. This desire for strength manifests in Chandlo wanting to consume bugsnax that he considers powerful for a variety of reasons. Chandlo's desire is deeply human—he wants to be strong to protect his boyfriend and the people he cares about, and this desire becomes externalized on the consumption of bugsnax. But of course, just because Chandlo can have a watermelon arm doesn't mean he's as big and strong as the extraordinarily large Mama Mewon. It's a grounding contrast to the exuberance and weirdness of changing bodies by feeding them food-inspired bugs. It's believable.

Worlds become believable when we experience the characters within it reacting in ways we understand or can relate to, or when the spaces and rules of a world holistically feel consistent and supportive of each other. Of course, characters aren't the only way to achieve this, but they are a very effective method for doing so. Believability is about a world that is constructed in such a way as to feel realistic, even if it's not, but it's also about relatable reactions to the various components of your world from the people and creatures who live in it.

Be Expansive/Open

Worldbuilding shouldn't be airtight. And by that I mean: it should be thoughtful and it should be intentional, but it doesn't need to be dense with detail. Not every detail needs to be articulated and not every nook and cranny needs to be explored—yet. Engaging and compelling worlds don't fill in all the details; they provide just enough to understand the world, but not too much where there's no room to let the audience's imagination run a little wild. Like using realism to generate believability, worlds need enough details to be coherent, but too much detail weighs them down and leaves no space for players to inject their own imagination into it.

Expansive worldbuilding invites players in for "co-authoring" the world and the story. "Co-authoring" means that you, as the game developer, are co-creating the story with your player (i.e., the player actions, decisions, and interpretations, whether in a branching narrative or not, are helping to determine the state of the story, character moments, and key bits about how the world functions). Certain games, because of the openness of their worldbuilding and the ambiguity of their storytelling, are extra rife for both co-authoring and fan theory-making. *Final Fantasy VIII* (Square Enix, 1999) in particular is rich with player-created theories on certain aspects of the world and the story. The popular "Squall is dead" theory revolves around the concept of whether or not the main character, Squall, died halfway through the game, resulting in the latter half occurring entirely as a sort of dream in the moments before he dies (an extremely prolonged death hallucination). Even the website dedicated to this fan theory (www.squalisdead. com) acknowledges that "there is no real 'proof', merely suggestions and hints. However, we hope this analysis will add meaning to the game for all players".[11] The point of the theory isn't whether or not it's true— it's that as a theory that isn't easily refuted by the game's worldbuilding and story, it's a fun exercise and possibility space for players to play in. It adds meaning to the game because players are able to engage with the theory and examine different possible repercussions to the game's events as so.

Of course, not all co-authoring is theory-making. Co-authoring allows for players' experiences and playthroughs to dictate aspects of the world and character identities, as well. In *Mass Effect 1–3* (BioWare, 2007–2012), players get to play Shepard as either paragon or renegade (or a mix of the two), creating a texture to Shepard's personality that is determined by how the player interprets and guides Shepard's actions. There's enough expansiveness in the worldbuilding (and Shepard's place in it) to allow for both versions of Shepard to exist and to be made more fully realized based on player decisions and actions.

SYNECDOCHE AND APOPHENIA

Co-authoring (or even just interpreting world details in specific ways) can be both a conscious or unconscious effort. Consciously, players are analyzing and making decisions about the world state and the characters that exist in it. And part of this process is guided by the concept of apophenia. Apophenia is the ability or tendency for people to distinguish patterns or meaning in an otherwise disconnected or random set of things. We consciously and unconsciously make meaning as we engage with video games (or anything, really), by determining and codifying patterns that appear significant to us. Being expansive and leaving intentional gaps in your worldbuilding provides useful fodder for letting players begin to stitch together meaning themselves.

A literary device that we can use to support apophenia and other versions of expansive symbol creation is synecdoche. Synecdoche describes when an element of something is used to represent the whole.[12] In an article for *GameIndustry.Biz*, I wrote about how I use synecdoche in my worldbuilding in *Grindstone* (Capybara Games, 2019) intentionally to create an expansive world that puts connection building into the hands of the players. *Grindstone* is a darkly humorous puzzle game where players play as a barbarian who mines treasure out of monsters' bodies, so when writing the bestiary entries for *Grindstone*, I deliberately used synecdoche as a way of sketching the outline of deeper politics, cultural touchpoints, and interpersonal dynamics in the game's world, versus burdening the limited text with too much detail.

In that article, I wrote, "Rather than explicitly stating and defining the entire world and how all of these creatures intersect, I wrote specific instances that could represent larger ideas or dynamics, letting this use of synecdoche help to create these sort of intentional gaps that are purposefully open for interpretation and player imagination".[13] Synecdoche, in its specificity but also in its symbology, is a reliable tactic for creating this openness or expansiveness, with expansive meaning that there is room for the world to grow, that the world is not so airtight that there aren't any pockets left for interpretation and imagination. Our tendency toward apophenia and the use of synecdoche creates an opportunity for us as worldbuilders to leave intentional gaps in places that invite player imagination and co-authoring in unexpected, but meaningful ways.

But even beyond creating intentional spaces for your audience to insert their own thoughts and ideas into the worldbuilding, expansive and open worldbuilding is just that: it's expansive, meaning that it can grow. Your worldbuilding should be able to grow as your game grows, either naturally through development, sequels, live service updates, transmedia, or in becoming a franchise. Having an airtight world means there are only so many ways in which to grow—or that growing it will require breaking parts of your worldbuilding, retconning and reshuffling events, histories, dynamics, and so forth. Plan for growth at the start by baking expansiveness into your worldbuilding.

Focus on Tangibility

Most writers have, at one point or another, heard the adage "show, don't tell". It's a common piece of writing advice centered around the idea that elements of your world and emotional states are more effective and resonant when your audiences simply aren't told about something, but rather are able to see the effects of it. This has origins in prose writing, meaning that even in entirely text-based formats, part of the craft of creating compelling worlds and stories is knowing how to show it in purely text formats.[14] In traditional prose writing, this looks something like: don't say a character is sad, show that they are sad in their actions, the way they speak, and so forth. Don't just say a word is hostile, show it in how the world responds to its inhabitants, its punishment system, and mechanisms for survival.

And while this also applies to video games, text-based or not, games have other tools at their disposal for showing rather than telling. Aspects like art (environment and character), audio design and soundscapes, and mechanics are all ways that we can further show the effects of our world in video games. It's for this reason that I like to focus on tangibility in my worldbuilding. Focusing on the concept of how concrete does this feel, and how much does this feel like I can touch it and interact with, is a helpful guiding tool for determining what is the best way to represent certain aspects of the worldbuilding in the game.

Kentucky Route Zero (Cardboard Company, 2013) is a deeply surrealist point-and-click adventure game about a delivery truck driver named Conway, who is trying to reach a destination for a delivery. The first scene of the game features Conway arriving at a horse-shaped gas station, where he needs to go into the basement to flip the breaker in order to power up a computer to find directions to the Zero. In the basement, Conway stumbles upon three people (Emily, Bob, Ben) playing a tabletop game. Visually, these characters are presented no different from Conway. Yet when Conway speaks to them, the game players respond oddly: Emily asks Bob if he heard something, and Bob tells Emily that no, he was studying the rules of the tabletop game they are playing. Without directly saying that Conway and the three characters aren't necessarily in the same realm of existence, the game is showing that there is already a bit of a slippage between realities in this world. The effectiveness of this short exchange is enriched by the visual language (they look the same) and mechanics (Conway interacts with them no different than other characters). And then the oddity of this world and this space is made even more explicit when the player flips the breaker, and the building is revealed to be a full horse, with half of it buried underground. The head of the horse is the gas station outside, whereas the basement the players are in is the torso, buried underground, creating a nice visual distinction of the duality of this world and ways in which the different realities slip toward and away from each other.

But, of course, what we can show in a video game is often determined not just by our worldbuilding, but by the development budget, timeline, and engine capabilities. Sometimes we want to show an effect of a magic system in our world, but we can't for a variety of reasons. Telling isn't the worst sin you can commit (in fact, sometimes telling is very useful and deliberate). Even aside from external factors like scope and budget, sometimes there is a need for just telling, especially in video games, where games writing often has to dual wield being flavorful with being functional and instructional. Telling can be tangible, as well. Showing is supremely effective, but that doesn't mean telling can't create a tangible touchpoint for players.

At the very start of *Kentucky Route Zero*, players are told that they are looking for the Zero, but that the Zero is a hard route to find. This text is instructional (find the Zero) and informative (the Zero is hard to find), and none of it is metaphorical or framed in any other literary device. It's a state of the world, and the player's obstacle is plainly told. Yet it's still effective in beginning to build the rules and logic for this world. The Zero is a difficult-to-find highway because of the surrealist slipstream of the world. Saying this plainly doesn't take away from how strange the game's world is, but rather begins to neatly stack up expectations for the game's world and story.

This is why I focus on creating tangible touchpoints, rather than just saying "show, don't tell". Sometimes telling can be really effective (and necessary) and can be done in evocative ways. So what's the golden rule for knowing when to show and when to tell? There isn't really one, except other than learning when you need either tool. Ask yourself: Is there a reason to quickly tell this now instead of finding a way to integrate it into the visual language and gameplay mechanisms of your world? There could very well be, such as pacing, relative level of importance, need for comprehension, and so forth. So much of game development is knowing where to invest resources and where a lighter touch is needed. For me, part of this decision comes down to: how important is what you're trying to communicate? The more crucial it is for coherence and world identity, the more likely I am to explore ways of showing the effects of it in the world. If it really matters, I want my audience to really feel it.

Find Inherent Pressures

The concept of worldbuilding as a story engine revolves around this idea that elements of your world should be exerting some sort of pressure on your characters and therefore on your players. This pressure often presents as conflict, or the obstacles that characters face in your world. An important distinction is necessary here for the word conflict. Conflict can be (and often is) a very important tool in storytelling, but its meaning often gets reduced down to violence or aggression-based gameplay and tensions. Conflict doesn't always mean violence, but it often does always mean some kind of pressure that your characters are feeling, be it an obstacle, some sort of drama, or any other way conflict can manifest in a space.

So when determining the major aspects of your world, the prevailing systems, and the key geographical features, consider what type of pressures these components are creating. In *The Outer Worlds* (Obsidian Entertainment, 2019), the sci-fi setting is constructed around the premise of corporations having created colonies in space built around the business in question. Planets do not belong to a civilization; they belong to a corporation. And this capitalism-as-rule is exerting a specific pressure on the characters in that world, namely in the variety of ways that they respond to and exist under the rule of their employer. One of the first major missions of the game is to speak to deserters in the Spacer's Choice corporation-colony on Edgewater. Edgewater, a colony of Spacer's Choice workers, requires more electrical power in order to support their life there. And the only way to do so is to redirect the power supply from a collective of deserters, who left Edgewater as a form of resistance to the horrific decisions that got made in the name of running an efficient business. Players are tasked with making the decision of whose power supply to cut off (as the player requires a power regulator from one of the colonies). The world-building here creates the moral quandary that players must confront, in terms of recognizing the ways in which the systems of power (Spacer's Choice controlling Edgewater) exert different pressures on the people there (both the workers of Edgewater and the deserters).

We can use the way we've built our world as a story engine to provide possible obstacles to our characters in really compelling ways. The Edgewater example from *The Outer Worlds* doesn't exclude violence-based conflict, but it's more focused on understanding the different pressures each group is experiencing and navigating the obstacles they both face. Worldbuilding is a way of setting up inherent pressures in the world that will then bear down on your characters to create meaningful character arcs and plot points that grow and evolve both your character and your world. But it will also set up missions, specific gameplay moments, as well as environment and character art and sound design. These pressures can also become the basis for specific mechanics, verbs, and interactions inherent to the gameplay of your world, what tools characters and players have for engaging with the pressures the worldbuilding is exerting is gameplay, and how characters respond to pressure and conflict is both worldbuilding texture and a basis for interactivity.

A QUICK NOTE ON LIVE GAMES

These key principles (particularly expansiveness) have also been instrumental in building a world that is sustainable for the development of live games or live service games. Live service games are games that have a consistent cycle of content updates provided to the game during its post-launch (the period of development time after the game has initially launched). Examples of live service games include PC and console games like *Fortnite* (Epic Games, 2017), but also can be commonly found in mobile, with games like *Genshin Impact* (miHoYo, 2020).

While I won't focus much more on live games at the moment (more in the case study on *Sea of Thieves*), I will mention that robust and expansive worldbuilding is integral to live games in order to create the story engines, modes, and evolution of mechanics that feel aligned with the game's identity and themes. Live games require lots of space for coherent evolution of their existing world and mechanics and focusing on worldbuilding (rather than focusing on plot-based storytelling) is an important method toward achieving this. Mobile live games in particular benefit from a world-first approach to narrative. In the chapter "Building Narrative in Mobile Games" in *Storytelling for New Technologies and Platforms: A Writer's Guide to Theme Parks, Virtual Reality, Board Games, Virtual Assistants, and More*, Bay Anapol writes that "The medium doesn't lend itself to traditionally storytelling or a plotted experience. Instead, it's about world creation".[15] Live games can include plot-based sequences and events, of course, but as an experience designed without an end, focusing rather on worldbuilding as a story engine provides a more consistent and naturally coherent way to generate these stories and characters.

WHAT IS IMMERSION?

Immersion is a funny concept to me. Referring to the ability to get pulled into a piece of media or play experience so fully as for the lines between reality and game to momentarily bleed and fall away, immersion is often sought as a hallmark of worldbuilding. Because of course, when you build believable worlds, with compelling characters, engaging stories, and provoking mechanics, it is often with the goal of achieving that level of investment.

But immersion is also a bit of a vague and nebulous concept. What does being "pulled in" actually mean? And how does one achieve this? To talk a bit more about immersion, let's take a look at Nordic LARP (live-action role playing), that heavily values immersion. While distinct from video games, Nordic LARP (and LARP in general) has a robust and rich methodology for approaching immersion in play. In the book *Larp, the Universe, and Everything*, character immersion is described as the effect of players feeling the feelings of their assumed characters (or taking on their personality).[16] Character immersion then becomes a total incorporation of the character, inhabiting that character so fully as to feel things as that character. This is an outcome of play and worldbuilding that has let player and character align with each other.

Immersion, to me, is best thought of when it is thought of as an outcome, rather than as a principle. It is a goal of worldbuilding and play experiences, one that can be desired (or not) but that is a subjective experience achieved through a set of principles and craft practice, rather than being a practice in and of itself. Players don't all follow the same path toward immersion. This is why "immersion" isn't listed on my key principles above. The key principles are aspects of craft that I can practice and that, when delivered in particular ways, can help achieve immersion for some people.

But above and beyond this, Jaakko Stenros in the chapter "Nordic Larp: Theater, Art and Game" in *Nordic Larp* (a different, but equally fascinating book on Nordic LARP) discusses the fact that there will always be friction between the ways in which the game world and our real-world overlap. But this friction isn't a problem. Instead, Stenros argues that "games and gaming cultures' performance or success in reaching one's goals is more valuable than the subjective experience of feeling your character's feelings".[17] Immersion is the result of a well-crafted world, but not all players will experience the same level of immersion in the same world, and that more so, certain games and their experiences may not even be striving for immersion. They could be striving for education or for encouraging a very specific experience, neither of which requires or necessitates immersion. Immersion is inherently personal and subjective, a result of both the game's affordances[18] and how players respond to and inhabit role play. And for me, this is true of video games, as well. Immersion can be a desired goal, but it isn't necessarily the only goal for worldbuilding.

This is why I treat this type of immersion as a goal and an outcome, rather than a principle of craft that I can practice and get better at. I can get better at constructing believable worlds, making those worlds expansive and places that invite co-authoring, and I can create worlds that players want to engage in by focusing on tangibility and pressures/conflicts inherent to those worlds. These are my tools for achieving immersion—if I want to delineate immersion as one of the goals for my worldbuilding. (More on worldbuilding goals in Chapter 3.)

And immersion doesn't have to be one of your goals! There are plenty of games that deliberately (and effectively) break the fourth wall.[19] *Doki Doki Literature Club* (Dan Salvato LLC, 2017) earned its reputation by leaning into visual novel dating sim tropes and then violently bucking them against the fourth wall by interrogating your computer as a mode of play. And then of course there's the ever-famous Psycho Mantis battle in *Metal Gear Solid* (Konami, 1998). Psycho Mantis purports to read the playable character's mind, and so the only way to defeat the boss is to unplug your controller and plug it into the second player controller port. Of course, to further complicate matters, fourth-wall breaking may actually enhance immersion for certain players, despite the two appearing at odds. Fourth-wall breaking may actually draw the player deeper into the game world by extending the boundaries of the game's world beyond its screen and into our real world (particularly with the Psycho Mantis fight). Creating meta-textual experiences, particularly in video games where the hardware and physical modes of play become incorporated into the game world, can actually layer the two worlds on top of each other. But, like typical immersion, this is subjective, an experience that can be mediated through specific aspects of creation.

It is worth noting, as well, that character and world immersion aren't the only types of immersion accessible to players, either. In the paper, "Four categories for meaningful discussion of immersion in video games", Mata Haggis-Burridge outlines the following ways in which immersion can be felt: systems immersion, spatial immersion, narrative/sequential immersion, and empathic/social immersion.[20] This overlaps with a few of the types of immersion noted in Nordic LARP, such as character and physical immersion. In an article on *First Person Scholar*, Sarah Lynne Bowman establishes a similar but crucially different set of categories for types of immersion often found in LARPs, which include character and physical immersion but are expanded to include "immersion into activity" and "immersion into game" as meaningfully different ways game audiences seek out immersion.[21] These categories can be expounded, also, when we consider technology like VR (virtual reality), where it might be helpful to consider immersion as either mental or physical.[22] These distinct categories are helpful in considering what we actually mean when we say "immersion" and how we can build our worlds to achieve them.

All of this is to say: immersion is a bit of a sticky subject, so if you are building your world with immersion as a desired goal, think about the type of immersion you want and which elements of your practice and craft can help achieve that outcome. But also, to keep in mind, that immersion isn't the only hallmark of successful worldbuilding, and to, as always, approach worldbuilding with the defined goals that matter to your game.

On that note: this is a good point for a gentle reminder that this book is, by design and by necessity, written and filtered through my perspective and should be taken as thought to chew on, to argue with, to pick and pull what works for you and what doesn't! I understand why some people would want to craft with a goal of immersion in mind (and if it helps them, that's excellent!). I'm just here to say that if you, like me, find the concept of immersion to be nebulous to deliberately plan for, then it is absolutely okay to throw that out the window. Use what works for you, discard what doesn't, and hone your craft in the way that achieves your goals.

NOTES

1. Totten, C.W. 2014. *An Architectural Approach to Level Design*. Boca Raton: CRC Press/Taylor & Francis.
2. For ease, I will use "conceptual worldbuilding" when referring specifically to the worldbuilding done in a world bible or other similar documentation, in concept and pre-production, that then informs the "practical worldbuilding", which is the expression of the world in implementation and development.

3. Like with making video games generally, creating a fictional world is any-thing but "simple", even if it looks that way on the surface.
4. Litore, S. 2017. Write Worlds Your Readers Won't Forget. Westmarch Publishing.
5. Think of a story engine as being exemplified in the procedural TV show format. A procedural offers up consistent ways to continue telling stories in that world, with repeated characters, because there is no shortage of poten-tial scenarios that arise out of the setting and set-up. TV shows like *X-Files* and *Supernatural*, both which utilize "monster-of-the-week" style episodes, are shows that contain story engines in their worldbuilding—monsters, aliens, and cryptids can all appear because the jobs of the main characters in both shows revolve around dealing with monsters and aliens.
6. Fernández-Vara, C. and M. Weise. 2020. Making Worlds into Games—A Methodology. World-Builders on World-Building: An Exploration of Subcreation ed. M. J.P. Wolf, 76. Boca Raton: CRC Press/Taylor & Francis.
7. Finley, T.K. *Narrative Tactics for Mobile and Social Games: Pocket-Sized Storytelling*. Boca Raton: CRC Press/Taylor & Francis.
8. Jemisin, N.K. 2015. Growing Your Iceberg: Crafting a Secondary World That Feels Ancient in 60 Minutes (Or Less). https://nkjemisin.com/wp-content/uploads/2015/08/WDWebinar.pdf.
9. In a Game Maker's Toolkit video, the word "credible" is used by the design-ers at IO Interactive when discussing how to blend usable game spaces with our understanding of how those spaces are constructed in the real world: https://youtu.be/RwlnCn2EB9o.
10. Hard sci-fi is the science fiction genre most concerned with creating worlds and technology that are realistic outcomes of current technology. But of course, hard sci-fi is not the only route toward believable sci-fi worlds.
11. Squall Is Dead. https://squallsdead.com/.
12. For example, when people say "the Crown" to refer to the British monar-chy. In this case, "the Crown" is representing the entirety of the monarchy, despite only referring to a singular part of monarchy.
13. Tremblay,K.2021.TellingStoryThroughGameplay.GameIndustry.Bizhttps://www.gamesindustry.biz/articles/2021–06–23-telling-story-through-gameplay#section-2.
14. For those interested, I gave a talk at NarraScope in 2020 on making text-based horror games and how to use the text-based format to emphasize and highlight atmosphere and to create tension: https://www.youtube.com/watch?v=ULk1gm0d6wY.
15. Anapol, B. 2022. Building Narrative in Mobile Games. Storytelling for New Technologies and Platforms. ed. Berger, R. 51. Boca Raton: CRC Press/Taylor & Francis.
16. Castellani, A. 2009. The Vademecum of the Karstic Style. *Larp, the Universe, and Everything* eds., 188. Haraldvangen: Knutepunkt Books https://nordiclarp.org/w/images/b/bf/2009-Larp.the.Universe.and.Everything.pdf.

17. Stenros, J. 2010. Nordic Larp as Theatre, Art and Gaming. *Nordic LARP* eds. Stenros, J. and M. Montola, 300. Fëa Livia: Nordic Larp. https://trepo.tuni. fi/bitstream/handle/10024/95123/nordic_larp_2010.pdf.
18. Hannah Nicklin, in her excellent book *Writing for Games: Theory & Practice*, drawing on *The Design of Everyday Things* by Don Norman, describes games' affordances as the specific qualities to video games as an art format (such as interactivity, which is not unique to video games but is specific to video games). I highly recommend reading Nicklin's book for an in-depth and insightful approach to writing for video games.
19. Breaking the fourth wall means acknowledging the audience as such, breaking the realities of immersion insofar as it eschews the current rules and logic of the world and drawing focus on is means of construction and existence.
20. Haggis-Burridge, M. 2020. Four Categories for Meaningful Discussion of Immersion in Video Games. https://pure.buas.nl/ws/portalfiles/portal/1228916/Haggis_Immersion_4CategoriesInVideoGames.pdf.
21. Bowman, S.L. 2017. Immersion into LARP: Theories of Embodied Narrative Experience. First Person Scholar. http://www.firstpersonscholar.com/immersion-into-larp/.
22. VR Studio. 2019. Immersion VR – Everything You Need To Know. https://mobfish.net/blog/immersion-vr/.

CHAPTER 2

A Cross-Discipline Breakdown of Worldbuilding

NOW THAT WE HAVE a common language for what worldbuilding is generally, I'd like to take a look at what aspects of a video game compose worldbuilding explicitly. This section isn't exhaustive, although I will try to be thorough, because its aim is to begin to peel back the layers of how worldbuilding is surfaced in a video game by looking at how certain job disciplines contribute to worldbuilding that is felt by the player (practical worldbuilding). There are aspects of each job discipline that I'm sure I will have missed, but that's okay—this book is meant to be a springboard into understanding and supporting your own cross-discipline approach to worldbuilding for video games, not an exhaustive guide on it.

While this section is an overview, Chapter 4 is dedicated to exploring a few of these larger components more in depth (and from a more holistic angle), so consider this chapter a primer on what each major job discipline consists of and the various worldbuilding tools available. Some areas will overlap, and that will be discussed in Chapter 4, as well. Just like with narrative and storytelling, everybody on a team contributes in some way to worldbuilding.

DOI: 10.1201/9781003345619-3

In this chapter, we'll look at:

- Narrative

- Gameplay

- Art

- UI

- Programming

- Audio

For each section, I'll use examples (some general, some highly specific) to help make the theory concrete, but bear in mind that these are just examples and are not the definitive way of worldbuilding. So let's dive in.

NARRATIVE

The narrative department (comprising game writers, narrative designers[1], technical narrative designers, and perhaps other job roles, including localization) is responsible for the explicit storytelling aspect of both games and their worldbuilding. Narrative is the way in which a story is told, and game writers and narrative designers have plenty of tools at their disposal for worldbuilding (not only traditional tools from other storytelling crafts, but also those from video games specifically).

Some (non-exhaustive) ways in which narrative can surface worldbuilding in a video game includes:

- Narrative collectibles

- Naming conventions

- Descriptions

- Characters

- Dialogue

Narrative Collectibles

Lore is probably the concept most associated with worldbuilding in video games (other than environmental storytelling, discussed later). But lore is also vague and gets applied to mean many different things depending on user and context. Is lore just the story? Is it background information? Is it character details? Mission anecdotes? Lore as a concept is vague, but I do think it can be a useful one when we specify what we mean when we use it, and consequently, what we want from it as a narrative device. In my experience and perspective, and for the purposes of this book, let's define lore as non-essential world details. What this means is that lore is the aspects of the characters, the story, and the world that aren't critical or necessary for player progression or story comprehension but are details that help provide texture and flavor, filling in missing beats and providing alternate perspectives to the world and story.

So with that definition established as a baseline for us, let's focus on one of the common tools we have for surfacing lore to players: narrative collectibles, namely in the form of text and audio logs. Text and audio logs are the ephemera that players find, and while they can be snippets of lore, text and audio logs can also be gameplay tools and important devices for delivery of main story plot points and character information. Text and audio logs don't have to be only lore, but they are a common device for offering lore because they are supplemental and easily returned to by players in menus.

System Shock (Looking Glass Technologies, 1994) is noted for being the first game to really popularize audio logs as a storytelling device. As the hacker navigates Citadel Station under SHODAN's control, they find emails and voice logs from the deceased, which add flavor and detail to the world of *System Shock*, but also do so in such a way as to stitch together the world's identity. And ever since audio and text logs have remained a reliable tool for both delivering main plot and worldbuilding. Text and audio logs often are found on NPCs or as collectibles in the environment, commonly given diegetic forms such as recording devices, computers, or papers and other physical ephemera found in the environment. Games like *The Elder Scrolls V: Skyrim* (Bethesda Game Studios, 2011) contain text logs in the forms of books that can be perused on in-game bookshelves, a doubling down of worldbuilding in the way these books explore what fictional literature, as well as recipes and other such ephemera, looks like and the role it serves. Collectibles generally are a good tool for surfacing hyper-specific elements of the world, ones that contain a bit more detail because they are static and can often be reviewed or read in down moments of play, rather than competing for the player's attention during gameplay-heavy sequences.

Control (Remedy Entertainment, 2019) uses text and audio logs incredibly well as a supplement to the absurd and strange worldbuilding of the game. Players play as Jesse Faden, who finds herself mysteriously in the Federal Bureau of Control, tracking down her brother and navigating paranormal phenomena. While the world of *Control* is steeped in brutalism, surrealism, and reality-defying mechanics, the text and audio logs hold their own as hyper-specific explorations into how this world functions. With the Dead Letters (letters confiscated by the Bureau that could potentially reveal information about paranormal events in civilian lives), players are offered glimpses into how the paranormal events that the Bureau is focused on bleed out and affect the rest of the world. These Dead Letters indicate how expansive *Control*'s world is in that the weird and the strange of this world isn't contained just to the Bureau but exists far beyond the seams of what players will ever see.

Malindy Hetfeld, in an expansive article called "Understanding worldbuilding in games" at *Eurogamer*, talks about how *Control*'s text logs are a crucial mechanic for understanding the world the game occurs in:

> The thing I enjoyed most about *Control*, for example, was finding correspondence from Bureau employees, not only because it helped an otherwise mostly deserted place come back to life, but also because it was crucial in helping me figure out what the Bureau even was.[2]

In *Control*, the text logs are not just lore (as is often a dismissive way of referring to audio and text logs)—these text logs are an important part of stitching together the world's (and therefore the game's) identity. *Control* establishes a surreal world that looks like ours but operates according to different rules, and consequently, information about this world is sparse. Bureau correspondence is a highly effective tool for answering questions about the world in a diegetic manner that feels believable. It's not a sticky note with a password stuck to a computer monitor, which is obviously placed for the player to find; they are documents believably left behind in the setting. And, as Hetfield points out, they make the world feel alive, full of people, drama, policy, and politics, even if in the game as Jesse players interact with a fraction of these characters.

Of course, narrative collectibles aren't just text or audio logs. *Control* makes liberal use of video logs from NPCs (such as instructional videos from Dr. Darling, the Head of Research), as well as the horrific puppet show "Threshold Kid" videos, a series of educational videos that were created to teach children at the Bureau. Video logs are an extension of audio and text logs, a presentation of world-rich storytelling with a different expression and integration into the game. The manner of presentation for video logs—VHS tapes, holograms, security cameras, and so forth—can also flesh out some of the worldbuilding, as well.

Even static collectible objects, paired with a name and an optional text description (both discussed in the next sections) can offer rich worldbuilding details. *Ghostwire: Tokyo* (Tango Gameworks, 2022) uses a variety of everyday objects (referred to as either relics or treasure) as part of its collectible systems. These relics range from being tiny model minivans to netsuke of spirits to Marimo moss balls. Whatever objects humans may have been carrying with them or stashed in a house can become a relic in *Ghostwire: Tokyo*. These relics can then be sold to a cat yokai called nekomata, who have vendor stalls spread throughout the game world. It's a nice way of providing a look into how the supernatural has blended into the everyday reality of this world. Finding each treasure is a combination of gameplay mechanics and level design created to highlight a sense of place and of the absence of the people from that place. Players find relics in a pile of clothes, next to abandoned bicycles, in empty homes. What is left in the wake of humanity is our everyday things, so finding these relics establish mini-vignettes of a specific person at a specific time. In addition to where and how players find them, each relic contains a blurb explaining meaning of it, as well as an audio cue of a cat meowing when players are nearby as a gameplay hint. Together the relics help stitch together the urban fantasy/supernatural nature of *Ghostwire: Tokyo*'s world, as well as creating a bit of a history of the people who lived there.

Naming Conventions

Similar to collectibles, naming conventions (and their associated descriptions, discussed next) are a great way of showcasing important elements of your world. The way in which things—items, weapons, places, people, buildings, countries—in your world get named has the potential to reveal so many layers of worldbuilding. Naming conventions can indicate major factions, the corporate structure of your world, who key figures are, what major values your world holds, what superstitions and curses exist, how items get passed down, religious pantheons and belief systems, and so forth. The names we give things—and how we determine those names—can indicate subtle aspects of a world.

The *Borderlands* (Gearbox, 2014–2019) franchise and subsequent related IP *Tiny Tina's Wonderlands* (Gearbox, 2022) use item naming conventions to indicate how corporations profit off of and are an integral part of the violence-soaked sci-fi world of Pandora. In *Borderlands*, there are a range of gun manufacturers: Hyperion, Torgue, Atlas, and so forth. This naming convention (and the fact that players can buy guns from vending machines) situates the role of corporations and capitalism in profiting off of and constructing the fabric of this world. Violence is king in the world of Pandora and knowing what type of gun you like is key to survival. So players can begin to learn these corporation names as shorthand for the types of guns they like to play with. A Hyperion-manufactured gun behaves differently than a Torgue-manufactured gun (because Torgue likes explosions so his guns deal explosions). All Dahl-manufactured weapons deal additional elemental damage. Tediore guns explode upon reload. The fact that mega corporations like Hyperion can produce weapons alongside explosion-obsessed individuals like Torgue shows the ways in which this a world constructed for and around violence.[3]

Tiny Tina's Wonderlands employs the frame device of a tabletop game set in the fictional world of Pandora, which provides even more room to let the naming conventions and playstyle of the weapons reflect the world. In *Wonderlands*, Tina is naming guns based on her fantasy world's interpretation of the guns that exist in her real world. There are Hyperius (Hyperion), Feriore (Tediore), and Dahlia (Dahl). These are versions of the existing corporations, ones Tina has twisted to fit her fantasy setting. She is worldbuilding on her reality, and this double layer of naming provides both the context of her real world (Pandora) and of her own fictional world (the Wonderlands).

Wonderlands features a ton of gear names that are obviously the result of Tina's adolescent, frenetic, bomb-loving mind when applied to a fantasy world, names like "Skillful Mood Ring of Supping", "Rumpy-Pumpy", "Courageous Wailing Banshee of Edginess", and "Bad Egg of Breathing", all ridiculous and flavorful in their own, perfect way. But there's also a gun called the "Swordsplosion of Blastoff" (obviously a Torgue shotgun) that features the flavor text: "Your sword is the sword that will pierce the heavens!" The swordsplosion shotgun, as you might expect (or not), shoots swords instead of shells, a wonderful collapsing of both the bombastic explosive nature of Torgue weapons and Tina's imagination of what a fantastical Torgue gun would be. Being able to invoke all of the worldbuilding that already exists for weapon manufacturers in *Borderlands* but then filtering them through Tina's perspective of how they would work for her fantastical tabletop campaign gives *Wonderlands* a really rich layering of meaning in the weapon naming.

Of course, weapons aren't the only place where naming conventions deliver worldbuilding. Collectibles, spells, items, objects, animals, plants, characters, towns, place names—they all create the texture of the world, and they all reveal important facets of the worldbuilding. How things get named reveal what is valued by that culture. Names reveal meaning, both of what they are and where they come from, in subtle and explicit ways. *Bugsnax*'s Snacktooth Island is filled with geographical and food-named locations (such as Snaxburg, Flavor Falls, Sugarpine Woods, etc.) reinforcing that this is a world constructed around consumption, and the land is both habitat and buffet. The names of planets in *Outer Wilds* (Mobius Digital, 2019) are indicative of what types of terrain and physical characteristics are hallmarks for each planet, such as Giant's Deep for the oceanic planet and Brittle Hollow for the planet that is literally crumbling beneath the player's feet.

Elden Ring (From Software, 2022) has a really robust world built up from individual elements, like enemies, text logs, and how the names of items, weapons, and spells reflect back the events of the game's history and the player's actions in it. For example, there is the "Flame of the Fell God", which is obtained from defeating a boss (Adan, the Thief of Fire). "Flame of the Fell God" is not just a good name in and itself (although it is), but it's also subtly creating a few references to certain aspects of the worldbuilding. First off, there's a magic system here, one that needs spells to be harnessed (while that seems obvious, how magic systems get harnessed and used is an important worldbuilding element of magic). Second off, there's the reference to a sort of pantheon, the Fell God, and a mythical history being interwoven here: Adan stole the spell from the guardian of the flame initially and now you, as the player, can harness the spell by stealing it from Adan after his defeat. The name of this spell is an encapsulation of a few beats of worldbuilding, a mini encyclopedia of meaning.

Elden Ring and the games like it are full of this kind of worldbuilding housed in the ways items, weapons, spells, collectibles, and so forth get named. In *Elden Ring*, there's also the Sword of St. Trina and St. Trina's Torch, both a reference to a sort of sainthood that exists in the game's worldbuilding.

There's Vyke's Dragonbolt, a reference to Vyke, Knight of the Roundtable Hold, and there's Radian Baldachin's Blessing, a boost to poise and a blessing from a deathbed companion. All of these are creating small pockets of personality and distinct worldbuilding flavor just in the name and associated description of the item. We understand more about pantheons, magic systems, the values of the world, and so forth through the naming conventions.

NEOLOGISMS AND PROPER NOUNS

Just as names are a robust way of introducing worldbuilding into artifacts, items, weapons/gear, and collectibles, they can also become a burden if infused with too much detail or flavor. Neologisms (new words) can be incredibly effective in creating an identity and a distinction for the thing it is referring to. For example, the word "Dovahkiin" in *Skyrim* means "dragon-born" in Dragon language, reifying the mythopoeia of the world of *Skyrim*. In the same vein, turning normal nouns into proper nouns can also create the same effect as neologisms. Proper nouns grant common nouns status and world-rich meaning by turning them into proper nouns. For example, *Destiny*'s (Bungie, 2014, 2017) two major forces of power in the world are the Darkness and the Light. Darkness and light are turned into proper nouns to denote that they are entities with importance in this world.

But overdoing the use of neologisms and proper nouns can become cumbersome if players need to constantly be remembering what they are referring to. Striking the right balance for neologisms and proper nouns being supportive and illustrative rather than cumbersome is an important part of using names to support worldbuilding. For example, in the chapter "Building a Universe" in *The Advanced Game Narrative Toolbox*, Danny Wadeson illustrates:

> Imagine being asked by an NPC to take the Mag-Wave to the Nexus to pick up some ProTEEN from the Hexchange before you set off on your Pilgrim-AGE in hope of finding not just the source of the Murkiness, but also yourself. Lots of made-up terms do not a brave new world make.[4]

Neologisms and proper nouns are useful world markers when used sparingly and effectively.

Descriptions

And of course, the meaning and world-richness of naming conventions gets compounded and reinforced by their descriptions. Sometimes purely function, sometimes more detailed (flavor text), description of items, weapons, gear, and so forth can also express elements of the world in highly specific snippets. This is particularly true of flavor text, which is more often about expressing the backstory behind an item, its function in the world, or the nature of the thing.

The weapon descriptions in *Destiny 1* and *2* are full of world flavor and detail, and are beloved for the detail and depth they contain. The pulse rifle "Bad Juju" contains the flavor text "If you believe your weapon wants to end all existence, then so it will", a quote attributed to in-universe character Toland, the Shattered. The "Glass Minuet" jumpship is flavored with the text "The Vault whispers of a world beyond". These lines are specific and full of personality and create references to the wealth of worldbuilding that exists in the *Destiny* universe.

Magic the Gathering (Wizards of the Coast, 1993–present) uses flavor text in juxtaposition with the card's ability to create both an identity for that card and to reveal a bit of worldbuilding. The artifact "Darksteel Plate" features the flavor text, a quote from the in-universe character Koth of the Hammer, "If there can be no victory, then I will fight forever". This, combined with the card's ability to grant a creature indestructibility, creates a really nice texture about who Koth of the Hammer is and the magic infused into the artifact. For a different example: The white land card "Temple of the False God" features the ability to activate that card to add two mana to the player's mana pool, but with the caveat of this card can only be activated if the player currently has five or more lands. This ability gets paired with the flavor text of "Those who bring nothing to the temple take nothing away". This pairing of gameplay ability and flavor text creates a specific texture to this land card: only players who have lands can use this land card to generate extra mana, while also indicating elements of worldbuilding in how offerings work in this specific pantheon. The instructional text (the description of the card's ability), when paired with the flavor text, creates highly specific instances of world flavor. The flavor text on its own would be interesting and compelling worldbuilding, but it is given more tangibility and focus when read after the ability text.

Strange Horticulture (Iceberg Interactive, 2022), an occult plant-identification game, uses the layering of description and flavor text as part of its puzzle system. A florist, the player is tasked with identifying the correct plant as requested by their clients. The requests come in the form of looking for plants to solve either physical ailments, like digestion issues or headaches, or to invoke the more ethereal attributes of the plant, such as plants that can help people identify lies, to lift curses, to fix broken hearts, and so forth. Each plant has its own description, which usually mostly just describes physical aspects of the plant, such as the shape and texture of the leaves, properties of its petals, the plant's odor, and so forth. But certain plants contain other sensory details, such as "The dark blue pearls are soft and feathery to the touch. My fingers ache from handling this plant" and "The leaves seem to have a mind of their own". (Of course, the names of the plants themselves—Shimmerlung, Solomon's Sceptre, Winterbore, Maiden's Sorrow—are all also creating a bit of worldbuilding texture.)

These descriptions of the plants then get paired with longer entries in a plant field guide, combining to create the solutions for the puzzles but also to flesh out the specifics of the world. When correctly identified via its encyclopedia entry, the Gilded Dendra, the feathery plant that aches to touch, is revealed to be so poisonous that even touch can cause pain. The same process is used to discover that Jacob's Worth, the leaves with a mind of their own, can point a wielder toward any person they wish to find. These details—both the mundane, purely descriptive ones and the more flavorful ones—create a specific tapestry of how plants and fungus exist in this world. The occult world is made tangible through these descriptions, in the mingling of mundanity and supernatural.

Characters

As much as I am taken by thrilling worlds, with alien vistas and the potential for new flora and fauna, I need characters. Characters are one of the most important vehicles for worldbuilding because we as an audience connect to characters. We form emotional bonds, we become invested in their struggles, and we care for people and creatures. It's this emotional connection that makes characters such an essential part of worldbuilding. The companions in *Mass Effect* (and their possible romance plotlines) are beloved by fans, and that's in large part because they are the emotional anchor points throughout the game's story and world. *Mass Effect* is known for creating loyalty missions for each of the companions. These are missions where the character asks you to help them out with a deeply personal problem. Through these highly specific missions, the characters of *Mass Effect* give meaning to the tensions in the world.

But even beyond just the emotional connection, characters are important representatives of aspects of the world. Characters are culture, they are loci of power, they have privilege or they don't have privilege, they react to the environment, and they have jobs. Worlds contain people and people reflect back all the nuances of how a world is constructed because of the way those constructions bear down and exert pressure on characters. The types of jobs that exist are the result of infrastructure from your world and what needs must be met. Worldbuilding is the ground that character and story grow out of, and that is because characters and worldbuilding exist in parallel with each other, not against.

To dig into this more, let's return to *Mass Effect*. In *Mass Effect*, the Quarians are responsible for creating the Geth as robot laborers. But when the Geth began to gain sentience, the Quarians attempted to fully exterminate them before they could revolt. In response, the Geth (learning violence from the Quarians) declared war on the Quarians. The war resulted in the Quarians fleeing on their ships (becoming the Migrant Fleet) and the Geth became insular, evolving their technology and growing hostile to any Non-Geth presence. This history saturates Tali'Zorah and gives context and dynamism to her as a companion on the Normandy. And furthermore, this history is keenly felt in *Mass Effect 2* (BioWare, 2010) when trying to obtain both Tali and Legion's loyalty. Tali is Quarian and Legion is Geth, and the tensions of their people, their histories, and their conflict are evoked in the ways both characters interact with each other, but also in how players attempt to obtain both (or either) of their loyalties. Because of the tensions they share with each other, gaining both Tali and Legion's loyalty involves making certain choices at the right time, otherwise reconciling the two is impossible. And that's because Tali and Legion are products of history, not just characters in service of the player, and this is an inseparable facet of what makes them both compelling characters.

Mass Effect's loyalty missions aren't just excellent character-building moments (even though they absolutely are). The loyalty missions also firmly situate the characters and their problems within the context of the world. In *Mass Effect 1*, Wrex's loyalty mission is about obtaining his family armor, a mission that invokes culture and history, as well as Wrex's personal thoughts and responsibilities in regard to his race. In the same game, Garrus's loyalty mission is about tracking down a geneticist related to black market organ harvesting. Wrex provides perspective into Krogan culture and the Krogan tensions with the Turians, whereas Garrus is a look into ethical quandaries in the world, and Tali and Legion are representatives of the Quarian-Geth war. But they are also characters, with differing wants and desires and opinions. They are not just representatives of the worlds they come from, but they give life and context to an aspect of that world.

Dialogue

Obviously what language your world speaks is a huge element of world-building. Famously, J.R.R. Tolkien created his story of Mordor and *The Lord of the Rings* after having created the Elvish language spoken there. In his letters, Tolkien said, "The invention of languages is the foundation. The 'stories' were made rather to provide a world for the languages than the reverse".[5] Language is an inseparable part of so many worlds, be it spoken, oral, gesture-based, or written (or a combination of all, or some other form of communication) that obviously what your language is means something about your world. An example of this would be the fictional language Simlish, which I'll discuss in the audio section at the end of this chapter, and of the Dragon language from *Skyrim* discussed above.

But dialogue doesn't need to be from a whole, brand-new language in order to be expressive of worldbuilding. NPCs or playable characters can talk about the world's history, its current climate, the tensions, the geography, the cities, and so forth. Characters have opinions on where they are from and where they currently are. Main quest dialogue is continually referencing world details as they pertain to the game's central story. For example, in *Titanfall 2* (Respawn, 2016), when the military titan BT says "Protocol one: link to Pilot. Protocol two: uphold the mission. Protocol three: protect the Pilot", players are given an immense amount of worldbuilding quickly. Additionally, when quest-giver NPCs request help from the playable character, particularly with side quests, they are situating their personal motivations within the context of the larger plot and game world.

Dialogue systems, in the ways they prioritize and assign value to choices to constitute how characters view and react to politics, morality, and so forth, are also adding texture and bringing worldbuilding into the story of the game. Games like *Mass Effect* that bake a morality system into the dialogue options are clearly constructing a reflection on what values are deemed morally upright (paragon) and which ones are more morally conflicted (renegade). The way these choices map to values in the world is clearly distinguished, creating a Commander Shepard who is viewed accordingly and thus occupies a slightly different role in the world's history. But conversation systems are also able to expose other values and elements of the worldbuilding, beyond just morality. Conversation systems can reveal any rules and values of the world they belong to by mapping choices accordingly. We'll further discuss different types of systems and their worldbuilding capabilities, as well as a deeper look into missions, in the gameplay section.

NPC barks, the disconnected lines of dialogue spoken by NPCs in games triggered by specific in-world events, are often used as a vehicle for providing a lens on how people respond and react to the game's world. NPCs can utter idle, disconnected lines or they can remark upon events of the world, or they can reference technology/magic systems, guilds/factions in power, and so forth. In *Tiny Tina's Wonderlands* some enemy skeletons will bark "I'm a talking skeleton, wooo, so scary", which is funny and also indicative of how Tina approaches constructing the world of the Wonderlands. Barks are a good worldbuilding tool because of how they exist naturally in the game world and because their purpose is to have NPCs create a living space. In the fantasy fighting game *Soul Calibur VI* (Bandai Namco Studios, 2018), each character has a host of victory lines they bark after winning a match. These lines are flavorful, character-centric, but often also reveal bits and pieces of the world these characters exist in. For example the character Nightmare, who wields the cursed Sword Edge that all combatants are fighting for, will ask "My sword ... do you still thirst?" after a victory, creating a specific texture to how the Soul Edge exists in this world as a distinct entity and Nightmare's bond to it. Dialogue doesn't need to be mission-centric to be an effective worldbuilding tool.

Dialogue can also be reflective of the world in other ways, such as through accent and dialect (discussed more in the audio section later). Phrases characters use can indicate what a world values and what it holds taboo. How do characters swear? How do they insult? How do they express joy? Idioms and turns of phrases can carry elements of worldbuilding in them by creating a lexicon built around shared vernacular. *Call of Juarez: Gunslinger* (Techland, 2013) uses dialogue to establish the wild west setting, as well as the mythology that often gets applied to cowboys in the wild west. *Call of Juarez: Gunslinger* is a wild west shooter and employs one of the main protagonists, Silas Greaves, as an unreliable narrator. Throughout the game, Silas is narrating the events as if he is telling the story to an audience. This frame device is a deliberate tool to evoke the ways in which cowboys in the wild west have become folk heroes. But players progress (and fail), Silas often contradicts himself or gets spoken over and corrected about versions of the events from others, and it creates a meta-layer around how we construct stories of heroes and how we turn events into legends through the act of storytelling. It creates an important texture to this world: yes, it's set in the wild west, but it's also about the act of mythmaking that occurs there, turning ordinary people into folk heroes through shared stories.

UNRELIABLE NARRATORS

Dialogue isn't the only avenue toward achieving unreliable narrators. *Alan Wake* (Remedy Entertainment, 2010) is a supernatural game following in-game horror writer, Alan Wake. Throughout the game, players can collect pages of Wake's upcoming novel, which details the story they're currently experiencing but that also contradicts itself. Through the collectibles, Wake becomes a bit of an unreliable narrator, which loops back in on creating tension and building distrust of both the characters and the world they inhabit.

Unreliable narrators are a good literary tool when used sparingly and effectively to enhance how characters (and the stories they have about themselves) are at odds with the game's world and how these characters actually fit into that world. This becomes especially resonant when the world is semi-constructed around the character's sense of self, as is exemplified in both Alan Wake, but also in *Call of Juarez: Gunslinger*. Both of these worlds exist in a heightened state as a direct result of who these characters are (a writer and a cowboy), so it makes sense that one of the tensions players experience in these games is between the character's concept of self and their telling of it and how the world contradicts that.

GAMEPLAY

I'm using "gameplay" here rather broadly to refer to the things that players do in a game. Gameplay is composed of actions and activities, or, generally, what the player does. It's the modes and rules of play, and defined broadly, gameplay creates the actions and experiences of players-as-characters in the world and creates the conditions to express the world's uniqueness and boundaries via systems and mechanics. When I talk about gameplay, I'm referring to all the different components and disciplines that focus on creating the interactions players will engage with in the course of play. So this can include: game design, narrative design, system design, level design, combat/encounter design, enemy/boss design, and so forth. The granularity of each role and responsibility depends on the size of the studio and the genre of the game, so for our purposes, let's think about gameplay holistically as the modes of play that can be engaged with in order to explore how gameplay intersects with worldbuilding.

In *Once Upon A Pixel: Storytelling and Worldbuilding in Video Games*, Eddie Paterson, Timothy Williams, and Will Cordner explain that "Storytelling techniques in video games are expansive and varied, and it is the role of play in bringing them to life".[6] This is true not just of storytelling, but of worldbuilding as well. Play—expressed via mechanics and other gameplay modes—is the mechanism by which players engage with and affect the world. And as such, gameplay creates pockets of access into the worldbuilding. How players navigate the world and the mechanics and systems by which they do so (traversal, combat, exploration, survival, etc.) are all aspects of the game's worldbuilding. The ways levels are constructed and puzzles are placed, the ways systems intersect and create consequences, and the ways in which quests and missions are structured are all stitching together the fabric of the world as the player engages with it and understands it. Gameplay helps bring the world to life.

Some specific tools gameplay has for expressing worldbuilding in video games include:

- Systems
- Mechanics
- Verbs
- Quests/missions
- Level design
- Enemies and creatures

Systems

Systems in games can be defined as a set of mechanics, or rules and logic, that are all working in a specific ecosystem. Or, to put it in simpler terms, systems design is about the relationships between the elements of your game. And there's a lot of room for systems in games (like conversation systems previously discussed, combat systems, romance systems, morality systems) to directly contribute to worldbuilding, since world-building is in effect also just a series of defined and interlocking systems that cascade and conflict in dynamic ways. What elements you include in the system is a direct result of the world, and how those systems respond to player's choice and action in turn creates the texture and feel of the world. *Dishonored*'s (Arkane Studios, 2012) chaos system implies the values the world holds for and against certain actions, that, essentially, lethality will create a more lethal world. The world of *Dishonored* is felt through the chaos system, as well as in the environmental art and storytelling.

Fire Emblem: Awakening's (Nintendo, 2012) relationship system is both story and gameplay-oriented. The relationship system is a chance for players to know each character better, by hearing more and more of their stories and how they relate to their teammates. But it also provides tactical boosts on the battlefield: characters with existing relationships provide buffs to each other when they are adjacent on the battlefield. The romance system includes many details of the world, including who can marry each other, what values exist in marriage for different characters, as well as how different tensions inherent in the world affect the ways in which characters relate to and understand each other. Additionally, it says something about the world in which these characters exist in, that connections provide literal strength and that people are stronger against evil together than they are individually.

Wildermyth (Worldwalker Games, 2019) is an RPG with procedural storytelling where the decisions players make change both the world and the ensemble of characters they are playing with. In *Wildermyth*, players start with farmers and then through a series of choices and tactics combat guide these characters into becoming heroes of their own adventures. Characters form romances, create legacies, and die, all of which feed into the history and next generation of characters that players can play with. Like other RPGs, its world is robust and filled to the brim with possible character backstories, conflicts, and world histories. And like simulation games (discussed below), the possibilities for these different elements to emerge and conflict are abundant. It's a world where the systems are worldbuilding, both literally and metaphorically.

Wildermyth isn't just a story about a cast of characters navigating conflict in the kingdom. It is also about how the stories of those characters (stories determined by the player's actions ticking against the many systems driving the game) become the game's world and history. The website for *Wildermyth* says that "over many lifetimes the myths you make will form your own legendary pantheon", indicating the clear way in which *Wildermyth* is constructing a world around mythopoeia based on a variety of procedural generative systems and player choice. *Wildermyth* isn't just about the current slate of characters—it's about how all the characters and the choices players make for them are creating a legendary history.

SIMULATION (WORLDBUILDING) GAMES

Simulation games are a subset of games designed to let players modify and interact with inputs and outputs of a system for different results. Often with simulation games we see games that simulate some aspects of our real world (or a certain aspect of the real world) as a way of providing accessible information about the inputs and outputs of the system. *The Sims* (Maxis, 2000–present) is a great example of this, as a simulation game that trades in our understanding of the real world to create a common set of inputs that players can tweak for a variety of systems-driven outputs. The simulation, with player modification, can result in exaggerations of everyday life that trades in grandiosity, hilarity, and tragedy.

There's also games like *Civilization* (Sid Meier/MicroProse/Activision/Firaxis Games, 1991–2016), which is about building a civilization all the way from prehistory to the far future. What inputs (levers to pull, choices to make, elements to tweak in the simulation set) create the texture of the world. Introducing new rules, new emperors, and new orders are all inputs that change the shape and flavor of the world. Like *Wildermyth*, the ways in which players interact with the various inputs available create outputs that are the literal building blocks of the world.

These games are literal worldbuilding games where players are constructing worlds or spaces, and all the levels of details therewithin, ranging from political systems and wars to interpersonal dynamics and family lineages. In discussing these sorts of games, Mark R. Johnson uses religion as an example to show how the underlying systems of simulation games directly create the sociological aspect of the worldbuilding: "For example, religious conflict might determine who can marry, and therefore who does marry, and therefore what nations form alliances, and therefore which go to war, and so forth".[7] The systems of simulation games are giving direct fodder for the texture of the worldbuilding, and worldbuilding provides the jumping-off points for systems to be built around.

Let's look at Gandhi in the *Civilization* series. Or more aptly, let's look at "Nuclear Gandhi", a popular way of referring to the fact that the famously peaceful leader would sometimes drop nukes and go to war in the game. While this used to be attributed to a programming technicality, Sid Meier clarified how this worked in his memoir, by explaining a few of the factors that went into Gandhi's war-faring tendencies: namely, that all characters shared the same script, so using nuclear weapons in war was an option available to any leader, regardless of their real-world counterpart's dogma; and that given India's predilection as a country toward scientific achievement also meant that, as far as the gameplay systems and data were concerned, India would be one of the first countries to develop nuclear weapons.[8] It's a fun example of how data sets and the rules governing systems can create (good and bad!) friction in the coherency of a world. Systems, and the possibilities contained therewithin, are the gameplay realization of the world's rules and logic, and simulation and worldbuilding style games explicitly make their worldbuilding literalized through their gameplay, which become rules for fictional sociopolitical systems.

Mechanics

Mechanics refer generally to the rules of the interactions players can perform in a video game and are a specific expression of a system. For example, *Fire Emblem: Awakening*'s relationship system mentioned above includes the conversation mechanics, but also includes battle mechanics, where pairing units together on the battlefield feeds back into the growth of their relationship. The mechanics are the ways in which players engage in the system. As mechanics represent a variety of ways (or the limitations!) that players can interact with the game world, it's easy to see how mechanics can give root to worldbuilding. Worldbuilding and mechanics have a reciprocal relationship. What you can do proves out the rules of the world, to some degree.[9] And what the rules of the world are determines what mechanics can and should look like. Simply put: what a player can do is a direct result of the worldbuilding, whether intentional or not.

In his excellent book *Situational Game Design*, Brian Upton discusses how games make meaning, and theorizes that, in video games, "Rather than meaning being seen as something that is transmitted, it's seen as something that's constructed".[10] While Upton is speaking of meaning-making generally, it's a lesson easily applied to how mechanics in games are constructing the worldbuilding (meaning) of the game. Worldbuilding can be static, but it's more often fluid. Everything the player does is in a feedback loop with the worldbuilding, constructing the meaning of specific actions in the context of this world. The things players do are, in part, constructing aspects of the world as those actions and mechanics create texture and a way of engaging with the world's various systems and rules.

Let's go back to comparing how *Tiny Tina's Wonderlands* and *Borderlands* utilize the same mechanics, but with different worldbuilding results. *Tiny Tina's Wonderlands* uses the same mechanics as *Borderlands* (both are first-person shooters with RPG elements), but *Wonderlands* takes these same set of mechanics and gives them a fantasy twist in a way that actually reveals a ton about the worldbuilding—both the explicit worldbuilding the player is engaging in, but also the worldbuilding from Tina, the bunker master (*Wonderlands'* version of a dungeon master). Tina's fantasy world still has guns, because Tina only knows a world with guns and they are an integral part of her understanding of what conflict is and how to resolve conflict.

But even beyond that, one of the most interesting changes *Wonderlands* made to the *Borderlands* formula was to swap out the grenade slot with a magic spell slot. While mechanically they are very similar (a secondary weapon type that is used to support the player's main weapons and play style), they offer very different insights into the worlds of each. Grenades make sense in the bombastic world of *Borderlands*, one based on violence and survival. But they make less sense in a fantasy tabletop version of this world. So grenades are swapped for magic spells, and while the same input triggers both, the effect is starkly different. This is also a particularly clear example of how in worldbuilding practice, technology and magic are often two sides of the same coin. Technology and magic systems exert the same sort of pressures on a world (How do they change a world? How do characters use them? What do they mean about power?), but they exist in different flavors of worlds. *Wonderlands* is able to make sense of its constructed world by leveraging and manipulating aspects of *Borderlands'* world.

While the *Wonderlands/Borderlands* example is of a mechanic that saturates the entirety of the gameplay, specific and unique mechanics can also be a really effective method of worldbuilding, particularly in action-adventure games where finding a way to express stories and world through actions is important for player comprehension. *Dishonored's* Heart is an example of a unique gameplay mechanic that is also an exceptional world-building device. The Heart is primarily a navigational mechanic, an item players can equip to guide them toward mystical relics, such as runes and bone charms (which are also incredibly flavorful and create a tangible texture to the mystical aspects of this occult, Victorian-punk world).

But because the Heart is a heart from a living human, it can also speak to Corvo. The Heart, when equipped, will reveal details about characters and locations, offering moody insights into the secrets people and places both carry with them. The Heart, while directing players toward relics, is also surfacing some of the many intricate details of the world of Dunwall. For example, of the Flooded Distract, the Heart says, "When the sea wall broke, many strange things were drowned and forgotten" and "These waters are greedy. They will never give back what they have taken". The Heart provides a moody introspection into the world of Dunwall, the parts that aren't necessarily seen but that are felt. This dialogue, combined with navigational mechanics, creates a compelling way of delivering world details and character moments to the player by directly surfacing elements related to the objects and locations Corvo interacts with. It combines place and story to reveal all of the specific details of the world of Dunwall contains.

Verbs

To go a bit more granular into mechanics, let's talk about verbs and how the rules of your world can dictate which verb sets characters even have available to them. While similar to mechanics, verbs are a highly specific expression of certain mechanics in game design. If exploration is a key system of a game, then traversal mechanics are an important part of how players go about exploring, and then verbs are the specific ways in which players move through an environment. What does it mean about a world if the verbs contained within the traversal mechanics focus on walking versus flying versus riding a horse versus web-slinging? Verbs can influence the worldbuilding in a few ways, including through dictating the rules of the world (characters can fly) or by indicating how conflicts get resolved in this world (shooting, negotiating, bare-knuckle brawling, kissing, etc.). Verbs are subtle, but important because they dictate how characters exist in and respond to the world.

Signs of the Sojourner (Echodog Games, 2020) is a deck-building game, with an explicit focus on using the card-based gameplay to build connections with NPCs, rather than defeating an opponent in battle. *Signs of the Sojourner* uses similar mechanics to other deck-building games like *Hearthstone* (Blizzard Entertainment, 2014), but with a different verb set in order to create an experience built around communication and community rather than violence and victory. Whereas in *Hearthstone* players' verbs are things like "attack", "defend", and so forth, *Signs of the Sojourner*'s verbs are, essentially, "connect" or "don't connect". The cards in the deck in *Signs of the Sojourner* have symbols on either end, and players must connect the correct symbols as they play cards in order to successfully navigate conversations with people who have different opinions of the world and the protagonist. While both *Hearthstone* and *Signs of the Sojourner* use the same set of mechanics (deck-building, card-based gameplay), the specific verbs they employ dictate different textures to their corresponding worlds. *Hearthstone* is an epic fantasy world filled with magic and might, whereas *Signs of the Sojourner* is a slice-of-a-life introspection about a character navigating their community.

These expressions of the world via verbs are subtle, but they create important signifiers for what the rules of the world are, how characters interact with each other, and what is valued or what is taboo. For example, if a character in *Hearthstone*'s verb suddenly switched to "convince" rather than "attack", this would indicate how that character views and wields power, what their privilege in the world is like, and how they situate themselves according to the values and taboos of the world. And on the flipside, violence being introduced into a game like *Signs of the Sojourner* indicates a social contract has been broken, that somebody is behaving anomalous, against the order of the world.

While considering how different action verbs can influence a world seems obvious (how is violence treated in this world? Who is allowed to behave violently? Are there repercussions for violence? And so forth), less action-focused verbs also are bountiful when considering how characters respond to conflict and tensions in a world. A game like *Coffee Talk* (Toge Productions, 2020) prioritizes verbs such as talking and making coffee as a way of getting to know the drama in the world and navigating the variety of needs of the NPCs. *Coffee Talk* is an urban fantasy game, revolving around the premise of humans, monsters, and creatures all coming to a late-night cafe to unwind. The game takes place after a war between all the different creatures of the world, and interspecies dynamics have settled into a casual, modern routine. At the very start of the game, it notes that there are many stories—of the elves that created start-ups, the dwarves that work in factories—that remain unknown in history, but that get told or shared over a drink, like a cup of coffee.

It's a world where violence has occurred but is no longer the main identifier for the world. Violence is in the past, and now this is a world that revolves around the minutiae of everyday life for these fantastical creatures, a world that can only be unearthed via making cups of coffee and asking patrons about their lives. So the verbs for *Coffee Talk* are: talking and making coffee. In the game, the second set of customers players meet are Baileys and Lua, an elf and a succubus who are having a secret relationship behind the backs of their less inclusive families. Learning about the ways in which this historical/cultural tension between elves and succubi exerts pressure on Lua and Baileys is available only via making the right drinks for them and giving them space to talk. Players cannot solve Lua and Baileys problems for them—but they can make coffee, listen, and talk to them. It would be a very different take on this urban fantasy world if players had a different slate of verbs available to them. This is a world where violence exists, but the verbs for contending with it aren't violence-based.

And even this subtle choice impacts how your world feels. *Hearthstone*, with its verbs focused on attacking and defending, is a world about heroes and villains amassing power, whereas *Coffee Talk*, with its verbs focused on talking and making coffee, is about the problems in people's daily lives. But this doesn't mean *Coffee Talk* is a world without its own issues (every world has its own tensions and pressures that get exerted on characters), but rather it means that players' paths toward engaging with those aspects of the world—and the prevalence of those aspects of the world—is just different.

Worldbuilding is the sum of its parts (no matter how small) rather than an individual flavor dotted along the way. And in addition to all the explicit ways worldbuilding is surfaced in a game, ensuring your verbs are also in line with the worldbuilding can help provide a coherent or resonant texture to your worldbuilding.

Quests/Missions

Quests (or missions, depending on your studio's vernacular), in addition to serving as vehicles for story and character development, are also adept at surfacing specific details from a game's worldbuilding. Quests, with their focus on resolving obstacles and progressing narrative forward, provide a direct link into examining the types of pressures your world-building is exerting on your characters. I'm using the word "pressures" here for the range it contains. There are a variety of different types of pressure your worldbuilding can exert and that can manifest in quests, such as resource collection (does your world have a particularly valuable resource that is integral for building a weapon, a potion, a cure, and so forth?), traversal (is moving between cities and places easy for everyone or for only specific people? why?), obstacle removal for NPCs (what obstacles exist in political infrastructures and social systems that people need help navigating or working against? Who has access to what structures?), and any other number of action-oriented requests that result from the unique ways in which your world is constructed. Quests are about obstacles and believable obstacles in stories come from the ways in which our worlds are constructed.

Main quests often show these conflicts in action and are an avenue for providing a direct look at the repercussions of world pressures on charac-ters. Main quests are, essentially, the main plot of the game, as they are the discrete beats of action and plot that get strung together to form the main path or bulk of the game. For our purposes here, I'm concerned with talk-ing about main quests as the discrete story/gameplay beats that comprise the main flow of the game.[11] As such, obviously quests have an inherent capacity in them for delivering worldbuilding as felt by the main charac-ters of your game.

Dishonored's world of Dunwall is an incredibly rich and detailed place, and its missions do an excellent job of putting the players as Corvo directly into turmoil, one that is a direct result of the political and resource-driven systems inherent to the worldbuilding. One of *Dishonored*'s most iconic missions is "Lady Boyle's Last Dinner Party", where Corvo is tasked with finding the correct Lady Boyle out of three possible ones amidst a costume party. This lavish costume party is an evocative contrast to the Dunwall players have experienced so far. Up until this point, Dunwall has been dark, hostile, overrun with the plague, and Corvo has focused on remain-ing as hidden as possible. But with "Lady Boyle's Last Dinner Party", Corvo is thrust directly into contact with the aristocrats of the world. This contrast—between the plague-ridden streets and the walled-off homes of luxury—is an important element of *Dishonored*'s game and story, and this mission sets up this contrast, in terms of story, gameplay, and environ-ment art, really well.

But, of course, there are side quests—optional story and gameplay beats—that, by their very nature, are excellent ways of delving into more niche aspects of a game's world and story. Through their hyper specificity and ability to explore a wider range of conflict and vignettes, side quests are an arena to explore a variety of pressures and aspects of your world, not all that need be fully related to the story your game is mainly telling. Because of this ability to be broader in focus, side quests add texture and difference to your world, and to the world as your playable character experiences it. They provide perspective into a variety of systems and forms of power and include specific insights into the different ways a world ticks. *The Witcher 3: Wild Hunt* (CD Projekt Red, 2015) is filled with a myriad of side quests that flesh out the world, from singing trolls, to ghosts, to assisting in wars. In an article on *GameInformer.com*, quest designer on *The Witcher 3: Wild Hunt* says that, "Aside from the obvious answer of giving players extra things to do, a world that only revolves around the main story feels dead".[12] Side quests make your world feel more robust by surfacing tensions and pressures (of varying degrees of severity) that exist, but also by illustrating that there is more to the world than just what exists in service of the main plot.

The *Witcher 3* quest "The Last Wish" is a beloved side quest, one that revolves around the romance between Geralt and Yennefer. In "The Last Wish", Yennefer wants to track down the djinn that bound the two of them together (in accordance to Geralt's last wish). It's an emotionally charged quest, focusing on the validity of the feelings they have for each, as well as directly exploring the ways in which elements of the world have consequences and repercussions on the people and creatures that live in it. As Yennefer and Geralt search for shipwrecks, they share adventures they experienced before, such as searching for golden dragons, which builds both the legacy of their relationship and the expansive boundaries of their world. It weaves nicely between showing (Geralt interacting explicitly with the magical elements of the world), as well as telling (sharing stories of past adventures) to create a tangible texture to the worldbuilding that is an inseparable part of their relationship. Geralt and Yennefer's romance isn't just a romance between two characters—it's a romance infused with specific elements from the world, in so much detail that their relationship would be unrecognizable in a different world. "The Last Wish" is just one of many quests in *The Witcher 3* that explores the magical and fantastical world, but it does so through the specific lens of how these elements can change and shape the characters.

Side quests are also great avenues to explore characters who aren't connected to or who are indifferent to the main character, as well. Not all NPCs need to exist in service of the playable character—and in fact, the worldbuilding that characters and their desires exude is more palpable, more believable, when they don't. NPCs with their own desires, their own conflicts, and their own opinions that are not in service to the playable character create texture and variety to the world, and using these NPCs for side quests provides us the opportunities to see the world more fully.

In the game *I Am Dead* (Hollow Ponds, 2020) players inhabit Morris, a recently deceased museum curator who is now tasked with protecting his home island from disaster. This involves Morris exploring the memories people have of fellow deceased beings (through hidden object gameplay), learning both about the people he shared a home with and what the world was like from their perspective. In the "Boats of Shelmerston" section, Morris learns about Samphire, a local fishfolk who has experienced the best and the worst of Shelmerston as one of the first fishfolk to integrate with humans on the island. Morris learns about who Samphire is, how people react to Samphire, and the tensions between humans and fishfolk—and none of this has any effect on Morris's goal of saving the island, whatsoever. Samphire does not exist for Morris, but rather Morris is learning about Samphire as somebody he shared a home with. And, in the course of play, Samphire rejects Morris's request for help to save the island. Samphire does not exist for Morris or for Morris's needs. Throughout the game, Morris is exposed to pockets of the small island town he didn't interact with explicitly and he learns more about his home and the people he shares it with in doing so. *I Am Dead* is as much about the island of Shelmerston as it is about the people whose memories the player is exploring, and this is possible because these NPCs don't exist in service to Morris—they had their own lives, often ones that didn't intersect with Morris's very much at all, and this is an important detail in making the world of Shelmerston feel believable and expansive.

Level Design

Level design is one of those disciplines, like art and narrative, that contributes a substantial amount to how worldbuilding is realized in video games. Level design, alongside level art or environmental art, builds the world that players move through, be it a dungeon, a building, a city street, or a forest (or any number of available in-game locations). Levels are literally the ground players walk on, the signposts they pass, the nitty gritty texture of the world, where art, story, and gameplay are all combined to create the experience of the world and of the game. So it's no surprise then that level design has its own set of worldbuilding practices (such as pacing, encounter design, and so forth), since level design is a direct link to the realization of worldbuilding through environmental storytelling (more on that later), pacing, and the construction of the spaces that compose the world.

Compelling level design comes at the intersection of spaces designed for movement and discovery, that are well paced in terms of interactions, tailored for engaging quest design, and offer insights into both place and story. In *An Architectural Approach to Level Design*, Totten says that "A world with a properly defined sense of place is a world that players can learn to use".[13] Like the concept of synecdoche, this idea that level design, in conjunction with level art, can create recurring symbols (motifs) that help generate an understanding of how to navigate different environments. Level design is the moment-to-moment understanding of how characters fit into and exist in the world, and as such, are excellent conduits for worldbuilding that is both relevant for story, but also for gameplay. Worldbuilding is not story, but rather the conditions and context in which stories arise, and so level design (in combination with level art) becomes an avenue for evocative stories based entirely on place. World-rich levels are like vignettes—they are specific, they are well paced and built, and can feel like mini-worlds all on their own.

The Game Maker's Toolkit has an excellent video titled "How Level Design Can Tell a Story", which focuses on how "level design can drive understanding, feeling, and identity" of a place and a story.[14] Environmental storytelling is an obvious example of how level design and level art can create a specificity in the places players visit (more on environmental storytelling in the environment art section later in this chapter). But even beyond that, level design drives how coherent and memorable a world is to players by creating all of the components of a place that makes it remarkable and unique, components like shops, markets, cave systems, the paths through a space, and so forth. The Game Maker's Toolkit discusses how even things like the scale of a place and the materials used in building can illustrate aspects of the people who then use those spaces.[15] Every aspect of how—and where—places are constructed exemplifies some element of worldbuilding, such as geographical features or how cities are built, and how the people and creatures of this world respond to these elements.

But even how characters—and therefore players—move through and use a space is indicative of the world, in the way that a character interacts with a space implies something about the relationship between person and space, and that relationship is often a nexus point of worldbuilding.

CITIES AS SOCIOLOGICAL MICROCOSMS

Cities in particular are a great worldbuilding tool in that they are an encapsulation of so many of the details often found in worldbuilding, such as political systems of power (are there police?), economy (are there shops?), group behaviors (what are the NPCs doing?), social and recreation (where are the NPCs hanging out?), religious (are there buildings or sigils of worship?), and so forth. As the Game Maker's Toolkit explains, the scale and type of materials used in construction speak about the resources available (and to whom), whereas shapes and scale also speak about the importance and use of different places.[16] Cities like Midgar in *Final Fantasy VII* (Square, 1997) are an excellent example of how a city space speaks to larger values and systems at play in the game's worldbuilding.

In *Final Fantasy VII*, Midgar is divided. Each neighborhood or sector of Midgar contains two types of neighborhoods: the one on the plate and the slums below. And both these distinct neighborhoods boast their own unique identity and flavor. For example, Sector 6's on-plate neighborhood is inaccessible, but in the Sector 6 slums exists the Wall Market, the entertainment district run by a seedy crime lord. The texture of Wall Market is vibrant and intentionally a contrast to the unseen, corporation-controlled on-plate neighborhoods. The distinct flavor of each neighborhood was something that was preserved and focused on in *Final Fantasy VII Remake* (Square Enix, 2020) as well. On Square Enix's website, remake co-director Naoki Hamaguchi talks about the work that went into recreating the iconic city over two decades later, particularly about how the team used worldbuilding elements to bring the city to life. He explains that knowing the "economic status of the different regions was invaluable in helping us define which elements of the environment could be shared across areas, and which should be region-specific–right down to the ratio of text on the posters!"[17] The incredible specificity of who lives in what sector and how that is reflected in what the sector looks like is part of what makes Midgar so iconic even today.

Then there's Sector 7, where the employees of Shinra live with their families on the plate, with the slums below being where the resistance group Avalanche runs their operation. This stark division of a city space is directly echoed in the game's themes and worldbuilding: Shinra, with their nuclear reactors and destructive, capitalist policies, are destroying the

Earth, which mainly affects the most impoverished citizens, particularly those in the slums below. Midgar reflects the state of *Final Fantasy VII*'s world brilliantly by creating a city that literally embodies the major conflicts (divisions) of the game.

In the above-mentioned post about remaking *Final Fantasy VII*, Hamaguchi spoke about the importance for them of showing life on the Sector 7 upper plate. Hamaguchi explained that they wanted to go deeper into Avalanche as a resistance group, so part of the way they did this was to create the Sector 7 upper-plate residential zone, which is home to a member of Avalanche's family.[18] This, of course, both fleshes out the world of Midgar, of *Final Fantasy VII*, as well as the characters, but it also provides an emotional connection to a part of the city that is going to be collapsed and destroyed. Highlighting this division between the upper plate (the residential area of Sector 7) and the slums (where Avalanche's headquarters are run and operated by Tifa) illustrates Midgar as representative of both the worldbuilding and the pressures that the tensions in the worldbuilding are exerting down on the players.

In his book *Virtual Cities: An Atlas and Exploration of Video Game Cities*, urbanist Konstantinos Dimopoulos notes that

> What's perhaps the most ingenious aspect of Midgar's design is that, when players are in it, it feels as if the city is the entire world … Only leaving the city reveals this elaborate setting to be a tiny black spot on the planet's face, and a monument to a strong rural-urban divide powered by Shinra's greed.[19]

Midgar is so robust, so resonant of the major themes of the game that even though it is only the starting area of the game, it feels like it's the entire universe.

To get into how level design can be used to create an understanding of a world (or many small worlds), let's look at *Outer Wilds*. *Outer Wilds* is a time-loop exploration game all about taking off in a physics-based spaceship to solve the mystery of why the solar system keeps exploding every 22 minutes. *Outer Wilds*'s level design is an ever-evolving sense of place based both on where players are, aka which planet, and at what time interval they're at in the time loop.

Let's look at the Hourglass Twins specifically here. The Hourglass Twins are two binary planets: Ember Twin, a rocky world, and Ash Twin, a sandy world. As the loop progresses, sand flows from Ash Twin to Ember

Twin, literally changing both the availability of spaces to explore and the level design of both planets. At the start of the loop, Ember Twin is fully exposed. Its bottom caverns are accessible, but notably, higher ones are more difficult or outright impossible to get to. So as the sand from Ash Twin begins to fill up the empty spaces of Ember Twin, certain areas become buried, while others are made available as the ground level rises. The changing level design provides a time-based puzzle system that must be navigated in order to fully explore Ember Twin.

But this isn't a one-way relationship, not where level design is concerned. As Ember Twin's terrain changes based on the level of sand, so too does Ash Twin's available puzzle pieces change. As the sand gets pulled into Ember Twin and away from Ash Twin, ruins become exposed on the shrinking, sandy planet. And while this is an incredible bit of worldbuilding (literally watching the sand wash away to reveal destroyed houses overrun with cacti), it's also a key part of progressing through the game. What makes this level design so brilliant is that *Outer Wilds* is not just about understanding where you are; it's about understanding when you are, as well. It's a really evocative piece of level design combined with puzzle design that is dictating rules and relationships about the world.

And this facet of its worldbuilding (players are stuck in a perpetual time loop as the universe constantly blows up) is realized brilliantly in this type of level design. Players are not just racing against a clock, they are working with the clock because they can only access specific areas at specific times, and some clues can only be found in combination of these highly curated and designed moments. But in addition to this type of level design creating intricate puzzles, it also deliberately creates the sense of place and rules of the world. It references a history (who lived in those buried houses on Ash Twin?), while also creating a tapestry of world rules and logic that generate both gameplay and stories. Level design, in this sense, is a story engine: as the accessible layout of the planets change, so too can different stories be generated. The world of *Outer Wilds* is dynamic and the level design of the Hourglass Twins wonderfully reflects that.

The much praised "Effect and Cause" level in *Titanfall 2* is another example of world-resonant level design. In "Effect and Cause", players need to traverse through a dilapidated research center in order to track down a character they were supposed to rendezvous with there. But because the facility is in ruins, the only way through the level is to hop back and forth in time. The ability to shift between time periods of this specific level creates an opportunity to explore the world in two different states: the present, which is currently all rubble and destruction, and the past, the working research center filled with NPCs and life.

The duality of this level is a nice moment of providing backstory (the research facility was developing a super weapon—The Fold Weapon, a supergun capable of destroying worlds—which then becomes the focus of the campaign) while involving the player in the mechanics of that back-story delivery. This level is illustrative of the type of world that created the Fold Weapon (the past version of the facility, which is sterile, clean, and bears all the hallmarks of a place removed from the research it is conduct-ing), but also of the consequences of such research (the collapsed and dan-gerous facility crawling with monsters in the present).

This weaving together of story and mechanics creates a really fun texture to the world, as the researchers and security guards in the past respond to the present version of Jack Cooper (the protagonist) time trav-eling to their world. There's an Easter egg in an audio log in this level, where if players interrupt the researcher delivering a lecture they can hear that lecturer stop and question them in an audio log in the present).[20] This moment ties the two worlds together, dictating how time travel works here and the repercussions of it. It's also a highly evocative setting to engage with the world's backstory in because it deliberately forces the player to experience it and not just consume it in codex-style log. The moment of creating the Fold Weapon warrants this level of expression, as well, since the world state that led to the weapon being made is an important contrast to the world that lives in the weapon's wake.

Of course, even the smaller, moment-to-moment aspects of being in a space, as dictated by level design, can feed into the world. In the survival game *Grounded* (Obsidian Entertainment, 2020), players are kids who have accidentally shrunk themselves down to the size of ants in their backyard. The scale of the grass around them, the size of the insect enemies, and so forth creates an immediate understanding of the world. The shape and size of these locations create wonderful gameplay moments (climbing trees is akin to climbing mountains, blades of grass offer both building materi-als and pathways through the backyard), as well as dictating the rules of this world. Finding discarded soda pop cans provides slight hydration to combat the thirst mechanic, as well as hiding spots from spiders and other aggressive insects. The scale and shape of these details in the landscape indicate gameplay use but also create specific touchpoints for the type of worldbuilding *Grounded* is built upon, namely that of turning mundane backyard locations and objects into fantastical lands to explore.

Enemies and Creatures

Enemy design is another way that designers (and animators and programmers) can make enemies both feel distinctive and highlight elements from the world they exist in. To talk about enemy design, let's look at both creatures and human enemies, starting with creatures.

Conceptual worldbuilding asks questions of what type of creatures are born from specific worlds. Creatures are responsive to environments, so the types of creatures found in specific places and their specific design is indicative of certain elements and rules of your world. For example, desert worlds tend to feature creatures evolved for little need for water (or the ability to store water), whereas creatures who live in darkness have evolved other ways of navigating in the dark. Their biology (and consequently their visual design) is either derived from world conditions (i.e., creatures are biologically responsive to the environments they live in), or the world is inferred from their design (i.e., a creature that inhabits certain biomes begins to establish a dialogue of what conditions that creature needs to survive and how/where the world provides those conditions speaks to the way the world is constructed generally). Creatures are deeply reflective and indicative of the spaces they inhabit, both explicitly and implicitly. This relationship between the world and creatures is important to making creatures that feel at home in your world.

Let's take a quick look at *Subnautica* (Unknown Worlds, 2014), a game full to the brim with terrifying and magnificent underwater creatures. A fully realized oceanic planet, *Subnautica* boasts an incredible range of distinct creatures with different designs to make the world feel believably constructed. There's the flat and wide Bladderfish, the adorable half-dolphin, half-squid Cuddlefish, the giant and long-legged Sea Trader, and the horrifying and quick Ghost Leviathan. So many of these creatures are distinct to specific environments, indicating relative level of safety (or danger), as well as availability of resources for the survival aspects of the game. For example, running into a Reaper Leviathan or a Ghost Leviathan indicates the entering of an extremely hostile part of the world.

It's this specificity that also can be used to create really memorable moments of distinction, as well. Since Reaper and Ghost Leviathans are aggressive carnivores and indicate less friendly waters, it's no surprise then that a player's first encounter with a Reefback Leviathan may be cause for concern. Reefbacks are passive leviathans that swim through relatively accessible and early level biomes in the open-world game, and given their size and the fragility of the protagonist, they are often initially terrifying. But the closer players get to the Reefbacks, the more it becomes obvious that they are not just passive, but are designed to be mini ecosystems within the game's world. Reefbacks move slowly and assuredly. They are found in the safer and more early-game biomes. Certain flora, like the brain coral, can be found on Reefbacks, prompting players to interact with the creatures to harvest resources or creatures that they need for the survival aspects of the game.

The Reefbacks, by being a neutral leviathan rather than an aggressive one, create a specific contrasting texture to the full world of *Subnautica*. This is an ocean world full of distinct and valuable creatures and fauna, and not all are what they appear to be. Since *Subnautica*'s progression is locked not behind quests and story points, but rather behind crafting loops that allow for further (and deeper) exploration, knowing where to reliably find certain resources (and creatures providing those resources) is important. *Subnautica* is also a survival game, where hunger and thirst mechanics must be dealt with to ensure you don't die. So the Reefback, while at first this terrifying sight because of its size and the precarity of your life, quickly becomes a bountiful treasure trove of flora, fauna, and coral, all of which are important elements either for survival mechanics or crafting loops, and which builds out the detail of what this alien world is like.

But, of course, the ways in which human enemies are designed and implemented into a game also feeds into the practical worldbuilding of the game. In video games with violence-based conflict, whom players are fighting against carries a lot of weight when it comes to both implicit and explicit worldbuilding. Conflicts exist in all sorts of manners in every type of believable world, and the opposing forces of conflict are stand-ins for some assumed values. Put another way: the factions that exist in the game world create values about what is important (and what is considered taboo) in the fictional world. Who is your playable character fighting against? Why? What are the competing motives? How do each provide an obstacle to the other? These sorts of questions are not just story-based but are evolutions of aspects of the worldbuilding (and another example of how worldbuilding can be generative of gameplay).

Let's take a look at a common enemy archetype, across a variety of game genres: grunts, or the default fodder enemies in games. Specifically, though, I want to look at a distinct flavor of grunts: bandits.[21] Narratively skinning grunts as "bandits" is already creating a specific texture to what the low-level enemies of this world are. Bandits are often low-tiered, villainous analogues to the player character's faction and they tend to represent a shift from societal norms; they work against established order for a variety of motivators (not necessarily villainous). But the point is that a bandit is often an opposition to order or law, both which are elements derived from worldbuilding. *The Outer Worlds* has its marauders and outlaws, humans who have turned against the established colonies, which represent the same ideological shift from accepted civilization and colonies as the term bandit. Bandits represent the outlawed, the reckless humans who shun the common or moral good and exist solely to antagonize the player. They represent a world with a schism, where there is a reason to turn against civilization. They are taboo and they hold values that reflect the sort of values already inherent in worldbuilding: in *The Outer Worlds*, the outlaws represent humans who have rejected the ethos of colonies founded by corporations on capitalist principles. In *Borderlands*, the bandits are humans who have embraced the incoherent violence of their sci-fi wild west world. And just as bandits are a narratively skinned low-level fodder for gameplay and worldbuilding, there are other types of human enemies that through their narrative identity can indicate rules and elements of your worldbuilding.

For example, let's look at *Skyrim*. *Skyrim* has bandits (they're a staple), but they also have the Afflicted, the Forsworn, Warlocks (and so forth). *Skyrim* features a host of human enemies who represent factions and ideological values inherent to the world. For our purposes, let's take a quick look at the Forsworn, a faction of humans devoted to a heretical faith. Their position as enemies, but also their belief system, bear a mark of difference. They are outcasts, but because of their unique faith they also provide the opportunity to drop a unique armor set (Armor of the Old Gods). The Forsworn provide a specific texture to the world: they represent a shift in values, a schism in religious ideology, and this is also represented in their gameplay. They're not just bandits, the villainous version of ordinary NPCs, but they are stand-ins for other aspects of the world, such as religious heresy and what being a heretic even means in this world.

ART

As mentioned with narrative and level design, art is one of those disciplines where its role in worldbuilding is obvious and immediately felt by players. Art determines the look and feel of the world, as well as those who inhabit the world, largely creating the atmosphere and the way the worldbuilding's themes and tones become realized to the player. When I talk about art here, I'm once again being fairly broad on purpose, but art for a video game includes roles such as character/creature artist, environment/level artist, UI artist, animator, as well as more specific specializations, such as foliage artist. All of these roles are involved in the visual construction of the world and work in tandem with narrative and gameplay to establish the tone and atmosphere of the world.

To focus on the discussion of how art creates the look and feel of a world, let's examine the following components of art in video games. Like with the other disciplines prior to it, this is general and not exhaustive but provides an important foundation and framework for discussing art and worldbuilding:

- Environment art
- Character art
- Creature art
- Animation
- Palettes

Special note: UI will follow as an entirely separate section.

Environment Art

Environment art is the literal visualization of the world. While this can range from wholesale world construction, such as with the moons like Europa in *Destiny 2* to specific instances of places, like the cities/towns like Megaton in *Fallout 3* (Bethesda Game Studios, 2008), environment art literally creates the fictional world and the places in the world. Environments are composed of so many details that are directly informed by (and in turn, directly inform) the worldbuilding. This includes the look and distribution of buildings, the flora and fauna, the distinctive geographical elements of the world and how these in turn influence what life exists there and what existence is like. Games like *The Legend of Zelda: Breath of the Wild*, *Skyrim*, *Mass Effect*, and so forth are creating whole new worlds and use distinctive geographic features, and placement of creatures and civilizations, within these ecological frameworks, to build a coherent, visual identity to the world.

Sable (Shedworks Game, 2021) is a stylistic and beautiful open-world exploration game, where players guide the titular character through a coming-of-age ritual that takes her outside of her home community and across the game's desert world. *Sable*'s world is open, it is expansive, and it is a sandbox for self-discovery, and so the environment is this lush, open world that clearly highlights landmarks on the horizon as guiding stars for Sable's journey. There are low and expansive desert fields and dunes, contrasted starkly against the quiet darkness of the petrified forest, which again is contrasted against the gigantic ribcages and bones of long-dead creatures, as tall and wide as many of the abandoned spaceships that also dot the land known as Midden. It is a flourishing and beautiful world built on top of ruins, complete with distinctive landmarks, floating hot air balloons signaling cartographers, and camps settled everywhere among the reclaimed ruins.

The world of *Sable* is composed of so many distinct cities and vistas because it's a game explicitly about exploring the world in order to understand how one fits into it. *Sable* features a rich history, full of characters with traditions and routines that are reflective of the world they exist in. How different people understand and work with their environment is a large part of the self-discovery of the game. Roles in the world of *Sable* are dictated by the type of mask worn. For example, cartographers boast the Cartographer Mask, and Sable can earn badges toward one of these masks by performing quests or tasks for people. To obtain the Climber Mask, Sable has to complete quests that has her climbing to unfathomable heights. To get the Beetle Mask, Sable has to access isolated pockets with specific berries to catch beetles. To get the Machinist Mask, Sable has to perform a variety of tasks, one including harvesting lightning crystals from the Crystal Plateau. To find herself and what role she wants to fulfill for her community and world, Sable has to traverse starkly different environments and interact with them in highly specific ways.

It's a deeply stylized, cell-shaded desert world, one that was born of the game's aesthetic vision, as well as technical constraints. *Sable*'s creative director Gregorios Kythreotis explains the balance between realizing a world's literal setting with the technical constraints that come with video games: "One of the key reasons the game is set in a desert is because we knew we couldn't make a really detailed open world at this scale".[22] The literal choice of what type of world to inhabit for *Sable* was a decision fundamentally driven by the technical opportunities and challenges of visually depicting certain types of spaces in a video game, at a specific technical and budgetary level.

But even beyond just visualizing the geographic and spatial layout of a world, environment art is also establishing a societal texture to the world, as well. Elements of environment art also include aspects like prop placement—where certain props get placed indicate the way in which characters and creatures interact with the world, where they build, and how they exist in these spaces. Architecture—not just of full cities, but individual buildings–indicates time period, as well as materials, resources, needs of housing, what is valued in how well taken care of different buildings are, class structure, and so forth. And graphic design, including elements such as advertisements, posters, graffiti, all indicate the sociological response to different systems in the world.

All of these elements, from geographical distinctions to how civilization is carved out in the world to the details and minutiae of the places, are all highlighting values and tensions within your world. What areas are well tended to versus not can indicate class divides, as well as political systems of powers (such as in *Dishonored*'s contrast between the rot of the street and the luxury of the mansions). But also lighting and other elements can indicate the level of friendliness or hostility in an environment (Night School Studio's *Afterparty* used a combination of dark spaces and neon lighting to indicate the unique textures of their version of hell, namely how hell is a combination of classical hell and a night club).[23]

To take a deeper look into this, let's dive into *Control* again. *Control*'s environment is distinctive and flavorful, with every detail stitching together the ominous and surreal atmosphere of the world of the Federal Bureau of Control, as well as the Old House. *Control* is a world with modern tech but it is purposefully retro in what the players interact with. This combination of Bakelite objects and brutalist architecture is extremely reminiscent of 1950s FBI buildings and Cold War paranoia, which is then contrasted against the oily basalt-like columns of the Old House, a place of power and violence. The way the environment reacts and changes is also a crucial part of the worldbuilding. Jesse Faden, as the newly appointed director, has the ability to reclaim control points, and in doing so, the Bureau responds and re-molds itself accordingly. The Bureau is not a static setting—it is responsive to Jesse and this is part of the mystery of the world that players as Jesse untangle in the game.

The lighting in *Control* is also surfacing specific aspects of the worldbuilding: the grainy, overexposed lighting of the Bureau is heavily contrasted with the red of the Hiss and the invading enemies, creating a clear contrast between the two aspects, but also letting them sit neatly on top of each other. The red lighting works so well because the Bureau is heavily overexposed and gray. They are contrasts, but they aren't at odds. Even the most surreal parts of *Control* feel logically connected, because the sterile brutalist architecture forms the foundation connecting the weirder and stranger places of the world. Related to this, the prop placement in *Control*, while a subtle element, is also incredibly detailed and specific. When investigating a lab overrun with mold, players descend hallways changed with mold and bacteria. Walls and floors are covered in the mold, distorting the actual architecture. As players descend, floor lamps are scattered throughout tight hallways, tipped over and shining small bursts of lights, mundane office furniture that is reminiscent of miner's lamps. These moldy hallways are lit with whatever was available, remarking on a resourcefulness of the Bureau employees, as well as a banality of these strange events.

CORPSES IN CAVES: ENVIRONMENTAL STORYTELLING

Environmental storytelling is perhaps one of the best-known features of video game worldbuilding. Composed of level design and level art (primarily), environmental storytelling is the act of creating mini-vignettes or static scenarios in a game that tells a contained story or implies a story. Corpses with a particular set of objects around it can tell the story of how that character died. Blood smears can lead to hidden rooms. Corpses are a great tool for suggesting events and providing minute texture to the worldbuilding, adding detail and history into the places they are found. The poses they form, the objects they are found near, the geographical formations they are found in—these all stitch together specific little vignettes that flesh out the history of the world. *Sea of Thieves* boasts an immense array of different skeleton corpses spread throughout its world, as shipwreck survivors or as pirates left stranded in caves, all creating the important understanding of the dangers of this world, particularly when alone.

But environmental storytelling is more than just corpses, of course. The ways in which props get placed in an environment, the graffiti added to walls, the arrangement of posters—all of these elements can tell mini-vignettes and create moments of a deeply intimate understanding of a space. Props, and how props get laid out, indicate how characters have previously interacted with that particular space. Like the placement of the floor lamps in *Control*, props have the ability to stitch together a specific understanding of normal use of a space, and then what a disruption of this normal use of space looks like.

Character Art

The way a video game realizes the look of its characters can indicate either major or subtle aspects of the worldbuilding. The appearance of the people in a world creates touchpoints for how those people fit into the world. Are they humanoid? Are they realistic? Are they highly stylized? While creating an emotional register for characters (how do they make audiences feel?[24]), they are already creating tonal aspects of the world. Both realistic and stylized presentations of characters create a tone and texture of the world they exist in. But further beyond that, some aspects of character art that are also conveying details of the worldbuilding include things such as how do these characters move, what are their gestures like, how do they dress, how do they adorn themselves, and so forth.

Let's look at Tali'Zorah in *Mass Effect* again. Tali's design is deeply evocative of where she comes from, both geographically and culturally, particularly with the mask that Quarians wear. As a result of the war with the Geth (the AI they created that turned sentient), Quarians fled their home world and recreated their civilization entirely on their fleet of ships (the Flotilla). But because the Quarians have lived in this sterile environment for so long, their immune systems have become compromised, forcing them to wear a protective mask and enviro-suit whenever they are away from the Flotilla. Even beyond Tali's distinctive mask, the look of her armor is meant to be reflective of the Geth. In *The Art of the Mass Effect Universe*, it's explained the Quarian armor was designed to be reflective of the influence the Geth (particularly their armature) had on the Quarians and vice versa.[25]

These details in Tali's character design (her mask and her armor) embody her culture and history, while also distinguishing her from the other companions on board the Normandy throughout the series. This distinguishing detail creates an important texture to the range of species in the world of *Mass Effect*, as well as the different ways in which alien locations, ships, and geography determine how a character looks. Each character's look and design in the series is deeply evocative of their species and everything that comes with how those species clash or co-exist.

For a different lens into the same concept, let's take a look at Mae and the other zoomorphic characters of *Night in the Woods* (Infinite Fall, 2017). *Night in the Woods* is a game about Mae returning to her hometown after dropping out of college, lost and depressed, where she discovers a deeply held secret in the coal-mining town. In a post-mortem on the game, co-creator Scott Benson talks about the game's concept being born partly out of a desire to see characters from where they came from as creators (namely, Western Pennsylvania and the Rust Belt).[26] Because of this impetus, Mae and her group of punk-rock inspired friends are deeply reflective of the ways in which people are shaped by the places they grow up in. In a review on *Destructoid*, Ray Porreca writes of Mae's friends: "Like Mae, they're all quirky and kind of weird: a fellowship of friends tied together by a shared existence in a dead-end town".[27] The visual design of these characters mark them all as outsiders in some sense, which reflects their personalities and also their relationships; they are characters who find comfort in each other at the margins of their small town, but who are also deeply reflective of said small town. It isn't their zoomorphism that makes them stand out—rather, that facet is the one thing uniting them with the small town. Instead it's their fashion, their makeup, their movement through space, that marks them as outsiders here.

This approach of realizing the world through the characters is also expressed in the story-driven game *Don't Wake the Night* (Brujeria @ Werk, 2019). *Don't Wake the Night* is a game about a group of witches who have summoned a spirit and is, at its heart, about community and accountability. Inspired by Guarani culture and spiritualism, players inhabit a spirit who can't talk to the characters, but who can influence the scene around them. Director Santo Aveiro-Ojeda explained the process behind the mask creation for each of the characters in the game and how each character was designed around a specific animal that is common in South America (such as alligators and capybaras).[28] This is represented in the masks each character possesses and highlights both the personality of the characters, but also their connection to the culture the game was inspired by and the storytelling that Aveiro-Ojeda was raised in.

CHARACTER CREATORS: BUILDING A MINI-WORLD FOR YOUR CHARACTER

While character creators are based on the very concept of letting the players insert themselves into the world of the game, character creators can actually be one of the very first aspects that begin stitching together the framework of a world. What elements are included and how these elements can be remixed and tweaked are already indicating important pillars about the world. What types of tattoos are available, anatomical features like horns and wings, skin textures of different creatures like scales or fur— all of these are already beginning to suggest the rules (and limits) of your world, such as creature types, rituals, cultural artifacts, and so forth.

Character creators typically don't just end with the visual appearance of a character, also. They ask players to pick traits or backstories. In *Mass Effect*, players select their character's pre-service history. These options include "Spacer", where both of Shepard's parents served in the military and so they are following in their footsteps; "Earthborn", where Shepard was an orphan on Earth and escaped by enlisting in the military; and finally there's "Colonist", where Shepard was raised on an Earth colony and is the survivor of a raid saved by the military, which they then join. While these pre-service choices really only change a few dialogue lines here and there and determine which backstory-related side mission players get, they create an important texture to the roleplay of that Shepard and their outlook on the world they exist in. Players are defining how their Shepard relates to the world's existing political systems and major historical events.

Fallout 3's character builder is also an excellent example of diegetic character creation. *Fallout 3* starts with the player's character being born and growing up before taking an aptitude test (G.O.A.T, or Generalized Occupational Aptitude Test). The results determine the player's job and three skills that are recommended for them based on that. The answers to questions during the G.O.A.T. are tallied and the results are fed back to the player, and it's wonderfully diegetic and builds out the efficacy of life in Vault 101. It creates a really vivid sense of place. This is a world that has grown accustomed to life in the Vaults and has an infrastructure for designating how each member of the society contributes to making life work in the Vaults. Since *Fallout 3* is a dystopian world, the G.O.A.T. implies the type of order and infrastructure that had to be built and developed to make society work in this new incarnation of our world.

Creature Art

Unlike in the gameplay section where I combined human characters and inhuman creatures under the same "Enemy Types" banner, I want to look at creatures separately when it comes to how art represents creatures and what this indicates about worldbuilding. Just as a creature's design and gameplay abilities can highlight key components of worldbuilding (or gesture toward a possible intentional gap in the worldbuilding), so too can its visual design.

Let's return to *Subnautica*, but this time to its sequel *Subnautica: Below Zero* (Unknown Worlds, 2019) and the Ventgarden. The Ventgarden is a passive, leviathan-class creature that looks like a combination between a bell tower and a jellyfish. Large, thin legs anchor the leviathan to the ground, while the top is a gorgeous, clear bulbous balloon. The Ventgardens are anchored over top of hydrothermal vents so that the hot water can flow straight up into the balloon portion of its body. This balloon portion is the "garden", as it's a nutrient-dense zone (thanks to the hot water from the vents) that gives life to coral and other flora that otherwise wouldn't be able to live in this particular biome. The Ventgarden is this beautiful oasis in a hostile biome, one that requires its specific place in the world to exist. The role of the Ventgard (an oasis in a hostile biome) creates a really nice texture to the world of *Subnautica: Below Zero*. Like the Reefback in the first game, the Ventgarden is a reliable place for certain resources and a passive leviathan, two subtle details in the richness that game provides in terms of how it realizes its underwater ecosystem.

Another example of creature art revealing fundamental aspects about the world is *The Gunk* (Image & Form Games, 2021). In *The Gunk*, players are scavengers who have to make an emergency landing on an unknown planet. In the course of trying to find the necessary materials to fuel their ship, they encounter the gunk, a hostile and corrupting organic material that is covering the entire planet. And from the gunk comes something called "gunk critters", aggressive enemies that are born from the hostile organic mass. The gunk and the gunk critters share a visual identity, the same black and reds and circular shapes are found in both, indicating an obvious relationship between the organic matter and the creatures it spawns. The look of the gunk and the gunk critters is a direct contrast to the natural flora and fauna of the planet. The planet itself, when cleared of the gunk, is lush and verdant, and the native creatures similarly boast vibrant colors, like pinks and blues. The greens and blues of the planet's natural environment is a direct counter to the shadowy reds and blacks of the gunk, creating a visual distinction that easily identifies the gunk as foreign and antagonistic to the environment.

Animation

Animation is an important, yet sometimes subtle tool in conveying certain aspects about how characters and creatures fit into your world. Animation is about creating believable movement—again, not necessarily realistic movement, but believable ones that are coherent and congruent with the world and game's tone. The way people, creatures, and things move creates a coherency regarding certain aspects of what it means to exist in a world. Are movements slow and methodical or fast and frenetic? Are they serious in tone or exaggerated or ridiculous? Are they silly or are they credible? The way something moves is illustrative of the way movement in your world works, and this in turn establishes tone, atmosphere, and potentially even theme.

Mariel Cartwright, lead animator on *Skullgirls* (Lab Zero Games, 2012) gave a talk called "Fluid and Powerful Animation within Frame Restrictions" in 2014, focused specifically on their hand-animated, 2D fighting game. Fighting games as a genre rely heavily on their animations for telegraphing character moves, and consequently, these animations become really robust centers of meaning, for both character and the world. Cartwright emphasizes, while talking about not needing to be confined to poses that are realistically possible for human bone structures, that good animations in fighting games make moves feel powerful,[29] and thus indicate certain rules and systems of your world, such as where power comes from, what types of power exist and are effective, and all these tactical nitty gritty details about how characters harness power in your world.

Mortal Kombat (Midway Games/NetherRealm Studios, 1992–2019) is a fighting game notorious for its extreme violence, particularly in each character's finishing move known as "fatalities". Mortal Kombat's fictional world comprises a multitude of realms, all of which follow the same rule of war: one realm can only conquer another realm by defeating each other's most decorated warriors in a tournament. It's a premise built specifically for competitive-style play, focused on a series of battles between warriors. And because it's a world that is borderline boundless in its creation of realms, the animations available to each character reflect this multitude of how warriors gain and remain powerful.

Cassie Cage, for example, is the daughter of Earth action movie star (Johnny Cage) and special forces soldier (Sonya Blade), and the combination of her quick movements and "selfie" fatalities creates an important distinction about both who Cassie is, but also how Earth's realms warriors behave and the values of Earth in contrast to the other realms. Cassie inhabits her mother's technical training and her father's irreverence, the type of personality that is emblematic of Earth's warriors in the game: they are serious contenders, but also humorous and provide a comedic edge to the darkness of the world. Compare this to D'Vorah, an insect-like warrior whose realm was absorbed in the villainous Outworld realm. D'Vorah's moveset includes all manner of insect-based body horror, in which she uses pincers and stingers against her opponents, but also includes one move where she opens her abdomen to release a swarm of bugs at her opponent. As Cassie strikes a pose for a camera, D'Vorah spits acidic poison on her opponents turning them into spider-like insects before they die, it's very obvious Cassie and D'Vorah are not from the same realm. Make no mistake, Cassie is just as strong as D'Vorah, just as fierce a competitor, and the difference in movesets and their corresponding animations are used to indicate how each character harnesses and wields power in very different ways as a result of where they come from.

In talking about the best practices used in animating *Skullgirls*, Cartwright explains that there are certain animations players might not see, but feel nonetheless.[30] And this a subtle, but important part of how animations contribute to worldbuilding. Even if you don't clock every frame, the details (both minute and bombastic) of how characters and creatures move create a feeling about the world, as well. Players can feel how powerful Cassie or D'Vorah are when playing as them, and players can see how powerful an opponent is based on the way they carry their bodies and move in a space.

But even more subtle aspects of character art, like facial animations, can create important touchpoints for a world. *The Last Stop* (Variable State, 2021) is a story-driven adventure game that follows three distinct characters: John, a doting father; Meena, a high-level intelligence officer with MI6; and Donna, a teenager constantly at odds with her immediate world. It's speculative in the way it weaves supernatural elements into the everyday lives of its three protagonists. And the character art of *The Last Stop* is stylized and particularly effective in letting the characters' faces have large and identifiable reactions to the strange events they encounter. With their character design maximizing reactions, we as an audience are given important indicators about what does and does not belong in this world. While each of the characters in *The Last Stop* are fashioned according to the contemporary settings, it is their facial animations and reactions that make space for the worldbuilding to shine: just based on their facial expressions alone, we can tell when something is an expected matter of course in their world, or totally foreign, a break in the common routine and understanding of how their world operates.

And finally, animations in background art are an effective way of surfacing specific details of worldbuilding. *Guacamelee!* (Drinkbox Studios, 2013), a game about guiding a luchador through the land of the dead, uses subtle animations and colors in the backgrounds, such as rain versus floating motes, to signal when players are in the land of the living or the land of the dead. In order to seamlessly support the fluid movement through the platforming action of *Guacamelee!*, focusing on subtle background changes and animations is a key way of building up what each world is like and how they differ from each other.

Palettes

Palettes are one tool that can be employed to help indicate an expressive tone and atmosphere of a world. These can be monochrome or limited color palettes or they can just be a selection of colors identified for a specific tone, but both approaches can be used to indicate atmosphere and key elements of the game's world.

Monochrome games, or limited palette games, use their color choice in highly specific and intentional ways. *Limbo* (Playdead, 2010), a game about a boy navigating a hostile world, uses its black and white palette to be highly evocative of a dark and oppressive world like in horror films. *Limbo* is a scary world, full of dangers in its shadows, and the black and white palette creates this pervading sense of fear and unease. Conversely, *Genesis Noir* (Feral Cat Den, 2021) also uses a mostly black and white palette but interrupts the monochrome with spots of gold. The black and white color evokes film noir conventions, while the gold offers a disruption to the genre, which is echoed nicely in the world design of *Genesis Noir*, where players inhabit a cosmological being who watched the woman they love get shot. *Genesis Noir* is a noir film as it follows jazz musicians in the 1920s caught amid a love triangle, but it's also about the Big Bang and the history of the entire world. The gold throughout the game is a nice indicator of this disruption of genre, an infusion of cosmological to the hard-boiled black and whites of the noir genre. Both palettes indicate something key about the world, whether it's by invoking a certain genre or indicating mood and tone.

In the story-driven game *A Mortician's Tale* (Laundry Bear Games), creative and art director Gabby DaRienzo spoke often about the soft purple palette that ended up becoming the distinctive visual style of the game. For DaRienzo, the soft purple tones were a deliberate choice to contrast against the otherwise visceral and grisly nature of preparing bodies for burial.[31] And while this was a choice designed to provide a bit of comfort, it also created an atmosphere for the slight worldbuilding we were employing in the game. Yes, *A Mortician's Tale* is about death and bodies and funeral practices, but it's also about the social, cultural, and personal responses we have to death. So rather than leaning into strict realism to prove a point, DaRienzo leaned into a limited color palette to provide quietness and a space for contemplation and introspection.

But of course, limited or monochrome color palettes aren't the only way to create indicators about a world. In a 2013 talk, Joseph Staten (writer and design director) and Chris Barrett (art director) spoke about the pillars they used to develop both the world that *Destiny* would take place in, as well as how that world would be realized visually. One of the ways they went about this process was determining the types of color palettes they could use that would communicate the feel and tone of the world. This included finding colors that blended futuristic elements with colors that look more aged, building up this concept of a mythical sci-fi world with roots in fantasy.[32] While subtle, these elements create a really important personality and distinction to the world.

Color theory is important for conveying aspects of the world, and the creatures and characters contained within, as well. Colors carry emotional weight with them, as well as pre-conceived notions of what different colors indicate. Red is often used for highlighting enemies, green for allies, and white for neutral NPCs. But colors can also indicate important elements of a world. For example, bright, caustic colors can indicate irradiated and dangerous areas, bright red lava indicates danger, whereas cool grays and greens can indicate safe zones in an environment. *Ark: Survival Evolved* (Studio Wildcard, 2015) uses color theory to indicate these sorts of environmental cues but also uses color theory to refer to the ways in which tech interjects into the prehistoric world. Earth tones create the texture of the natural world, the world ruled by dinosaurs and weapons made of natural resources, whereas vibrant and prismatic colors, such as teals, indicate sci-fi technology and a break from the natural world. A switch in palette is an effective way to indicate a shift in environment. In games, light blues and darker palettes are an obvious indicator of night versus day (particularly in games like *Sable* where the ability to see and understand the world is changed significantly in the day or nighttime). DaRienzo explains that the use of color theory for gameplay is also effective worldbuilding. Speaking of *Mirror's Edge* (DICE, 2008), they said:

> the stark contrast between the very clean, white world of *Mirror's Edge* and the bright red doors, rails, interactive objects that the protagonist can use for parkouring helps establish that she is NOT part of this clean world and is actively using its environment to rebel against it.[33]

This use of contrasting palettes indicates both a structure of the world and Faith's response and relationship to that structure.

UI

UI, or user interfaces, determines the way players interact with the game space and the game world directly. While UI is a specialization of video game art, I wanted to focus on it separately since there are so many specific aspects of UI art that contribute to worldbuilding directly and distinctively. UI can either be diegetic or not, but even non-diegetic UI contributes significantly to worldbuilding. Noreen Rana, principal UX Designer at absurd:joy and having worked on UI for games such as *Far Cry 5* and *Guacamelee 2*, explains that,

> The biggest misconception is that 'No UI' is the best UI–the idea that a minimal or fully diegetic UI is better for a game is commonly misconstrued as successful design. If the user does not feel any friction with your UI, then it's successful.[34]

UI is the interface that is the bridge for players to engage in the world of the video game so naturally it is going to be evocative of the worldbuilding.

Some key (but, as always, non-exhaustive) ways UI contributes to worldbuilding includes:

- HUDs

- Menus

- Quest Logs

- Maps

HUDs

HUDs (heads-up displays) are a critical component of most video games. They indicate necessary gameplay elements, like health meters, ammo capacity, enemies, damage, etc. HUDs relay crucial game information to players, and as such are an element of the game that all players interface with and thus provides a natural opportunity for worldbuilding. HUDs become the intersection of where we as players meet the game world. Some HUDs are diegetic, others are not. And as with other components discussed, diegetic HUDs aren't necessarily more evocative of the worlds they inhabit than non-diegetic ones, they just provide different avenues toward worldbuilding.

A Short Hike (adamgryu, 2019) is a game about a bird, Claire, trying to hike to the tallest mountain to get cell reception. To indicate Claire's stamina meter, *A Short Hike* uses feathers. The more feathers players have, the more stamina Claire has. Which makes sense because she's a bird, after all. But we see these feathers neatly lined up at the bottom of the screen, clearly designed for player access and symbolic of Claire's ability to fly, but not a direct 1:1 representation of Claire (non-diegetic). Even still, these feathers are telling players something important about the rules of the world: Claire can only fly provided she has enough feathers. This isn't a world where being a bird gives her untapped ability to fly wherever she wants. Rather, this world contains rules about flight, and Claire (and the player) has to contend with those rules.

Conversely, the ammo counter on *Halo*'s (Bungie/343 Industries, 2001–present) assault rifle appears on the gun itself, accessible to both player and Master Chief. This diegetic ammo counter speaks volumes about what is important in this world: namely, fighting against the Covenant in an attempt to save everyone. The ammo counter is presented to players where they are naturally looking (at their weapons and the enemies in front of them), reinforcing the importance of fighting and war in this world. Halo is the type of world where the difference between an abundance of ammo and no ammo means something for survival, so it is presented in a place of importance to reflect that.

Both *A Short Hike*'s feathers and *Halo*'s ammo counter add flavor and texture to the world, supporting tone and atmosphere. We understand the world a bit more innately because of the way both of these examples surface key information to us. What matters for Claire is her ability to climb, and what matters for Master Chief is his ability to be an unstoppable force against the Covenant.

Menus

Starting with *Dead Space* (Visceral Games, 2008) and *Fallout 3* as two games that really popularized a certain standard of diegetic menu and UI, the concept of finding clever ways of integrating a game's menu into the game's world has become more common. *Dead Space* placed the menu in-game as if the playable character, Isaac, was looking at it himself (this diegetic menu is also supported in-game by Isaac's health meter being indicated as a series of lights on the back of his suit). And *Fallout*'s menu is contained in the PIP boy, a device worn on the playable character's forearm. Both of these are incredible moments of establishing the character firmly in the world and reflecting what's important from the world back onto the characters.

But even when menus are not designed diegetically, there are still a lot of subtle ways the design of a menu can imply details about worldbuilding. *Tunic* (Lifeformed, 2022) features a menu that was both fourth-wall breaking and highly evocative of the worldbuilding. *Tunic*'s menu takes the shape of an old video game manual that is written in an initially incomprehensible in-game language. It features diagrams, maps, pictures of enemies, tips for beating them, and how to use weapons—everything players would expect to locate in an old NES game manual.

And while it's wonderfully fourth-wall breaking, it also speaks volumes about the type of world *Tunic* is. *Tunic*'s menu is referencing a history of video games and an inspirational legacy for the development of the game, and it is wonderfully evocative of the type of world *Tunic* is. *Tunic* is a love letter to Zelda games, but one that stands on its own two feet and introduces a lush fantasy world. The language of the manual also unfolds as players explore the game world more and learn more about the land, implying a 1:1 connection between the protagonist and the player: they're both exploring this world together, learning together, even if the wrapper that contains it walks the line between being earnest and self-referential.

"UI GAMES" AND WORLDS TOLD IN INTERFACES

There are certain games that are colloquially referred to as "UI games"– that is, a game where the majority of the experience and gameplay is centralized in the game's UI. These types of games can take a variety of shapes and forms, like desktop games such as *Hypnospace Outlaw* (Tendershoot, 2019), where players navigate an alternate reality 1999 GeoCities inspired web, or *A Normal Lost Phone* (Accidental Queens, 2017), where players riffle through a lost cell phone's interface. These games are highly evocative of the worlds they exist in because they transport players directly into a diegetic UI that constitutes the entirety of the world.

But then there are games that create alien interfaces and have their players interact entirely with the world through these interfaces. One really evocative game in this style is *In Other Waters* (Jump Over The Age, 2020), where players inhabit an AI helping a xenobiologist categorize and explore an alien planet. Noreen Rana explains why *In Other Waters* is so effective in using the UI as the main mode of play:

> The world builds around you as you help your biologist friend explore new terrain, discover new organisms and piece together the story's mystery. It's imperative the UI and UX succeed in harmony together to ensure you're spending more time being engrossed in deep diving (hah) into the details of new species and terrain and not fighting a clunky set of controls.[35]

In Other Waters works so well because players are controlling the AI, so it makes sense that the main way they'd engage with the xenobiologist is through the interface of systems. Playing as an AI, players do not have a corporeal form to navigate the world through, so instead the understanding of the world is presented through the lens of interfaces that are congruent with being an AI. Players can set course directions, analyze samples, and draw narrative conclusions based on collected evidence and analyzed geographical features. The mechanics and verbs are entirely UI-based, which is a direct 1:1 with what this world is about.

In Other Waters is a gorgeous game that also uses palette choices deliberately and intentionally to create a differing sense of space as players explore deeper and further. A change in the UI palette color indicates a change in biome, creating a visual distinction that an AI might not otherwise have. As discussed in the art section, palettes are a commonly accepted way of indicating new and distinct environments, and the same is true of *In Other Waters*, even if those biomes are only ever reflected in the UI.

Quest Logs

Quest logs house all the information players need about their in-progress (and completed) missions, quests, and challenges. Quest logs most commonly live in menus, and while they are often written in the language of the game's world, they aren't always diegetic. But just like menus and HUDs, quest logs provide an opportunity to indicate worldbuilding to a variety of degrees based on each game's need.

To talk about quest logs, I want to talk about *Grindstone*. When we introduced a second challenge type into *Grindstone*, we also took the opportunity to redesign the way in which we were presenting the challenges and the quest log. While *Grindstone* doesn't feature quests or missions in the traditional sense, we wanted to make sure that players could still access their challenges as if they were missions. And when we introduced a secondary NPC to give out these challenges, having the presentation of the challenges look distinct and reflect the characters associated with each challenge type became even more important.

So the existing challenges were given by the Howling Wolf Inn's bartender, Lagr, whereas the new challenges were being given by Döttie and Harry, the playable character's wife and son. For the Döttie and Harry challenges, we knew we wanted them to look fun and silly, like something a toddler made for his parents. So they're ripped off pieces of paper, adorned with stickers, and scribbles meant to mimic children's writing. This caused us to then rethink how we were presenting the challenges from Lagr. Since she is the bartender of the game, we thought it'd be fun and diegetic to have the challenges appear as if they were written on the back of Howling Wolf Inn coasters. This way, when players access the quest log in the game, it's clear which NPC the player needs to return to in order to complete finished challenges.

For us, the visual presentation of the quest log was a good opportunity to showcase small aspects of this world, one specifically focused on the small-town nature of *Grindstone*. Other games do this excellently, as well. In *Bugsnax*, players play as a reporter invited to the island by the explorer Elizabert Megafig (and who turns out to be missing when they arrive). And since players are a reporter, the quest log (in fact, the entire menu) is housed inside of a notebook. Quests are housed inside this diegetic notebook, featured as to-dos and notes to self. Notebooks-as-menus are a common way of presenting menus for worlds where this makes sense, and it fits seamlessly and effortlessly into both story and gameplay.

But of course, the lack of a quest log can also be a significant choice for worldbuilding. *Elden Ring* does not feature map markers or a quest log, creating an experience where players are encouraged to explore and uncover important elements from the world at their own pace. The lack of a quest log here forces players into a role of needing to remember the NPCs and locations and quests that are appealing to them and creates a play experience based around a personal and intimate understanding of the world. It creates a really purposeful element of the game's world, based on exploration, hostility, and knowledge of the place.

Maps

Maps are, along with fictional languages, probably one of the first elements most people think of when they think of worldbuilding. And for good reason—when we create fictional worlds, there's a high chance we're also building at least a crude map alongside it. Maps are beautiful artifacts of a world, a lush and visual way to see the world we've created. So it's no surprise then that maps (both full maps and mini-maps) are an important tool in worldbuilding for video games. And as with everything in this section, maps don't have to be diegetic to be supportive of worldbuilding! Non-diegetic maps are able to contribute to tone, atmosphere, and a sense of place just as much as diegetic ones, they just do so differently.

So first let's take a look at diegetic maps by talking about *Firewatch* (Campo Santo, 2016). In *Firewatch* players inhabit Henry, a man who has recently started working as a park ranger at a national park. The map players are given is an object that Henry holds in the game—you see his hand holding the area map, one that is designed and recreated to look exactly like national park maps. Granted, *Firewatch* is a realistic game set in our world, but that feeling of place and understanding where we are is affected by the UI choices made in the game. *Firewatch*'s area map is an actual map that players pull out, complete with Henry's hands visible as he holds the map up against the backdrop of the national park the game takes place in. Alongside the map, in Henry's other hand, is a compass, providing a believable and necessary detail to navigating the otherwise overwhelming national park. It's details like this that work together to quietly evoke both how this place feels and how the rules work in this place: we know national parks are huge and that safe navigation in them requires the pairing of both a map you can read and a compass that can direct you, and *Firewatch* includes this effortlessly.

CARTO'S MAPS AS GAMEPLAY

Carto (Sunhead Games, 2020) is a game about the titular character trying to find her grandmother in a charming world. A top-down game, *Carto*'s main form of navigation is finding and connecting pieces of maps to extend the play area. Finding a new piece of map and connecting that to the existing map opens up the world for Carto, introducing new NPCs, quest items, more map pieces, and even holds the solutions to map-based puzzles. It's a wonderful game that uses cartography as its core mechanic. Map pieces only fit together at certain edges (water edges must connect to water edges, forests to forests, etc.), so these map-based puzzles provide the fodder for a lot of fun and detailed spatial puzzles about finding your way in a large, unfamiliar world. It reinforces both Carto's determination and her navigating a new and familiar world.

What I find really charming about *Carto* is the way the worldbuilding is designed to continually reflect itself. This is a world where people can get lost, houses can go missing, and danger can strike, but the way through it is forward and through building a deeper understanding of the land and the world and all the possibilities that exist therewithin. It's a really wonderful form of using cartography and maps as the main mechanic for both puzzles and progression. As Carto unravels the larger world around her, so too do we as players understand the full boundaries of this world.

For non-diegetic maps that are still effective worldbuilding tools, let's talk about *Skyrim*'s map. It's beautifully constructed, and it exists in the style and the flavor of the world, but it is not necessarily an in-world object. Players access it through a menu, and there is no indication that the player character is simultaneously accessing the map at the same time. But through its visual design and gameplay elements, it's able to communicate important aesthetic and tonal details of the world. It can be argued that this does heighten immersion because it is not at odds with the aesthetics of the game world, even though it's not a map that your playable character literally holds like the map in *Firewatch*.

Similar to *Skyrim* is *Elden Ring*. *Elden Ring*'s map is a gorgeously detailed map meant to look like old cartography paper. And while *Elden Ring*'s map isn't diegetic and it is aesthetically evoking the world around it, it's also deceptive. The initial focus and zoom of the map is tight, showing an area that's not necessarily gigantic, but detailed and enticing. Then as players progress through the game, the ability to zoom out illustrates that the map is actually exponentially larger and more robust than it initially seemed. *Elden Ring* is huge. It's a massive, sprawling world, the depths of which are actually initially withheld from the player (not with just a UI fog, but with clever use of map zooms and focus). *Elden Ring*'s map isn't just aesthetic flavor, it indicates a mythic world, one of epic proportions, where it's easy to believe that monsters lurk and heroic battles await. But it also creates a moment of awe (or terror or frustration) when the full scope of the map is revealed, a sense of the sublime that is reflected in the world's history and details.

CREATING MAPS

Map creation goes hand-in-hand with worldbuilding. A quick search about how to get started worldbuilding will often yield plenty of results for crafting your world's unique map. And that's because maps are important visualizations of your world. Depending on the depth of your world, maps can contain an incredible wealth of information about the world: the geography, yes, but also how cities make use of the geography, how country/state lines get implemented, what the superstitions of the time are ("here be dragons"), and so forth. Maps can chart a world, as well as how people respond to and exist in a world. Maps aren't just a reflection of a physical world—they highlight relationships between various aspects of that world, socially and politically.

Since this is a book about how game writers and narrative designers can better collaborate with other disciplines in worldbuilding, I'll keep this section short and focused not on how to visually construct a map, but rather how design can support the map-creation process. Remember that maps are illustrative of your world from a geographical perspective, but can also be full of sociological information about the world, as well. From a design and story perspective, it can be useful to consider who made the map, why, what their relationship is to the place being mapped, and so forth. Like any other diegetic worldbuilding ephemera or documentation, maps are not neutral. They are subjective representations of how the world is understood by whoever is creating the map, so having answers to these questions creates more believable maps that reflect a world full of history and tensions, worlds that are full of texture.

PROGRAMMING

Programmers and engineers (along with designers) determine how everything in the game world actually works, how things feel, what actions are available to players, and how certain technical constraints can create opportunities for signature worldbuilding moments. Programming brings worlds (and everything in worlds) to life, which in turn also has a huge effect on how elements of the game's world feels. Programming can also provide creative solutions to technical obstacles that in turn have a direct effect on what the world looks like, plays like, or feels like.

A few components of practical worldbuilding that programmers directly contribute to that dictates important elements of how a game's worldbuilding works are:

- Boundaries

- AI behaviors

- World simulation

- Physics

Boundaries

Game worlds, no matter how expansive and open, cannot simply stretch on forever and ever. So the concept of boundaries refers to the ways in which programmers create walls (either diegetic or not)[36] around the game world. These boundaries contain the gameplay space and can either be seamlessly integrated into the world, or not. But if they are diegetic, there are lots of ways boundaries can reinforce worldbuilding or introduce a new aspect of it.

Some games use literal walls or fences to keep players within the game's boundaries. Like many other games, *Ark: Survival Evolved* uses a literal holographic wall that players can bump up against. This holographic wall at first is incredibly jarring (especially because it's invisible until players are right up against it). But as the world unfolds around the players and they learn more about the setting and the history of the island they are on, the holographic wall becomes a coherent aspect of the game's worldbuilding. In fact, this holographic wall is often one of the very few clues and evidence toward the game's larger setting and the mysteries within it.

But, of course, literal walls are not the only way to create boundaries that are coherent with the worldbuilding. Other games use the world's geographical features to contain the world within its technical boundaries, such as mountains or untraversable water. *Legend of Zelda: Breath of the Wild* (Nintendo, 2017) makes use of its varied biomes and geographic features as boundaries. Gameplay space is contained within the traversal environment, with mountains often acting as de facto walls. Other games prevent the player from leaving a gameplay area, usually with a character dialogue indicating some in-world reason for why the character doesn't want to go that way. While this is a forced boundary, the narrative reasoning for it can sometimes provide a small hint at world details. The *Assassin's Creed* (Ubisoft, 2007–present) games make use of the fact that players are inhabiting historic assassins' memories by presenting a "Desynchronization Warning" whenever players veer out of bounds. This warning is deeply diegetic, despite just being a text warning accompanied with visual distortions, because it references the technology being used to place the protagonists into the body of their ancestral assassins.

Each game has its own flavor for this, and each version of it contributes something particular to that game's world. How you create a boundary creates a tangible texture to the world that can be a locus of meaning. For example, *Subnautica* uses a diegetic game boundary that is deeply evocative of the world of the game. In a post-mortem talk about the game at GDC, Unknown World's Jonas Boetel talks about how despite being an underwater open-world game, they couldn't just build an infinite body of water (they needed to put some reigns on player exploration), but they still wanted the feeling of complete openness. So they used the game's worldbuilding, and clever programming, as a solution. The further players swim outward (horizontally, because in *Subnautica* vertical exploration is just as important when it comes to mapping the entire game world), the darker the water gets and the more dangerous it becomes. This area is referred to as the Crater Edge. Rather than putting up an artificial wall or simply warning players they were going out of bounds, *Subnautica* opted to use its terrifying sea creatures as a fence.[37]

The further you swim out in the Crater Edge, it becomes darker, more barren, and filled with ghost leviathans that gate player's exploration by eating them whole. And while players contend with ghost leviathans in other areas of the game, Crater Edge ghost leviathans are slightly different: they continually respawn, ensuring players cannot progress beyond Crater Edge. This solution to a technical problem ended up creating a wonderful layer of worldbuilding: don't go to Crater Edge, not because there's a wall there and nothing more players can do but because ghost leviathans will literally eat you. It's a perfect "here be dragons" moment that adds a wonderful texture to the world of *Subnautica*.

AI Behaviors

We discussed the ways in which the design of enemies and creatures can highlight specific aspects of the worldbuilding already. And the same is true of how the AI for those enemies is created. Video game AI is a robust field that is focused on creating NPCs, enemies, and creatures that behave believably and purposefully, to varying levels of complexity and fidelity. The ways AI-driven NPCs or creatures move about in their respective worlds are illustrative of some of the rules and internal logic patterns of those worlds. AI need not be robust to be effective at worldbuilding. It just needs to be purposeful.

AI behaviors contribute to a sense of place by making it feel alive. The way the NPCs and creatures move around imply certain rules of the world, such as movement and biology, and can contribute to the tone and atmosphere of a world. They make it feel a certain way and that feeling is a direct link to certain aspects of worldbuilding. Is this a crowded world? Is this an erratic, whimsical world? Or is it a somber, slower world? Is this a world where everybody flies or is it an ocean world? AI can (and should) reflect all of these elements, dictating how this world operates.

Let's talk about *Alien: Isolation* (Creative Assembly, 2014). The alien's AI in *Alien: Isolation* is contributing heavily to the survival horror worldbuilding of the game (and is a hallmark feature of what makes the game so good). Built in the *Alien* universe and following Ripley's daughter, *Alien: Isolation* is a world full of terror, tension, and yes, isolation. To really heighten the sense of being hunted and of trying to survive, Creative Assembly built the alien AI to be dynamic, rather than scripted. And "dynamic" here means that the alien's AI doesn't follow a prescribed or authored path in terms of where it will be and what it will do. Instead, the alien's AI is responsive and reactive to what the player does. It follows, it can create traps, and it changes where players find it. Notably, dying to the alien in one spot in the game doesn't guarantee that the alien will then be there when players revisit that same spot, making finding solutions for surviving a real think-on-your-toes moment versus the standard experience of memorizing the enemy's patterns and movements to get past it. It's an intelligent AI system that is directly contributing to the terror in the worldbuilding: the alien is intelligent and this world is hostile, no matter how contained of a space it is.

In an interview *PC Games N*, lead designer Gary Napper and lead artist Jude Bond spoke about the interplay between realizing this sort of claustrophobic world and the alien AI. Bond explains that

> We needed that sense of unknown things to deliver horror that was actually horrific. You need to be able to go 'what's in those shadows around the corner? I don't know' – and you're right, you don't know, we're not going to tell you and you're going to have to go and find out.[38]

The alien's AI represents the exact aspects of the worldbuilding that are so important to the game's tone: there are dangers in space that we do not know how to contend with, and they could be anywhere.

But of course, a dynamic and hostile AI isn't the only way to realize aspects of a game's worldbuilding via creatures. The vibrancy and the feel of the world of *Bugsnax* is brought to life by the sheer variety and distinctions of the different AI behaviors. Each bugsnax behaves differently, reacting to both the environment and player according to a set of internal logic. These AI behaviors are designated into "attributes" for each bugsnax, which is viewable by the player in the menu. Some attributes for bugsnax include: "aggressive" (they will attack the player and the snack trap, so therefore they usually require being stunned before they can be captured); "burrowing" (they will dig and hide underground from the player); "spicy" (they will set the player and other flammable objects on fire); and so forth. There are also "breakable" bugsnax that break into a handful of smaller bugsnax, like the Scoopy Banoopy that breaks into a Scoopy, a

Cheery, and a Banopper, all of which have their own distinct attribute set. And even beyond just their attributes, the bugsnax follow different paths in their environments, ones that players can learn and intercept in order to catch the bugsnax—or to use the bugsnax against each other. This path memorization is a hallmark of stealth mechanics in games, one that works to create a believable movement pattern of enemies and creatures.

In *Bugsnax*, each of these attributes (and there are many more than I've mentioned) can be mixed together to create a large variety of ways in which the bugsnax AI react and behave, creating a place that feels alive with believable snackable bugs. The bugsnax all feel distinct, and ones that are related (like the red and yellow Peelbugs, which are just slices of lemons and limes linked up to create a worm-like creature) feel related and believable because of both their visual design and also that their AI behaves the same way, with some minor differences. The bugsnax are the point of the world of the game—they are the defining feature—so having the variety of AI behaviors helps create a world that feels believable and full of very different bugs that are also snacks.

World Simulation

World simulation (things like lighting and weather systems) create a concrete sense of place via building a world that moves and breathes all on its own. World simulation includes the various ways in which programmers build out believability or a sense of place into a setting. This includes elements like lighting tools, weather simulation, day/night cycles, and even breakable objects. The ways in which all of these elements function within a game space is very directly (like environment art and level design) creating the world, but they are also creating the way a world feels to inhabit.

Sea of Thieves boasts a really robust and interactive weather system, as well as a day/night cycle. The game world is very full and very dynamic. There are fog banks that creep across the map, obscuring player ships and islands alike. There is a hurricane that roams, threatening to sink ships with its torrential rain and vicious waves. And each interweaves with gameplay in specific and compelling ways. Fog can be great cover to lose pursuing pirates in. There is a certain rare fish that can only be caught at a shipwreck during a hurricane. Deliveries need to be made on time. The world reacts to the weather and the time of day believably.

But even beyond that, there's the way in which players can begin to read the game's sky. There are certain world events that can happen in the game (for example, a skeleton fort that is currently active for all players to raid, or a Kraken that can strike sailing ships). These major world events are signaled by a large cloud formation, such as a skeleton's skull-shaped cloud or a galleon-shaped cloud. But only one of these major world events can be active on the server at a single time. So what this means is seeing a cloud world event in the sky indicates that the waters are clear of a Kraken. But the second that cloud formation goes down, the threat of a Kraken emerges. Knowing how to read the world events creates this really cool and concrete setting where players know how to respond to the world's various set pieces and activities based on exposure and experience.

This type of dynamic world simulation means that the world of *Sea of Thieves* not only feels alive but is also following its own internal logic. There are rules to how the world operates (when Krakens appear, when certain fish show up) and the simulation of the world surfaces these details.

SHADERS: WHERE ART AND PROGRAMMING MEET

Shaders are tools artists and programmers (depending on your studio) can use to, essentially, render different pixels from what already exists. Shaders can be used to create shadows, lighting, different palette treatments, and so much more. They are an incredibly useful tool for creating in-engine effects, like weather systems and day/night cycles (as well as a host of other applications). A critical part of the fantasy of *Sea of Thieves*, and supporting this pirate fantasy with a believable and reactive world, is the water. The game largely focuses on sailing ships, and the way in which the water behaves and looks is no small part of creating the specifics of that world. In a chat on the Rare YouTube channel, Andy Dennison (Software Director) and Mark Lucas (Senior Software Engineer) discuss the rendering and shader work that went into creating the believable and reactive water of the game. Dennison and Lucas talk about the way light hitting the water was an important part of creating this experience, that the way the water reflected the morning sun or the night moon, created a really believable and distinctive feel to the water.[39] Believable water signals a distinction between different areas of the world (the water in The Wilds is very different from the water in the Shores of Plenty), providing tangible touchpoints to the variety of landscapes in a mostly water-based game.

In a talk titled "Shading the World of Anthem", technical artist Ben Cloward talks about the shaders they created for *Anthem* (BioWare, 2019). *Anthem* features this lush alien world with impressively realized and distinct environments. There are swamps, alien structures, cave systems, forests, and so forth. These diverse environments are then also compounded by day/night cycles and dynamic weather systems. But shaders in Anthem are also creating specific details of the game's world. Cloward mentions a specific shader to create a bioluminescent bacterium that can only be seen at nighttime,[40] which creates a highly specific sense of place and rules for the flora and fauna of this world. Shaders are able to create important in-engine distinctions for the feel and look of a digital world by providing the means to explore difference and distinction in various settings.

Physics

Physics in a game is just like physics in the real world: it's the rules that determine how material objects exist and interact. And it can be used in both extremely hilarious ways, like in *Octodad: Deadliest Catch* (Young Horses, 2014), a game about walking around as an octopus in a suit and tie, or in extremely impressive ways, like in *Kerbal Space Program* (Squad/ Blitworks, 2011) that is about launching rockets into space and then learning about the laws of motion in outer space. The way physics works in games absolutely influences worldbuilding: it can add an element of goofiness, of terror, of realism, all of which create an important and undeniable texture and tone of your game.

PHYSICS GAMES AND STRANGE WORLDS

Physics games are games where their main gameplay and identity are derived from physics-based play. And because of this hook, they tend to be lighter and more humorous in their worldbuilding (although, obviously, physics games are not exclusively comedic). But the use of extreme physics to generate playful mechanics means that the physics become a sort of story engine for their world by focusing on play, story, and worldbuilding as supportive of the physics-based play.

For example, there's *What the Golf?* (Triband, 2019). *What the Golf?* is a weird physics-based golf game, where the ball and putter are not always just a ball and a putter. In one level, the player could be hitting office chairs or a moving truck or even donuts. The physics of the game contributes heavily to the absurd worldbuilding by quickly onboarding players to the concept that in this world even couches are golf balls. The variety of different types of clubs and golf balls available creates the texture of this world. It's weird and the only boundaries of it are … well, there aren't any boundaries, and that's sort of the point.

Outer Wilds is a good example for how physics can be used as a way to make various aspects of a world (i.e., different planets) feel distinctive from each other, as well as driving unique gameplay for that area. The game's planets and moons each have their own physics (and, of course, the ship also is a physics object). Every planet in the game is a simulated physics object[41], and so every planet behaves in a slightly different way to each other. They can interact with each other, with a moon (Attlerock) exerting gravity on its planet (Timber Hearth). They can break in specific ways. And they can change what it means to traverse that space—especially when it comes to landing a physics-based spaceship on a planet.

In an interview for *Rock, Paper, Shotgun*, creative director Alex Beachum and producer Loan Verneau talk about the way in which the planet Brittle Hollow is constructed. Brittle Hollow is a planet that is literally falling apart, hemorrhaging pieces of itself as it rotates with its volcanic moon. Because the moon has its own orbit and spin, it is launching meteors at different times and different speeds toward Brittle Hollow—meaning that Brittle Hollow never breaks in quite the same way each time[42]. This procedural, physics-based destruction of the planet creates a really believable feel to exploring Brittle Hollow. Learning paths through the planet means it can be harder to learn the way based on how the planet crumbles. Like Attlerock exerting its own gravity on Timber Hearth, the procedural way Brittle Hollow breaks creates a really cool and believable aspect of the world and one that feeds directly into the exploration-based gameplay. *Outer Wilds* is about exploring and connecting clues in the environment together, so having the environment behave in specific ways is an important element of the worldbuilding for the game. Each planet feels real and alive.

Outer Wilds has each planet and moon operating according to an individually internally consistent logic that is also available to the player to explore at their directive, at any point within the repeating time loop. It's a technical marvel, one that is so crucial to the magnificent worldbuilding the game offers. *Outer Wilds* doesn't just say it's this incredibly detailed, natural world where a mystery happened; it shows it in every way it can, through character, through level design, and through its meticulously detailed and planned physics.

AUDIO

Audio design (a discipline including roles such as sound designers, foley designers, and voice designers) determines how the world and the people in it sound, both which have a direct impact on tone, atmosphere, and general mood of your world. Audio is so incredibly important for the feel and realization of a world. Most memorable landscapes, cities, and places have a soundscape innately associated with them, be it natural sounds such as water rushing or the chirp of wildlife or human-made sounds like cars honking, crowd chatter, and so forth. Places are full of sounds, and which ones get included and omitted creates the soundscape of a place, providing an insight into details of your world (such as creatures, human infrastructure, geography, and so forth). Sounds, whether we are fully keyed into them or not, are a huge part of how we understand where we are. Sounds can indicate elements of the city, the geography, the people, the technology, and so forth. Just like how different palettes can indicate a shift in biome or day/night cycle, so too can the soundscape. Distinct places contain familiar sounds that build a memorable understanding of a space.

Em Halberstadt gave a GDC talk about how the sound design told the story of *Night in the Woods*. At the start of the talk, Halberstadt states that "[*Night in the Woods*] is a story about a place and a time"[43] and that the soundscape was created to firmly root players in the setting. Halberstadt goes on to explain that this was done via making the setting feel "alive", with things like awkward silences, overlapping dialogue that all contribute to a sort of chaos. The ways in which characters speak to each other (and the sound associated with this communication) helps create the world of *Night in the Woods*, one built for its zoomorphic characters primarily. The world of *Night in the Woods* is very much alive, and the soundscape of the game contributes heavily to that feeling: it feels like a small town filled with people just living their lives. What the world of *Night in the Woods* sounds like matters just as much as what the players do or say because that game is so very much about its setting (as noted in the earlier mention of *Night in the Woods*, the game is driven as much by how characters exist in small towns as much as it is about the mysterious plot).

In addition to creating the texture and familiarity of a place, soundscapes situate players in a specific time, even if it's designed to be new or unrecognizable. Sound of technology, like computers, phones ringing, and dial-up intonations (or lack therefore), can recreate a modern soundscape compared to horse hooves on cobblestones, town crier shouts, and so forth. The common adage in sound design is that the best sound design is the one audiences don't even notice because it's working so effectively to place them in the world.

A few (as always, non-exhaustive) ways in which audio design contributes to worldbuilding includes:

- Sound effects
- Foley
- Soundtracks
- Voice design/direction

Sound Effects

Sound effects, particularly diegetic ones, are a layer of worldbuilding provided through the soundscape of the game. Sound effects are the sounds that are distinct from speech and music in media. Sound effects for video games can range from sounds from weapons, from the environment, from creatures, UI, and so forth. Anything—and indeed, most things—emit a sound, particularly a distinct sound that helps root players in a place.

Michelle Hwu, lead audio designer at Beans and former voice designer on *Watch Dogs: Legion*, talks about *Returnal* (Housemarque, 2021) as an example where the soundscape is created via a lot of compiled sound effect details. Of *Returnal*, Hwu says,

> There are so many details in how the aliens, fauna, weather, gameplay objects, and weapons sound. The game also uses 3D audio effectively and changes whether or not you are playing in first or third person view. From the sound of rain on your helmet to hearing the location of where creatures exist are both extremely immersive in *Returnal*.[44]

The soundscape of *Returnal* is an important part in understanding how the world of *Returnal* ticks. As an action game focused on difficult combat, understanding the sounds associated with specific objects and enemies creates a shorthand that can help players effectively navigate the world they are in. Knowing the world of *Returnal* is knowing how to survive.

Sound effects can include sounds recreated with foley (discussed later), but can also be audio cues used for gameplay, as well. In video games, audio cues are sounds that chime in relation to a specific in-game trigger, such as reloading or an ammo pick up, but it also extends to creatures and ambiances, as well. Most things in our world have a sound, so it stands to reason that most things in a fictional video game world will also have a sound. Hwu explains the importance of sound design in creating important aspects of the world, and how much space this encompasses: "Sound is often needed for things in the world like gameplay objects, ambiances, characters, and UI. When an object emits a sound, it not only gives aural feedback, but the object itself becomes more tangible to players."[45] And something being tangible helps anchor players into that space, creating a believable setting that players can interact with. Sound stitches together important elements of how players understand a place and the things that live or exist in that space, creating both worldbuilding texture and gameplay understanding.

While I mentioned above diegetic sound effects as things like ammo pickups, I want to focus on a slightly different example: *Wandersong* (Greg Lobanov/A Shell in the Pit, 2018). *Wandersong* is a lovely game where you play as a bard who uses music to interact with the world around him. From a radial wheel players select different notes, and these notes operate as the gameplay interactions. Different notes are related to different colors, and selecting a note of the same color as certain gameplay objects allows players to interact with it. For example, singing a green note at a bird that's also singing a green note allows players to use the bird to jump higher. In an interview with *GameDeveloper.com*, *Wandersong* lead developer Greg Lobanov explains that "...everything in the world reacts to the music. Everything is just kind of like connected with each other and reacting to each other".[46] The world is not just given life by the soundscape; the world of *Wandersong* reacts and responds to musical notes and audio cues. It is given life, coherency, gameplay, and story. This creates a world that is core to *Wandersong*: it's a game about a bard saving the world through music, so of course the individual sound effects are creating the personality of the world and defining what players experiences in that world are like.

But even beyond diegetic examples, non-diegetic audio cues and sound effects build the distinctive world soundscape, as well. In *Wandersong*, there are audio cues and sound effects associated with so much beyond just the musical notes players are selecting. When players do effectively use their bird buddy to jump higher, there's a sparkle sound effect that feels magical and that compounds the charming awe of the moment and the way the game's world works. Similarly, the sound effect from items creates an auditory register of the game, which helps to build the atmosphere and tone of the world. Non-diegetic sound effects, like chimes that suggest an important object is nearby or the audio cue associated with placing a waymarker, also help create the soundscape of the place and therefore offer subtle, but important, worldbuilding elements that are integral for gameplay and story. These sound effects can indicate tone and mood, such as the magical sparkle sounds in *Wandersong*, but they can also indicate types of instruments available to this world (discussed more in the soundtrack section), speech of inhabitants (discussed more in the voice design/direction section), as well as specific nuances of what rules objects or people obey in this world.

Composer and sound designer Priscilla Snow talks about their use of "audio palettes", a form of curating and creating sounds based on a similar feel and composition in order to stitch together a coherent identity based on consistency. Snow explained that for *Patrick's Parabox* (Patrick Traynor, 2022), a puzzle game about navigating boxes inside of boxes, they used "almost zero organic sounds, because everything about the game was super clean/simple/unnatural/mathematic".[47] The use of non-organic sounds was to stitch together a soundscape indicative of a simple, non-organic world. The types of sounds used are creating an auditory identity to the game and its world.

AMBIANCE

A worthwhile distinction from sound effects (and soundtracks, discussed at the end of this section) is ambiances. Ambiances are the sounds that exist in the backdrop of a game, like the sound of rain Hwu mentioned when talking about *Returnal*. Ambiance is distinct from sound effects for gameplay objects (such as ammo pickups of the bird response chirp in *Wandersong*). While a subtle aspect of game audio, ambiance serves a crucial role in developing and maintaining the experience of being in a space.

In an article on *GameDeveloper.com*, audio director Rob Bridgett explains that

> Ambience generally hints at a world just outside what can be seen and experienced on screen. It performs the functional task of making a scene feel real and continuous, no matter what other effects are layered on top of it.[48]

Ambiances are the continual background sound that flesh out the world and indicate atmosphere; ambiance is the soundscape of a place in its most subtle, but integral, form. *Legend of Zelda: Breath of the Wild* ambiance includes rushing water, the din of birds and insects, wind, and so forth, creating the subtle layer of organic sounds that firmly situate the player in the natural world.

Foley

Foley is the reproduction of sounds we hear every day (like footsteps), done in post-production. And the goal of foley is keenly aligned with our purposes as worldbuilders: foley helps build the environmental soundscape, building layers of what the game sounds like by distinguishing specific sounds in relation to people, creatures, and environments. It is built up of subtle and specific sounds that create believable and identifiable soundscapes. While foley is the technique for creating specific types of sound effects, it's useful to talk about on its own given its prevalence and specificity.

This specificity is also a tool that we can use toward a goal of immersion. Foley is important for immersion in particular because foley is about creating a believable soundscape for the place players are transported to. The right fall of footsteps, the way doors creak, exchange of coins, the whirr of a computer—all these sounds add texture that situates players in a familiar context and they make that context feel alive and real. Foley can also be used to create a soundscape that is unfamiliar, as well, but that is still a believable and tangible place. Strange footsteps, wet squishes in a dry environment, and wind howls are all hallmarks of horror, and they work because they introduce an unexpected element in an otherwise familiar soundscape. They disrupt what audiences expect of a setting, inviting in unease and the sense that something here is wrong.

To dig further into this, let's look at *Soma* (Frictional Games, 2015). *Soma* is a horror game with two distinct settings for its sci-fi, existential terrifying experience. There's the interior station, a metallic setting similar to many sci-fi locales. But then there's also the underwater setting, the seabed on which the station is housed. Both of these spaces have distinct soundscapes, informed partially by the different qualities foley in each environment denote. Footsteps, monster movements, light crackles—these all sound different depending on which of the two main settings players find themselves in. Samuel Justice, the audio director on *Soma*, describes the process for creating these two distinct soundscapes for the game: "From the get-go we knew that these two soundscapes had to contrast with each other heavily, so if we were to turn off the visuals, you could instantly tell where you were".[49] To do so they recorded in the spaces they wanted to mimic. For the interior station space, they recorded footsteps in a massively open hall to recreate the correct reverb and echo of footsteps. And for the underwater sections, they literally recorded the necessary sounds underwater.[50] Doing so helps to create an undeniable sense of exactly where players are. But this also makes it easy to disrupt a player's familiarity with the space. Knowing how the interior space should—and does—sound makes it easy to then disrupt that soundscape when a monster is approaching. And it builds the understanding of this world: both are like our real world but with very, very important distinctions, and those distinctions come across in the way foley gets implemented.

SPATIAL AUDIO, FOLEY, AND WORLDBUILDING IN VR

Like video games played on console, PC, or mobile, VR experiences are highly collaborative in the ways in which they approach worldbuilding. The same set of principles apply—believability, use of synecdoche, and so forth—but the ways in which these elements are highlighted and maximized can be changed in VR. Like video games, good VR understands all of the tools it has for creating vivid and immersive experiences. For example, environment design is hugely important to VR, especially in conveying a believable sense of space that players can move through, which involves understanding how players interact with VR spaces, as well as designing for scale and pacing.

One of these tools that plays a key role for VR worldbuilding is audio, particularly spatial audio and foley. Spatial audio places the soundscape in the environment rather than centralized on the player. This means that players are able to move around the space, with the audio locked to its environmental position and not following the player. The Oculus website describes spatial audio as a way to "mimic acoustic behavior in the real world"[51], offering a highly realistic and immersive experience. This recreates a highly realistic soundscape for a space that players can physically move through while in VR.

To take a look into sound design and VR, let's talk about *Half-Life: Alyx* (Valve, 2020). The sound design for the latest release in the beloved franchise highlights and emphasizes both gameplay (it provides a way to direct gaze and attention) and is also key in returning to and paying tribute to the iconic world of *Half-Life*. In an interview for *A Sound Effect*, sound designers Roland Shaw, Dave Feise, Kelly Thornton, and composer Mike Morasky talk about some of the decisions they made with regard to audio design for the game, including aspects like intentionally using foley to sell the player as having a physical presence in the world (despite players only being able to see their hands, a common immersion road bump in VR), to emphasizing creatures that are both familiar and otherworldly, and to bringing to life an environment full of sounds of lights buzzing, creatures breathing, and other strong sound indicators for a believably full place.[52] This emphasis on specific sounds in specific moments (for example, creatures breathing in idle situations) creates both tension and provides an anchor point for the believability of the world. The sounds sell the world of *Half-Life: Alyx* by creating a familiarity of the space (lights buzzing), but they intentionally disrupt this with sounds of the creature breathing.

Soundtrack

As with sound effects, both diegetic and non-diegetic soundtracks have the capacity to build the world via contributing to atmosphere, mood, and tone. Diegetic soundtracks, obviously, contribute to worldbuilding by providing a glimpse into what the soundscape of the world literally is. Musical scores have the ability to punctuate a moment and create an anchor point in both time and place, especially when worldbuilding within our existing real world. The choice of soundtrack, in modern, fantastical, and sci-fi worlds, all create small pockets of meaning. What instruments are available? What materials are instruments made out of? What is the popular music? What atmosphere is this harkening to? How does music get shared? All of these are elements of worldbuilding, which can have a massive effect on selecting soundtrack styles to compliment aspects of a world.

Kentucky Route Zero uses key musical moments as a way to highlight significant scenarios and to integrate the point of song into the game's story and themes. Act 1 features a moment of guiding Conway, the main character, to a farmhouse to try and find a path onto the Zero (the mythical and surreal highway in the game). Specifically, Conways can access the Zero via an old CRT tv. But the tv is busted and so Conway has to leave the farmhouse in search of somebody to repair the tv. And as Conway begins the trek back down the switchbacking hill, a bluegrass song ("You've Got to Walk" by The Bedquilt Ramblers) begins to play, growing louder and louder. As players continue their trek downhill, the scene shifts focus from the farmhouse and Conway's descent to a silhouetted bluegrass band in the forefront, as if they are on a stage and players are standing backstage behind them. This scene is a pivotal one because it showcases how fluid and surreal the boundaries of this world are—both in the game and the meta layers between game and player. Up until this point the game has been weird, it's been slightly ominous and off-putting, but it hasn't gone entirely off the rails. The scene with The Bedquilt Ramblers establishes a stage-like presence and indicates a shift in the world: the boundaries of this game are far from tight and realities are able to slip in and out of each effortlessly.

In an interview with *Rock, Paper, Shotgun, Kentucky Route Zero* co-creator and writer Jake Elliott talks the role of bluegrass music in the game. Elliott says,

> ...one of the big sources of inspiration we were drawing from is the culture of Kentucky itself. Bluegrass music. Which is mostly based on hymns. It's mostly these folk arrangements of hymns. Most of the hymns are about death, which is so weird. Death, either the fear of death and the fear of god or death as a relief because you don't have to work anymore.[53]

Kentucky Route Zero is a game about powerless people struggling with economic recessions and how they navigate these hard times set in an extremely specific time in place. And this musical moment from The Bedquilt Ramblers underscores this theme by drawing in the associations of Bluegrass music, with its history of being associated with the problems of everyday people, providing the texture of Kentucky's history, folklore, and music, as well as beginning to tip into the surrealist nature of the game's setting.

LEITMOTIFS

Leitmotifs (a short, recurring musical phrase often associated with key characters, themes, or storytelling moments) have a long history of being used to build narrative context and world information. Leitmotifs are snippets of song, audio cues, and other auditory signals that can create a recurring texture to your world. Leitmotifs can signal danger, calm, friendliness, etc., but they create an important connection and understanding to how sound is indicating aspects of the game and its world.

The Legend of Zelda: Breath of the Wild uses leitmotifs effectively and intentionally to help establish key moments in a game with a quieter soundscape compared to its predecessors. In the YouTube video, "Hidden Music References You Didn't Know About in *Breath of the Wild*", Xalem walks through the various ways leitmotifs are used in *Breath of the Wild* and the effect they have on both the gameplay experience and the world.[54] In particular, the video focuses on Zelda's lullaby as the recurring leitmotif. It's familiar, and it's calming and creates a distinction around Zelda's presence in this world and what her presence means for the world. In *Final Fantasy VII*, Sephiroth's "One-Winged Angel" also signals both his presence but also his role in the game's world, a violent, righteous force with the mistaken belief of his being the last remaining Cetra, an ancient race. In contrast to Sephiroth, Aeris's theme is full of magic and calmness, resonating with both hope and sadness, a direct contrast to Sephiroth's intense and violent leitmotif. Aeris is the last Cetra, and the melancholy brightness of her leitmotif signals this about her presence in the world.[55]

Whereas the musical moments in *Kentucky Route Zero* are often used to further push the boundaries of the game's reality, soundtracks can be effective worldbuilding tools in other ways. *Death Stranding* (Kojima Productions, 2019) uses its melodic soundtrack to signal moments of reprieve. A game built on navigating a post-apocalyptic world of isolation and paranatural hostility, *Death Stranding*'s use of original soundtrack builds the musical mood for the game. The soundtrack is moody, introspective, and contemporary, and juxtaposes modern sound with the natural, decayed, and futuristic world of *Death Stranding*. It harkens to a world that once was but is no longer, while still building the thematic and melodic tone of the game. The soundtrack is also layered well between the game's crucial diegetic audio cues, sound effects, and ambiances, such as rainfall, BB crying, and other environmental signifiers that are important for safely traversing the ruinous world. The melodic soundtrack provides a respite between other audio triggers that warn of danger, providing both a sense of place and a sense of safety.

Voice Design/Direction

Voice design (alongside voice direction) refers to the work done by audio designers/engineers, as well as voice directors, and is focused on recording, cleaning up, and implementing the recorded dialogue of the game. Voice direction in and of itself has an obvious impact on worldbuilding:

is your world serious in tone, and therefore, the direction for voice acting will lean into gravitas, potentially realism, and other vocal distinctions that support a more serious, somber world? Or is it more off-beat, more cartoonish and satirical, and then will the voice direction lean more into exaggerated and over-the-top performances? Is it comedic, and thus your voice direction will be honed to deliver jokes in either a slapstick or dry manner? How you choose to cast for voice acting also determines elements about your world. Do your actors have accents? What dialects are spoken? What details about who exists in the world are the voice design and direction suggesting?

Let's look at SHODAN's voice in the *System Shock* series. SHODAN's voice is distinct and establishes the world in rather quick ways. SHODAN is the digitized voice of a space station in duress. It's the voice of an AI that has decided it is smarter and more powerful than humanity. It is the voice of disaster and fear, as well as the mundane voice of a ship's AI designed to process data and run the routines for the ship. In combination with the poetic nature of the writing, SHODAN becomes this terrifying villain that represents the major schisms in the world of *System Shock*: that something this powerful can be created and that those in charge can weaponize it. SHODAN's voice is the world in *System Shock* because SHODAN controls Citadel Station.

Like SHODAN, the world of *Bastion* (Supergiant Games, 2011) is also made distinct and recognizable by the voice acting. Logan Cunningham voice acts the narrator in *Bastion*, but the narrator is not just a narrator in *Bastion*. The narrator is, in so many ways, the identity of the world of *Bastion*. Cunningham's acting creates the texture of the world, one that is rough and dangerous, but also buffeted by this narrator-as-guide, somebody who (metaphorically) holds your hand through play and moving on from catastrophe. Cunningham's narrated descriptions of the world provide texture and details to the space, amplifying unique and specific aspects, and like the Heart in *Dishonored*, it provides an additional layer of meaning and understanding to the world articulated through the speech and cadence of the acting. The Heart's voice is melodic, ethereal, relating it to the occult aspects of *Dishonored's* world, just as Cunningham's distinctive voice creates a sense of intimacy to the world of *Bastion*.

But above and beyond traditional voice acting, the sound of your language also matters. For example, *The Sims* is widely known for its distinctive NPC language Simlish. An interview on *TechRadar* with one of the actors credited for creating Simlish, Gerri Lawlor, delves into the history of how the fake language was created with its roots in improv. Simlish wasn't initially designed as a full language set, but over the course of the same two actors (Lawlor and Stephen Kearin) repeatedly performing the improv-born language, a loose set of vocabulary began to take root:

> While Simlish wasn't initially tracked as a language, both performers sneaking the same words in again and again meant that, as the series grew, certain words became tracked and Lawlor and Kearin found themselves reading scripts for a language they co-created out of improvisation.[56]

And the world of *The Sims* wouldn't be the same without Simlish, and the way its ludicrousness provides a backdrop to the ludicrousness of the dollhouse-style play (of kitchen fires and dead ghost husbands).

Let's look at a different example. *Jett: The Far Shore* (Superbrothers, 2021) created a fictional language out of the process of trying to develop the music for the game. Composer Priscilla Snow talks about how the fictional language in *Jett: The Far Shore* was the result of them creating soulfège notes to accompany the strings that would comprise the choir music of the game. As Snow mapped these soulfège notes, a natural sort of vowel and sound shape emerged prompting Snow to continue to grow the language, which then got turned into the vocals for the music that the whole endeavor grew out of.[57] The sound of the language in both *The Sims* and *Jett: The Far Shore*[58] is creating an identifiable distinction for the type of worlds these two very distinct games take place in: *The Sims* is a whimsical simulation of everyday life, whereas *Jett: The Far Shore* is an atmospheric exploration of a mythical place.

CREATING A FICTIONAL LANGUAGE

Rather than include this in the dialogue section of this chapter, I wanted to wait to talk about creating a fictional language until having had the chance to discuss both the written and oral components of language. And so now that time is upon us!

Language construction indicates a lot about the world, particularly that of the people, creatures, and species that inhabit that world. And video games all use fictional languages for different purposes, from providing a history and a texture to a species or to indicating a specific time in the past or future.

In the far future sci-fi games *Nier* (Cavia, 2010), *Nier Replicant* (Square Enix, 2021), and *Nier Automata* (Platinum Games Inc., 2017), there is the Chaos language, which notably is expressed in the game's soundtrack lyrics. The Chaos language was constructed to "sound as if our modern languages had drifted away for thousands of years to finally become indistinguishable"[59], and building lyrics out of this language created a really haunting and specific sense of place and time. It's familiar, yet different, and creates a discordant, yet epic layer to the game's worldbuilding.[60]

In *Skyrim*, the Dragon language isn't just a worldbuilding detail: it's also a gameplay mechanic. Playing as a dragonborn, the ability to harness dragon shouts as abilities creates a really powerful moment of weaving worldbuilding and gameplay together. But even just in its pure language form, the Dragon language contains specific details that are robust with meaning. For example, the sound of these shouts was meant to mimic the forcefulness with which a dragon would shout, whereas the runes of the language were designed to look as if they could be scrawled by a dragon's claw.[61] Both the Dragon language and the Chaos language are creating key distinctions about the worlds they exist in, whether it be a legacy and a history or an avenue toward fleshing out mythical creatures.

Not every game needs a robust fictional language, complete with grammar structures, idioms, and so forth. Language is deeply expressive of culture and even in minimal forms can carry a lot of weight and meaning. So consider which elements of a new language your game requires and which ones won't serve your game. Like the language in *Jett: The Far Shore*, or *Nier*'s Chaos language or *Skyrim*'s dragon shouts, the sound of a language can be incredibly important. Or maybe the focus is more on sentence structure and what this implies about how that species relates to themselves and others. For example, the Elcor in *Mass Effect* prefix everything they say with their emotional tone (such as "pleased greeting" or "temptingly"), as a direct juxtaposition to the monotone vocals of their speech. This syntactical element of their language implies a relationship between Elcor speech and how they have learned to communicate as a species and with other species.

When looking at creating a fictional language, whether as a fully fledged one or not, there are a few elements that are worth keeping in mind, such as considering what type of slang and idioms exist in the language, how it's spoken and what biological features are required for that language to be spoken, whether the people or creatures speaking this language require it to be written down (and if so, how do they write it down and where?), or is it passed orally, and so forth. Language is more than just the alphabet and sounds; language carries culture, and it carries meaning of how people interact and share information with each other and with future generations.

CASE STUDY: A WORLD WITHOUT WORDS IN *GRIS*

GRIS (Nomada Studios, 2018) is a gorgeous 2D platformer that forefronts its worldbuilding—and it does so without any written words or other traditional narrative devices. A colorful, meditative platformer, *GRIS* relies almost entirely on its art, audio, and gameplay to build the world and the story. *GRIS* is about restoration on a few levels. It is a game about dealing with an unspoken grief and a nebulous pain, and it is set in a dull, destroyed world that the player restores to life with a flurry of watercolors intimately bound up with its platformer mechanics. *GRIS* presents a crumbled, ruined world and crumbled, ruined protagonist to navigate it. Armed with only her dress, she sets out restoring the broken world, and, surprise, this restoration of a place becomes a symbol of a restoration of herself.

GRIS starts with melody. The soft, melancholic vocalizing combines with sounds of wind rushing as the camera zooms in on the playable character, waking up in the palm of a stone hand. The vocalizing is soon revealed to be coming from the main character, and as she sings, the hand cracks and crumbles at the same time as she clutches her throat, communicating that the power of her voice is hampered. The music swells to a crescendo as the playable character falls, eventually fading out to minimal gameplay and sound effects. At first, the only sounds are the soft footsteps as the playable character begins to walk and jump again. Additional whimsical notes return only once the character has fully found her feet (literally and metaphorically). Sound continues to be an important element in communicating the state of this world, particularly in how the playable character can interact with distinct flora by singing notes, which awakens the flora, reinstating a sort of life to the world while also solving the platforming puzzles by changing the terrain.

In addition to the ways in which sound communicates world states, so too does color. This initial world of *GRIS* is all monochrome, blacks, whites, and grays disrupted only by the blue of the protagonist's hair. This use of palette is an integral aspect of rebuilding the broken world in *GRIS*. The rebuilding of this world is marked by an infusion of color to it. In addition to the palette building new biomes and fleshing out the world, when and where certain colors get used is also important. The game starts with a black and white world devoid of color. It indicates an empty, ruined world, but it also creates a slower, melancholic atmosphere. This is not a black and white world that is alive like *Limbo* (albeit *Limbo* is alive with monsters). This is a black and white world that is ruined, that is destroyed, that is devoid of color *and* life. The monochrome color palette indicates a world that once was but is no more, which is reinforced with all of the crumbling architecture, buildings that were once opulent are now destroyed, pale versions of their former selves.

The first color introduced to the world is red and indicates the real start of the adventure for the protagonist, a character who has realized her goal and how to achieve it. This is also when the protagonist begins to face danger. The dusty reds indicate that this world is being restored—and that restoration also includes the threats that existed in this world. A concentration of red, filling the screen, accompanied with an orchestral swell, is associated with sandstorms, a weather system that the protagonist must hunker down during or be swept away by.

And as more colors get added into the palette, so too do more sounds (the chirps of birds accompany biomes full of reactive plants and flowers). Soft, muted greens and blues intersplice with the reds and blacks, showcasing a world that is beginning to be full again, and one that grows more alive with environmental interactions. Geometric plants change their shapes in response to the protagonist's proximity, illustrating a world where both its flora and fauna are alive. Color is life, indicated by both audio and gameplay.

It's not just the gorgeous watercolor art laid on top of gray-scale ruins and biomes stripped of their lushness—the mechanics are matching the pace, as well. As in most platformers, the playable character has abilities that adapt to the level design of the platforming puzzles. And for *GRIS* these abilities don't come in the form of gained weapons or external tools but are rather inherent to her: her dress is the tool, the gameplay mechanic that adapts and allows her to gain new skills to reach new heights. This world does not need a hero with a sword. It needs someone to tend to it.

I had one moment in *GRIS* that I will never forget. I was playing and I missed a jump (as I am extremely want to do). And as I fell, I was crushed—I was already fairly high up, didn't know where my last checkpoint was, and was already feeling exhausted by the thought of having to possibly re-do a significant amount of the progress I made. (I've had this problem before.) But when I fell, instead of dying, or being reset to an earlier checkpoint, the floor below my character reached up to her, protected her fall, and let me continue on almost exactly where I was, albeit just a little bit lower. It was so gentle. This world didn't want me to fail. This game wasn't about failing and getting stronger or smarter. This game was about rebuilding this world and yourself, with gentleness and understanding, and a possible moment of failure in the gameplay reflected that. This isn't a world without friction, but the friction comes from restoring a ruined world back to life and all of the conflict and danger inherent to a world that is alive.

Through sound, art, and gameplay, *GRIS* weaves a moving tale of recovering from pain, navigating grief, and learning how to find strength again in oneself, backed by a world that breathes to the same rhythm as the protagonist. The way in which the playable character restores order to the world while also restoring strength in herself is a beautiful moment of resonance. As she gets stronger, she can navigate the ruined world better, but the world is also growing stronger, also restored to color. And rather than breathing life into the world making it only more hostile or aggressive, it also makes the world sing more. It's not about overcoming a hostile world. It's about restoring both. The world and the character are in step with each other, both returning to a former glory the more you progress through the game. And it's really, truly wonderful.

NOTES

1. This section is primarily focused on storytelling, so that means most of the examples here are more in the vein of storytelling and writing rather than narrative design. While some narrative design is included in this section, more narrative design is included in the gameplay section, along with other elements of game design.
2. Hetfield, M. 2020. Understanding world-building in games. Eurogamer. https://www.eurogamer.net/understanding-world-building-in-games.
3. In my book *Ain't No Place For a Hero: Borderlands*, I delve deeper into the gun manufacturers themselves and the way the guns challenge what the idea of a hero even is in the world of *Borderlands*. These conventions are gameplay driven (they quickly tell you the gameplay difference between two similar pistols), but they are also sneakily surfacing a lot of worldbuilding and world tensions to the player, as well.
4. Wadeson, D. 2019. Building a Universe. The Advanced Game Narrative Toolbox. ed. T. Heussner, 43. Boca Raton: CRC Press/Taylor & Francis.
5. Tritel, B. 1984. Language and Prehistory of the Elves. New York Times. https://www.nytimes.com/1984/05/24/books/language-and-prehistory-of-the-elves.html.

6. Paterson, E., T.Williams, and W. Cordner. 2019. Once Upon A Pixel: Storytelling and Worldbuilding in Video Games. Boca Raton: CRC Press/Taylor & Francis.

7. Johnson, M.R. 2020. The Place of Culture, Society, and Politics in Video Game World-building. World-Builders on World-Building: An Exploration of Subcreation ed. M. J.P. Wolf, 116. Boca Raton: CRC Press/Taylor & Francis.

8. Walker, I. 2020. Civilization Creator Shoots Down Our Memories of a Nuke-Happy Gandhi. Kotaku. https://kotaku.com/civilization-creator-shoots-down-our-memories-of-a-nuke-1845006305.

9. Sometimes worldbuilders need to work from mechanics as the starting point. Not all games are developed with a world first. Some games have their worldbuilding follow the basic gameplay loop and set of mechanics, whereas others have worldbuilding occurring alongside concept and pre-production, where major mechanics are being determined. Emily Short has an excellent blog post about questions to ask yourself if you find yourself in a position of worldbuilding based on mechanics: https://emshort.blog/2018/03/13/not-exactly-mailbag-worldbuilding-from-a-mechanic/.

10. Upton. B. 2018. Situational Game Design. Boca Raton: CRC Press/Taylor & Francis.

11. The distinction for "main quest" is more common in RPGs, where main quests are set apart from side quests, but the concept of a quest is easily applied to non-RPGs as well, when looking at quests through the vein of: what are the discrete units of story/gameplay beats that constitute the game's main components?

12. Game Informer Editorial. 2017. Side Quest Syndrome: Designing The Road Less Traveled. Game Informer. https://www.gameinformer.com/b/features/archive/2017/02/09/side-quest-syndrome-designing-the-road-less-travelled.aspx.

13. Totten, C.W. 2014. An Architectural Approach to Level Design. Boca Raton: CRC Press/Taylor & Francis.

14. Game Maker's Toolkit. 2020. How Level Design Can Tell A Story. Game Maker's Toolkit. https://youtu.be/RwlnCn2EB9o.

15. Game Maker's Toolkit. 2020. How Level Design Can Tell A Story. Game Maker's Toolkit. https://youtu.be/RwlnCn2EB9o.

16. Game Maker's Toolkit. 2020. How Level Design Can Tell A Story. Game Maker's Toolkit. https://youtu.be/RwlnCn2EB9o.

17. Hamaguchi, N. 2020. The Architects of Midgar: How We Rebuilt Final Fantasy VII Remake's City of Mako. Square Enix. https://www.square-enix-games.com/en_EU/news/final-fantasy-vii-remake-designing-midgar.

18. Hamaguchi, N. 2020. The Architects of Midgar: How We Rebuilt Final Fantasy VII Remake's City of Mako. Square Enix. https://www.square-enix-games.com/en_EU/news/final-fantasy-vii-remake-designing-midgar.

19. Dimoploulos, K. 2020. Virtual Cities: An Atlas & Exploration of Video Game Cities. Countryman Press.

20. For a breakdown of the design of "Effect and Cause", check out this video interview on the Game Brain YouTube Channel with Jake Keating, the designer of the level. It is also a really great breakdown of the ways in which the worldbuilding in this level is interdisciplinary, across level design, level art, and narrative: https://youtu.be/hPczwsRkVGk.

21. Grunts aren't exclusively bandits, as well. Grunts could be low-level aliens, for example, or generic soldier. Bandits is just the example I want to explore here.

22. Kerr, C. 2022. How Shedworks Refined the Art of Sable in Pursuit of Readability. GameDeveloper.com https://www.gamedeveloper.com/ gdc2022/how-shedworks-refined-the-art-of-sable-in-pursuit-of-readability.

23. Pascual, R. 2019. The Art of Afterparty: The Devil's In The Details. GDC. https:// youtu.be/Dzx1r1z6NqY?list=PL2e4mYbwSTba88_D6lbTYwUa2YooFoUYe.

24. While I won't get much into that there, Chris Solarski investigates how emotional registers are created in characters via the use of primary shapes in his book *Interactive Stories and Video Game Art* (CRC Press, 2017).

25. Hudson, C., D. Watts and C. Hepler. 2012. The Art of Mass Effect Universe. Milwaukie: Dark Horse Comics.

26. Benson, Scott. 2018. Nuke Possum Springs: A Night In The Woods Design Postmortem. GDC. https://youtu.be/Xzhe45Q8780?list=PL2e4mYbwSTbb iX2uwspn0xiYb8_P_cTAr.

27. Porreca, R. Review: Night in the Woods. Destructoid. https://www.destruc-toid.com/reviews/review-night-in-the-woods/.

28. Aveiro-Ojeda, S. Making Witches Talk in Don't Wake the Night. GDC. https://youtu.be/n_A4cGmY62w?list=PL2e4mYbwSTbZDaXUhtM-tvuHCZzeNMi7C.

29. Cartwright, M. 2014. Making Fluid and Powerful Animations for Skullgirls. GDC. https://youtu.be/Mw0h9WmBlsw?list=PL2e4mYbwS Tba88_D6lbTYwUa2YooFoUYe.

30. Cartwright, M. 2014. Making Fluid and Powerful Animations for Skullgirls. GDC. https://youtu.be/Mw0h9WmBlsw?list=PL2e4mYbwS Tba88_D6lbTYwUa2YooFoUYe.

31. DaRienzo, G. 2018. A Mortician's Tale: A Different View On How Games Treat Death. GDC. https://www.youtube.com/watch?v=zEl0b_9BmE4.

32. Staten, J. and C. Barret. 2014. Building a Brave New World. GDC. https:// www.youtube.com/watch?v=ZiDbv7nftM8.

33. From a personal interview for this book.

34. From a personal interview for this book.

35. From a personal interview for this book.

36. The term "invisible wall" is often used here to refer to a boundary that players can't see but that prevents them from leaving the contained space anyways.

37. Boetel, J. 2019. Subnautica Postmortem. GDC. https://www.youtube.com/ watch?v=fkjY_R7zQsM.

38. Hogarty, S. 2020. How Creative Assembly Designed Alien: Isolation's Terrifyingly Clever Xenomorph. PC Games N. https://www.pcgamesn.com/interview-creative-assembly-alien-isolations-terrifying-alien-ai.
39. Dennison, A. and M. Lucas. 2017. Sea of Thieves Inn-side Story #3: Engineering Great Water. Rare Ltd. https://youtu.be/9nxlmCq4220.
40. Cloward, B. 2019. Shading the World of Anthem. GDC. https://youtu.be/IjQWRjWZGn0.
41. Mobius Digital. 2016. Greetings from Outer Wilds Ventures! Fig. https://www.fig.co/campaigns/outer-wilds/updates/57.
42. Wiltshire, A. 2019. How Outer Wilds Built A Planet Which Falls Apart. Rock, Paper, Shotgun. https://www.rockpapershotgun.com/how-outer-wilds-built-a-planet-which-falls-apart.
43. Halberstadt, E. 2018. How Sound Tells The Story of Night in the Woods. GDC. https://youtu.be/CEJ6Mfd9Ic0?list=PL2e4mYbwSTbYGfRe55GM0LloQR0wi6l70.
44. From a personal interview for this book.
45. From a personal interview for this book.
46. Francis, B. 2018. Behind the Colorful Music Wheel of Wandersong. GameDeveloper.com https://www.gamedeveloper.com/design/behind-the-colorful-music-wheel-of-i-wandersong-i-.
47. In a person interview for this book.
48. Bridgett, R. 2007. Why Ambient Sound Matters To Your Game. GameDeveloper.com https://www.gamedeveloper.com/design/why-ambient-sound-matters-to-your-game.
49. Justice, S. 2015. SOMA – Behind the Sound. Frictional Games. https://frictionalgames.blogspot.com/2015/09/soma-behind-sound.html.
50. Justice, S. 2015. SOMA – Behind the Sound. Frictional Games. https://frictionalgames.blogspot.com/2015/09/soma-behind-sound.html.
51. Thakur, A. Spatial Audio for Cinematic VR and 360 Videos. Oculus.
52. Walden. J. 2020. Designing Half-Life: Alyx's Superb Sound. A Sound Effect. https://www.asoundeffect.com/half-life-alyx-vr-sound/.
53. Grayson, N. 2013. Interview: Kentucky Route Zero's Mountain of Meanings. Rock, Paper, Shotgun. https://www.rockpapershotgun.com/interview-kentucky-route-zeros-mountain-of-meanings.
54. Xalem. 2020. Hidden Music References You Didn't Know About in Breath of the Wild. Xalem. https://www.youtube.com/watch?v=tmlpHKuxEes.
55. For a great exploration of leitmotifs in video games, check out Jason M. Yu's discussion of leitmotifs in *Undertale* (Toby Fox, 2015). http://jasonyu.me/undertale-part-1/.
56. Hood, V. 2020. Simlish: How An Improv Game Gave Us The Most Recognizable Language in Gaming. TechRadar. https://www.techradar.com/uk/news/simlish-how-an-improv-game-turned-into-the-most-recognisable-language-in-gaming.

57. Castronuovo, C. 2021. Jett: The Far Shore's Fictional Language Started Life As Gibberish Choral Music. Daily Nation Today. https://dailynation today.com/jett-the-far-shores-fictional-language-started-life-as-gibberish-choral-music/.

58. While the *Jett* example isn't voice design as we may typically think of it, it does prove the point about how much audio and sound designers are able to contribute to worldbuilding, especially when brought on early enough in the game development's cycle.

59. Hertzog, C. 2020. NieR Replicant Singer Emi Evans Talks Music, Chaos Language, and More. PlayStation.Blog. https://blog.playstation.com/2020/12/18/nier-replicant-singer-emi-evans-talks-music-chaos-language-and-more/.

60. Like Simlish and the language in *Jett: The Far Shore*, the Chaos language was the direct result of audio's role in development, in which the singer Emi Evan created the language when writing the lyrics to the songs composed by Keiichi Okabe for the game.

61. Wilhelm, P. 2021. How Bethesda Game Studios Made Skyrim's Dragon Language. Bethesda. https://elderscrolls.bethesda.net/en/article/1rL4bCSc N6RYXaXQb4ownj/how-bethesda-game-studios-made-skyrims-dragon-language.

CHAPTER 3

How to Get Started Creating a World

T HE CONCEPTUAL PHASE OF worldbuilding, despite the importance it serves as a story engine and as the groundwork for mechanics, is a practice best done with careful consideration and intentionality. It's easy for conceptual worldbuilding to become a hyper fixation, an overly detailed deep dive with far more information than is useful (both in terms of what can be applied to games, but also creating a document that is cumbersome to navigate or that others on your team won't use). It's fun to see all the ways in which your world can grow and expand but knowing when to stop worldbuilding in concept and when to start finding avenues toward expressing that worldbuilding in your game is an important skill to craft as part of your worldbuilding practice. (I say this sympathetically—we all do it, to some degree.)

But even knowing the capacity for conceptual worldbuilding to become a vortex you never want to leave, it is still important. So part of the craft of early stage worldbuilding is finding a path toward formats and documents that give you the space to do what you need, but that have built-in guard rails to prevent you from spending too much time in the nebulous space of conceptual space. Worldbuilding, to me, is a practice that continues past a world bible and into development, as solutions, implementations, and expressions of worldbuilding can change and provide new highlights or textures to your existing conceptual worldbuilding.

DOI: 10.1201/9781003345619-4

With that in mind, let's take a look at some practices that have been helpful for me in focusing and formalizing my worldbuilding process, especially when in the conceptual phase of worldbuilding.

GOALS

Even before you get to writing your world bible (which I will detail out next), I always emphasize establishing the goals you need your world to fulfill. In general, I advocate for having goals attached to most documents that I work on, whether they are high-level like narrative direction docs or detail-oriented, like design feature briefs. Goals are both targets and guard rails, and as such they serve as the backbone to validate your decisions and questions against. They are what you're striving to achieve and they are a helpful tool to help you stay on task, to avoid going too far into the weeds, and to help make decisions, particularly with competing ideas or plateaued feedback. Goals are also crucial for collaboration, so that everyone can make decisions within their respective domains that are coherent and aligned.

The goals that I set for myself are very project oriented and that's because the goals of your world should be designed in support of the type of game you're making, its genre, playstyle, audience, tone, etc. A few example goals could be as follows:

- The world should grow in response to the game's lifecycle (for a live game).

- The world should build on existing characters while still providing space for new ones (for a sequel).

- The world should include a variety of opinions about the current technology (for a sci-fi game about technology).

These are vague because as mentioned the goals of your worldbuilding are inherently tied to the goals of your game and they should be reflected in each other. You don't necessarily want to build a world that is myopically focused on one faction's motivations and desires if your game is supposed to be a multiplayer game. Nor do you want to design a world that has one giant problem to be solved and a clear path toward a solution if your game is going to be a live game with an undefined end. Of course there is always nuance to this, but that's why having a well defined and agreed upon goal is important.

WORLDBUILDING WITHIN IP

Often, as video game developers, we'll find ourselves working on an established IP, or intellectual property. This can take two common forms. The first is an established video game IP within that studio (such as *Mass Effect*) that contains a lot of existing worldbuilding already. The other version is an established IP outside of video games, such as *Star Wars* or *D&D*. More commonly when we say IP writers, it's in reference to the second form, but the approach to both can be similar creatively, with different stakeholders and constraints/opportunities attached.

Just because you are working within an established IP doesn't mean there isn't room for some expansive worldbuilding for finding pockets of the existing universe to expand and grow. Of course, whether or not you are able to do this comes down to clear vision and approvals from the IP holders. But working on IP offers many opportunities for exciting worldbuilding within existing worlds. Mary Kenney, senior writer at Insomniac Games on titles such as *Wolverine* and *Spider-man: Miles Morales* and comics writer in existing IPs, explains that when she approaches worldbuilding in an established IP, she "look[s] for the blank spaces—where are the settings that have been mentioned but never seen? Same for characters and cultures".[1] This approach allows for worldbuilding that is consistent with the canon but still allows space for building out or expanding on existing places, characters, or concepts. Likewise, Eric Stirpē, lead writer at Remedy Entertainment and former game developer at Telltale Games with Kenney, says to spend "some time thinking about what in the IP emotionally resonates with you. What themes and aspects do you think you are uniquely qualified to explore?"[2] Both Kenney and Stirpē's tips focus on the opportunities that exist for worldbuilding in established IPs: there are pockets in worldbuilding, either locations/characters or thematics that can be expanded on, fleshed out, and given deeper meaning and significance in any world, it's just a matter of locating them and aligning it with your goals and craft. Of course, to do so, you have to be extremely familiar with the IP and respect the IP in order to know what makes it work and where it can be believably expanded.

Find the goals that matter to your game and then share those goals with the whole team so everyone is aligned and understands what you all are trying to achieve with your worldbuilding in your respective domains. Goals also provide the common ground so that different job disciplines can stay aligned on what needs to be accomplished in the variety of ways that worldbuilding is created and supported in a video game.

And one of the most useful tools for staying aligned (when done right) is a world bible.

WORLD BIBLE

A world bible is the document commonly used to house all the major worldbuilding decisions, particularly from a narrative perspective. The world bible is where the key components of the world start to crystalize, and it is where you need to document the important decisions. This is commonly where worldbuilding runs the risk of becoming overbearing or cumbersome. You need to be able to document the necessary parts with enough detail that others on the team can effectively work in co-creating the world, but you also don't want to over document and become stuck in a cycle of adding too much detail that makes using the world bible cumbersome and difficult.

Even in its smallest iteration, a world bible is often far larger than a player will ever see and that's okay! The trick is creating a world bible that is useful to the team when approached with questions (e.g., what style of fashion would characters from this region of our world wear?), while not becoming fixated on creating an unusable, 1000-page tome that the team is beholden to by chains. World bibles should work for your production and game, not against them. And, in my experience, finding what type of detail in a world bible works for your team is a process of asking what different questions need to be asked and answered.

In their chapter, Fernández-Vara and Weise explain the ways in which a good world bible (or game bible) can be utilized by game designers:

> A good game bible will also function as systems design reference guide, providing the context for the world's rules of cause and effect. On a properly managed story-focused game project, the world logic organically informs the game logic and vice versa.[3]

For Fernández-Vara and Weise (and which I agree with), a world bible isn't just a reference document used by narrative: when done well, it is a natural part of the process for determining systems, verbs, and other mechanics that the players engage with. Since worldbuilding is touched by every job discipline, and since worldbuilding is a process that continues throughout development, it makes sense then that your world bible should be a living document that is usable by everybody on the project.

Okay, so now let's take a look at my world bible template.

World Bible Template

Please take from this what works for you and absolutely discard what doesn't. It's so very easy to get lost in writing a world bible, but more words don't make it a better bible. You'll notice in my template there's a *lot* there and that probably seems antithetical to the advice I just gave. But it's because this is a template that I pick and choose what I need from, rather than filling out every single section in excruciating detail. Part of the craft of worldbuilding is determining which aspects you need to know really well, which ones you only need a little bit of detail in, and which ones don't need to be included at all. I'll ask others on my team what areas they want/need detail in, and I'll do a pass myself on which sections are needed and which ones aren't.

I never, ever use this full template. But I do pull what I need from it, so I hope you can do the same with it (Table 3.1).

TABLE 3.1   World Bible Template

Name of place	Questions to consider here: • Is the name important for players? • Is the name important for the civilization? • Does the name need meaning or is it purely functional?
Overview	A quick summary of your world conveying the most crucial facts that others need to be able to find at a glance.
Tone	A quick explanation of the tone of your world used to guide decisions and answers below.
Physical geography	• What effect does the geography have on civilization? • On politics? • On religion? • On biology? • On technology? • What type of resources are abundant here? • What type of resources are scarce here? • How does this abundancy/scarcity affect civilization? On politics? On religion? On biology? • Are there important sound qualities to this place?
Unique creatures	• How have creatures adapted to the physical geography described above? • How do civilizations respond to these creatures? • How might these creatures sound?

(Continued)

TABLE 3.1 (*Continued*)   World Bible Template

Civilization	• Who are the main people of this place? • What unites them? (A common cause, a common need, etc.) • What causes dissent? • What is the "thing" (value, concept, etc.) that people in this civilization value the most? • Is this place generally harmonious? Generally rebellious? • Who feels safe here? • Who doesn't feel safe here? • Where do people live? • How is this civilization viewed by outsiders? • What type of entertainment exists here? • What type of sport exists here? • What language(s) do they speak? Dialects? Accents? Note: These questions are about the civilization more holistically versus individual people.
Technology	• What is the technology level of this place? • Is technology commonplace or special? • Is technology fundamental to the world's organization or entertainment? • Who has control of the technology? • Who is the technology primarily helping? • What gaps exist in the technology? • What are the trade-offs that exist in the technology? • How has the technology changed the geography? Political systems? Religion? People's lives?
Magic	• Does magic exist? • How does magic work? • Is magic cosmological or geographical or some other explanation? • Are there trade-offs to magic? • Who can use magic? Who can't? • How does society view magic? Note: A lot of the same questions about technology can apply to magic, and vice versa!
The people	• How do people relate to each other? • What causes personal friction? (Good and bad) • What causes conformity? (Good and bad) • What taboos exist in relationships? • What is the typical family dynamic? • What are the beauty norms? Note: These questions are about the individual people, rather than the holistic concept of their civilization.

(Continued)

TABLE 3.1 (*Continued*)   World Bible Template

Infrastructure	• How do people travel in this world? • What does this say about the world? • What divisions exist in who can access various types of infrastructure?
Religion	• What religions exist? • Who practices which ones? • Where do people practice their religions? • How do different religions feel about each other? • What type of music is associated with this religion(s)? • What does this music say about religion(s)?
History	• What are the major moments in this place's history? Wars? Inventions? Labor policies? Public figures? Resistances? Entertainment milestones? Weddings? Deaths? • How are these major moments viewed by the civilization as a whole? • How are they viewed by different individuals? • How is the place's history viewed by outsiders?
Secrets	• What secrets exist in this world? • Between characters? • Between ruling bodies? • From history? • In the geography? • In the creatures? • What do these secrets mean for the future of this world and the people in it?

REMINDERS WHEN WORLDBUILDING

And finally, I wanted to share a shortlist checklist of reminders that I use when worldbuilding. These aren't exhaustive but are useful aspects for myself to keep in mind when I'm deep in my world bible or in writing or designing based off of my world bible. I use them to help guide me throughout a production, so perhaps they will be helpful as a guide for you, as well.

- Identify your conflicts (personal, external, political, etc.).

- Find the details that matter.

- Use synecdoche as shorthand.

- Show the effects in the world.

- Know what you need to tell.

- Don't over document (intentional gaps are good).

- Watch how many neologisms you use (for clarity and comprehension).

- Consider art requirements.

- Don't forget the sound of your world.

- Play the build!

NOTES

1. From a personal interview for this book.
2. From a personal interview for this book.
3. Fernández-Vara, C and M. Weise. 2020. Making Worlds Into Games— A Methodology. World-Builders on World-Building: An Exploration of Subcreation ed. M. J.P. Wolf, 76. Boca Raton: CRC Press/Taylor & Francis.

CHAPTER 4

Collaboration in Worldbuilding

A Series of Deeper Dives

N OW THAT WE'VE USED Chapters 1 and 2 to establish a lot of common ground (what worldbuilding is, why it's important, and how each job discipline contributes to worldbuilding) and used Chapter 3 to establish some practical tips for beginning worldbuilding practices, it's time for a series of deeper dives. There's a good chance that while reading the overviews of how different job roles contribute to worldbuilding that you were aware of the ways in which the same elements overlap. Level design and environment art are closely intertwined. AI and animation work together to bring creatures and people to life. Characters (and their dialogue) are created by narrative, but also by art and by sound. Nothing is, strictly speaking, neatly only one element. Because video games are an inherently collaborative art form, the ways in which the various components that contribute to worldbuilding intersect are also quite collaborative.

With that in mind, this chapter is going to be a deep dive into various aspects of how a world can be felt and realized in a video game—and the cross-discipline approach involved for each. If Chapter 3 was about understanding your tools for beginning the process of conceptual worldbuilding, then this chapter is about examining the ways in which the worldbuilding process can be expressed in video games by looking at in-depth examples.

DOI: 10.1201/9781003345619-5

We'll look at elements like creating characters, creating the environment, determining how a world feels, and get into the details of how each is built to reflect a world and all the ways different job roles intersect in the creation of it. This is a mix of concept and of implementation, but it will illustrate how the collaborative nature of video game development works when applied to something like worldbuilding since work on a video game is rarely done in total isolation.

BUILDING THE HEART OF A WORLD

When we think of worldbuilding in fiction, it's probably not far off to assume that most of us think of geographical or historical or systemic aspects, such as hierarchies, political systems, cultural traditions, religious beliefs, what type of recreation exists, what sort of technology exists, and so forth. Which makes sense because those, along with geographical distinctions and the cosmological rules that come along with creating new planets and universes, are the building blocks of a world. A world contains rules and the above examples of various infrastructures constitute the ways in which civilizations operate according to different rules.

But we are humans. And the way we interface with infrastructure and world systems is through ourselves. When I say "ourselves", I mean our bodies, as well as our mental and emotional facilities; or, to put it another way, we understand a world through our lived experiences of existing in it. A political system is engaging insofar as it exerts a pressure on the people of the world. Geographical anomalies are terrifying or challenging because of the way they disrupt our expected routines. A mountain range separating two villages becomes compelling when it makes sharing goods and resources a dangerous trek or endeavor worthy of challenge. The way people[1] react to a world makes the world matter.

This is why characters are an incredibly important part of worldbuilding. Characters are the heartbeat of any believable world. They are the emotional anchors we have to the world, as well as the ways in which the meticulous worldbuilding becomes concrete and flavorful. People have reactions. They have opinions. And their actions are incredibly motivated by how they feel about systems of power, social injustice, and geographical challenges. Characters are our way into caring about the world on a level that moves us and engages us.

All of the *Mass Effect* fanfiction that exists proves this to be true. We care about the universe in that game because we care about Wrex, Garrus,

Liara, and so forth.[2] We understand the world because we understand the tensions characters carry with them and the way these different tensions affect how they relate to each other—and to us as Commander Shepard. The characters are both individuals with wants, desires, and flaws, as well as representatives of their own worlds within the galaxy. They bring cultural conflict, they bring different modes of approaching conflict resolution and relating to each other, and they bring baggage, influenced by a personal as well as a societal history. Relating to each character and understanding each character means understanding the world they contain, both as people and as people from a specific place.

Characters don't need to be intricately robust to have this effect, either. NPCs we encounter in play spaces or mission-giver NPCs that are light on detail but high on flavor are also capable of providing tangible anchor points for the world they exist in. Every overheard snippet of dialogue from two random NPCs in a place, such as on Citadel Station in *Mass Effect*, is also contributing to the texture of the world they inhabit. People—and therefor characters—are inherently informed by where they are from and where they are. No matter their level of detail or involvement, characters are providing some aspect of insight into the world they exist in, whether it's the way they speak, where they live, how they feel about their home, or even what they need from you, the playable character (if they need anything at all).

In video games, characters are touched by every single job discipline. Characters need dialogue, emotional landscapes, plots to participate in, and goals to achieve. But also characters need to be realized in the environment. They need animations to move and art to be visualized. They need gameplay verbs to determine how they can interact with the world around them, and they need whatever those verbs are to be programmed. They need audio, whether full VO, audio cues, leitmotifs, or soundtracks to compose the tone of their role in the world. Characters are a village unto themself when it comes to bringing them to life.[3]

Let's do a deep dive into *What Remains of Edith Finch* (Giant Sparrow, 2017) to examine more in depth all the ways a character is brought to life by different job disciplines and how these components contribute to worldbuilding.

What Remains of Edith Finch's Ensemble Cast

What Remains of Edith Finch is a game where each character contains a world all on their own (both literally and metaphorically). In *What Remains of Edith Finch*, you follow the titular character Edith as she explores her family home. But the game isn't just about Edith nor are you only inhabiting Edith's psyche. The game is about Edith's family and the legacy of family in this world. And this is presented immediately in the game's map. The map isn't a floor-by-floor layout of the Tim Burton-esque house, a Frankensteined building reflective of the way the Finch family grew and grew over the years. Instead, the map is a family tree, one which only gets filled out after playing through the vignette of that family member. This is a small, but extremely effective detail that sets the stage for the entire game: Players are not just exploring a house—they're exploring how the house reflects character. And while exploring the house, each bedroom is far bigger and grander than can be contained by the walls that surround it because they are reflective of the person who lived in that room.

The game takes place in a gorgeous, surreal, and lovingly crafted house as its setting, which serves the purpose of creating place through character. Each room of the house is a shrine to a Finch family member and is created to reflect that individual's personality first and foremost. All the particular details of each room, including layout, aesthetic, and paraphernalia stitch together the personality of the room's inhabitant. Details such as an ant farm or a movie poster function as synecdoche: they are details representing both who this character is and how they exist in the world. And that's an important aspect of the game: these rooms aren't just reflections of character, they're also reflections of the type of world each character lived in.

Let's start by looking at Molly Finch, the first character whose room players explore. Molly is a 10-year-old girl whose story revolves around her hunger after being sent to bed without dinner. Her room is full of sweetness and pink things. There's a picture of Molly smiling in a pink-laced dress with white frills. She's cute, but somebody (presumably Molly) has drawn cat ears on her with a black marker. It's the picture of a normal kid that creates a nice contrast to how weird Molly's story gets. As players inhabit Molly's final adventure, they begin by scouring her room for something to eat and end up with Molly transforming into a variety of animals in search of food. She's a cat, jumping through tree branches and then she's a shark searching for prey. The walls of her room expand and float away as Molly's imagination tries to solve the issue of her rumbling stomach.

The details in the environment, the gameplay that transforms from limber cat to awkward shark, the dialogue, and the sound design, all work together to create a startling vivid sense of who Molly is and how she sees her world. Her world is not confined to the bounds of her physical self or location—no, her world far exceeds who she is and where she is, allowing her to transport herself into a large, fantastical vista. Moreso, Molly's world is not scary. She is free to grow her confidence and her sense of self, and the world is a place for her to explore, not be confined by. And this is a wonderful element of the worldbuilding that gets carried through for each Finch family member: the world is what they understand it to be, so the world (and worldbuilding) is different for each character. Molly's world is fantastical, it is meant to be her playground, and she approaches it with bravado and eagerness, even in the face of fatal danger.

As a contrast to Molly, there's Barbara Finch. Like Molly, Barbara's world far exceeds the boundaries of her house, but in a different way. A once famous scream queen turned restaurant server, Barbara was a Hollywood actor, somebody who knew how big the world was. But the flavor of Barbara's world is different from Molly's. Where Molly's world is surreal and fantastical, it is real to Molly. She is the cat in her imagination. But for Barbara, there's always a layer of distance. Barbara knows special effects and she knows how fictional worlds are made, which is reflected in her room, full of film props, and posters, and even contains a mural of the Hollywood sign, but with the word "Hollywood" replaced with "Barbara". Barbara's world is actually quite small because expansive worlds are just fictions to Barbara.

Barbara's vignette has players flipping through the pages of a horror comic. Barbara is used to her life being distilled through digestible media (movies) so having her gameplay exist through a comic book is nicely evocative of this. At first, players are simply following the pages of the comic as it talks about Barbara trying to get her scream back in time for a convention, but as her world descends into real-life terror, control is transferred to the player to guide a comic-book version of Barbara through panels. It is dripping with horror tropes (even *Halloween*'s iconic theme song), all developing the ways in which Barbara's world of being a scream queen is now oozing into her real life. What's so evocative about this is how it shows that the world contains layers of realness for Barbara, with "reality" often being a media construct. Power being cut, ill-timed storms: these are tropes in Barbara's world. Because Barbara understands her real world to actually be quite mundane and boring compared to the worlds she's inhabited in her movies, she's unprepared for the horror waiting for her in her own home. Despite living in the same house, Barbara's reality is very different from Molly's reality.

Finally, let's compare Molly and Barbara's rooms to Lewis's room and story. Whereas Molly and Barbara inhabited worlds that were far bigger than both of them, Lewis's world was actually oppressively and frighteningly small. Lewis's bedroom is in the addition tacked onto the house, the spiral upward that was added as the Finch family continued to grow and grow. Lewis's room is a typical teen's room in the early aughts: black light, weed paraphernalia, and neon bar signs. Angst and displacement from reality ooze in the details that constitute Lewis's room. His story follows his psychiatrist describing how she understood Lewis, somebody who worked at a cannery while newly sober after having sought help for substance abuse. Lewis is described as finding his world to be monotonous, and the gameplay begins with the repetition of grabbing a fish, chopping its head off, sliding it up, and then grabbing another one. Lewis's world is small.

But as Lewis continues this monotony of chopping fish, his mind begins to wander to greater and grander things. He imagines a kingdom and people in it, people who adore him and worship him. A princess (or prince, player's choice) who loves Lewis. A world that far exceeds the bounds of the current boring and tedious one he finds himself in daily. What's really cool about this vignette is the dual inputs players need to manage: on a controller, players use the right thumb stick to chop the fish and continue the motions of his day job, but the left thumb stick gets used to move the fictional version of him in his head. Lewis inhabits two worlds at the start that are totally distinct. At first, players contend with both actions: exploring the fictional world in his head and continuing the motions of his job at the cannery. But eventually the fiction takes over the screen, bleeding from imagination into Lewis's reality so thoroughly that he becomes lost to the physical world, consumed entirely in the kingdom he created in his mind.

Where Molly's world grew because of her active imagination and youthful intensity, and Barbara's world grew because she understood how media could fake new realities, Lewis's world grew out of a sense of desperation: lost within the physical world, Lewis's mind created a new world for him, an entire kingdom to make him happy. All these vignettes are heartbreaking and highly intimate. No story could be displaced onto a different character because each room and vignette are so specific to how that character fits into the world around them.

What Remains of Edith Finch is a wonderful confluence of different elements used to create memorable characters in a slightly surreal and deeply emotional world. It's level design (the space of the room), unique mechanics and verbs (the mini-game aspect of each vignette), UI and environment art (the map and the look of each room), character art (the characters themselves), audio (the VO for each character), and narrative (the stories about each character's death) all coming together to create these highly specific moments of place and person. The stories of each character are supported by the details of their bedrooms, which are in turn realized through the gameplay mechanics of the individual mini-game vignette. Each character looks different, acts different, and exists in a different world from each other. This is psychological worldbuilding, and a supremely effective one because *What Remains of Edith Finch* is all about digging through a family tree like an archeologist, unearthing secrets in order to understand family better. Simply put, the characters *are* the world.

Neo Cab's Fashion Representing a World in Flux

Fashion is an important part of expressing details of the world to players. Fashion can indicate social strata, political allegiances, accessibility of technology, and so forth. Fashion is directly derived from materials available in a world and constructed in ways to reflect a variety of societal values (or taboos). Fashion is so personal, but it is also sociological, belonging to groups, and is also reflective of how people choose to identify themselves as a part of or as distinct from these groups.

In a GDC talk in 2019, Victoria Tran (community director at Innersloth, former community developer at KitFox Games) talks about the importance of fashion in video games, by focusing on how fashion can be either "a mechanic or an information-rich piece of storytelling".[4] Tran stresses the distinction, and it's a worthwhile note here, that fashion isn't just simply clothes. Fashion is a trend, a style, a compilation of clothes in an expressive sense. And the fashion of a character can be super dense with information. This information can be about personality traits and what values the character holds, yes, but fashion also contains information about the world, in terms of what the differences in fashion is implying about place in society (and all the baggage that comes with occupying a place in society). Tran also points out that bad fashion can clash tonally with a game world, in fact detracting from the atmosphere.[5] Fashion needs to fit the world and how the character exists in the world.

MAKEUP STYLES AND TATTOOS REFLECT BACK THE WORLD

I briefly touched on this in the Character Creator boxed article in Chapter 2, but makeup, like fashion, can also convey important and subtle cues about the game world.[6] Do the people in your world wear makeup? Do certain people wear makeup and others don't? What is makeup made from? What does makeup signify? Related, what does beauty mean and signify in your world? What makeup styles exist (everyday, Avant Garde, cultural, etc.)? Makeup is similar to the effect of tattooing and can be used to indicate specific things about a world and how characters choose to express themselves or their culture. Moxxi from *Borderlands* is a great example of this. Moxxi is a bar owner, somebody who is violent and charismatic and isn't shy about her sexuality. She speaks in sultry tones, rife with innuendo, and also sports the face makeup of a clown. It's the exact type of whiplash you expect from the irreverent nature of *Borderlands'* Mad Max-inspired world.

And in the same vein, tattoos are also an important element of worldbuilding. Tattoos can be cultural, they can be aesthetic, and they can also be political. Faith's eye tattoo in *Mirror's Edge* is her runner tag, establishing her as a member of an illegal courier group, one which is integral to transporting information beneath the surveillance of the city's law enforcement. *Mirror's Edge* is a world built around resisting an oppressive regime, and Faith's eye tattoo is a clear signal of her dedication to resisting these structures. Without even digging too deep into the political systems of the game's world, the very act of Faith deciding to tattoo her eye with her runner tag already speaks volumes about the stance she feels she needs to visibly take given the political machinations of her world.

An important note (and something we will discuss in more detail in Chapter 5) is how tattoos and makeup can also be cultural expressions from real cultures and how to be mindful of not appropriating these forms of traditional, sacred, or cultural expression. Tattoos, makeup, and other forms of adornment are powerful tools of expression—in both our real world and our fictional worlds—and care is required for how we treat them, particularly in the ways in which we examine (or fail to examine) our assumed biases in what we use as inspiration from the real world.

To talk a bit further about fashion, let's look at *Neo Cab* (Chance Agency, 2019). *Neo Cab* is a futuristic game where players inhabit Lina, a human cab driver in a world of automation. It is a game that thematically revolves around the sociopolitical tensions that come from a place transitioning from human labor to purely automated labor. As Lina, players encounter a lot of different people in the form of clients, and each one is visually loaded with detail that indicates where they situate themselves in their changing world.

This liminal world space has a direct repercussion on its characters. In a talk "*Neo Cab*—Anatomy of a Character", writing lead Paula Rogers talks about the process for creating characters in *Neo Cab* and the thematic underpinning revolving around the concept of staying human in a world that is becoming more and more automated.[7] And *Neo Cab*'s fashion of its pax (in-game term for passengers) indicates a variety of levels of tech adoption and how characters fit into a world that is leaning so fully into automation (and who struggles to stay human during it all). Some characters are dressed in modern outfits (a suit and tie, no tech in sight), whereas others have bioluminescent jewelry and hair adornments, mech arms, holo screens in front of their eyes, and so forth. The range of fashion in *Neo Cab* is deeply reflective of the division of Los Ojos: some people are fully transitioning into the new world of automation, whereas others are resisting full automation and tech adoption.

Notably, *Neo Cab* features characters (and particularly Lina) wearing a bracelet, something called a Feelgrid. It's a described as a "biofeedback device",[8] and it alerts the wearer to their current emotional state. This is part of the core gameplay of *Neo Cab*: Lina needs to maintain control of her emotions to be able to chat with her pax and receive both intel about her missing friend and a good tip. The Feelgrid is an accessory that is both practical and stylish, and it indicates a lot about the world it is a part of, namely, that knowing your emotional register to be able to "know yourself" is a common enough problem in this world to be exploited. It's also deeply indicative of the way the fictional world of Los Ojos is in flux. This is a world caught between two states, between the old world centered around human labor and a new world of automation. And with the Feelgrid, even understanding your emotions is something that is getting automated. The Feelgrid, as a piece of fashion but also a gameplay device, encapsulates this tension perfectly. Humans and human emotions are messy, but the Feelgrid is an attempt to quantify them and to make them data that can be processed and responded to as if we are no longer human. *Neo Cab* doesn't just present a world in flux via its story or gameplay but uses every moment to reinforce this world state, including the range of fashion.

Character Sheet Template

Like the world bible template I provided in Chapter 3, I'm including Table 4.1 as a character sheet template as well. These templates are helpful starting points for collaboration with other departments, particularly art, audio, and gameplay, when it comes to realizing how our characters should look, sound, and behave in the game world.

My template is quite large, but I don't use every aspect of it for every game or character. It's a starting point, one where I can pull out what's necessary for myself and for my collaborators to start developing our game's characters and how they operate in our fictional world. I like to ask my collaborators in other disciplines what they need from a character sheet (such as what details or references would be helpful for artists or sound designers, what gameplay designers and programmers need to know about movement, etc.) and use that to inform which aspects of this template will be relevant. Additionally, some aspects will be more important for main characters, less important for side characters.

So, as always with templates, use what serves you and don't stress about the parts that aren't useful for your current project. Craft is about knowing the tools available to you and selecting the right ones for the right moment.

DETERMINING THE FEEL OF A WORLD

The rules of your world are not just lines in a world bible dictating the relationships between infrastructures and characters. The rules of your world in a video game are constituted by how gameplay and programming realize the state of the world and what can and cannot be done. How you build your

TABLE 4.1 Character Sheet Template

Basics

Name

Inspiration

Bio

Physical appearance

Gender

Age

Race/Ethnicity

Economic status

Role in Game/Story

Story/Plot involvement

Relationships with others

How do they come across to strangers?

How do they come across to people who know them?

Internal Characterization

Personality

Zodiac sign

(Continued)

TABLE 4.1 (*Continued*)   Character Sheet Template

Alignment

Motivation

Governing trait

Conflicting trait

Greatest strength

Weakest strength

Breaking point

Extroverted or introverted

Strongest dream

Strongest fear

What makes them laugh

What makes them cry

Dark secret

Relationship to External World

Religious/Spiritual beliefs

Attitude toward government

Attitude toward law

Attitude toward cultural norms

Belongs to subculture(s)

Love life

Family

Behavior toward strangers

Behavior toward family

How they speak

Speaking style

Words they use a lot

Words they use when they are angry

Words they use when they are happy

Words they never use

Misc

Education

Current job

Favorite food

Favorite clothing

Habits/rituals

game technically makes certain elements easier or impossible to support in a video game, which in turn then becomes key for what types of stories a game can tell and how we can express our worldbuilding to the player.

These rules and states also dictate what your world feels like to exist in. The feel of your world is composed not just of the visuals and the atmosphere, but of what you can actually do in the world. The way characters move, where they move to, how they interact with the environment or other NPCs, the way the world is presented: all of these aspects are creating how your world feels to your audience. And largely, this feel is created from a combination of all disciplines, but notably from gameplay and programming since the mechanics (and how those mechanics are implemented) determine the feel of existing in this place.

It's important to consider how we want characters to be able to exist in a world and what that world feels like to exist in. Is it easy to move around? Is it difficult? What does traversal mean to your character and thus what does it represent of the world's state? What you can do directly informs how you think of the place you are in. Is it restrictive, is it open? Why? And while these elements can come from narrative or art direction, they can also come from either gameplay requirements or technical solutions.

To discuss how the feel of the world is created through both art/narrative direction and engineering solutions, let's take a look at the horror genre.

Silent Hill's Fog and *The Medium's* Semi-Fixed Cameras

The technical constraints that exist in a game (because of engine, because of budget, because of scope, etc.) can lead to unique worldbuilding scenarios. To explore that concept, let's look at *Silent Hill* (Konami, 1999). Specifically, let's talk about *Silent Hill's* original use of fog. While the fog is now a signature and iconic part of the *Silent Hill* franchise, it was originally implemented because of the game's draw distance (a term to describe how far objects can be rendered in a 3D world). For objects beyond the draw distance available, the *Silent Hill* developers covered it with fog. While implemented to contain the world space to what could be rendered closest to the player's proximity, the fog became an integral element of *Silent Hill's* creepy, tense atmosphere and worldbuilding. This is a world where the lines between reality shift, where monsters lurk, and the fog is emblematic of that.

The rules of the world of *Silent Hill* hinge entirely upon the game's survival horror genre. It is meant to be unsettling and terrifying, not from cheap jump scares, but from deep, rooting, psychological fears. And we see this illustrated in the use of fog, which limits player visibility severely.

This limiting of visibility creates an incredibly tense atmosphere, even if the player is safe in that exact moment. It doesn't matter whether or not monsters are immediately present—the world feels tense to even just exist in. In the *Silent Hill* entry in *Virtual Cities: An Atlas and Exploration of Video Game Cities*, Dimoploulos also shares an appreciation of how *Silent Hill*'s technical constraints create the haunting atmosphere of the world: "Muddy, low-res textures, limited visibility, and a camera prone to switching to disorienting, expressionistic angels enhance the dramatic effect of the already bleak atmosphere".[9] These technical aspects of constructing the game are creating signature moments for the look and feel of this world. This is a hostile world, in both known and unknown ways. And while the technical combines with the visual in poignant ways, the effects of *Silent Hill*'s tense, disturbing world are also present in the mechanics and verbs available to players, as well as the art direction and narrative and sound design affordances.

In addition to the fog, there's the iconic static sound effect of *Silent Hill*, the terrifyingly identifiable indicator of when a monster is nearby. This clever use of sound makes the fog even more scary because now it is something that hides horrendous monsters like Pyramid Head. These monsters become even more terrifying when a player's best chance to protect themself is to run away or to hide. And then add onto that character motivation for needing to be here, for not just turning around and leaving this spooky place for good, and you have a world built on isolation. It's all working together to create the masterfully terrifying world of *Silent Hill*, focused on heavily emphasizing what it feels like to exist in this particular part of the world.

Silent Hill has so many more tricks up its sleeves in determining how this world feels to exist in. As with fog, camera controls (or the lack thereof) were also a staple in early survival horror games like *Silent Hill* and *Resident Evil* (Capcom, 1996–present). Fixed camera controls refer to the fact that in early survival horror games, players could not manually rotate the camera to adjust their field of vision or focal points. Successful horror (particularly in film) has a history in wrenching control away from their audience. Control means power and power is the antithesis to feeling afraid. So it's no surprise that when translating horror tropes and conventions to video games, a lot of mechanical and technical effort was focused on how to instill feelings of powerlessness in a medium so heavily about power fantasies and being powerful.[10]

And while modern games have mostly moved away from fixed camera controls as technical capabilities grew, there's been an aesthetic and genre-motivated desire to return to them in some horror games. *The Medium* (Bloober Team, 2021) made use of semi-fixed cameras to highlight both the tension that type of camera provides, as well as allowing them to highlight the "dual reality" of the game.[11] *The Medium* is a game about a woman, Marianne, who can essentially astral project to a version of reality inhabited by the dead. *The Medium* then has players explore both sides of Marianne's reality as she investigates the origins of her power at an abandoned resort. The use of semi-fixed camera for the dual reality (Marianne is shown in both fully rendered worlds, split-screen style, as the player controls her through both versions of her reality) highlights and cements Marianne's fractured self and both the strength she draws from her abilities, but also the way it can be used to harm her. It's cinematic, but it's also effective on a mechanical level: as modern players, we are used to being able to control the camera. With that taken away, we are more at mercy of the game's tension and terror.

These mechanical and technical aspects are incredibly evocative of the world they are presenting to players, and layer nicely with the art, audio, and narrative elements of the story and the worldbuilding.

NEXT GEN TECH DRIVING NEW WORLDS

The Medium is effective at building an atmospheric horror game, not just because of its clever use of semi-fixed cameras, but also because of the way its next gen tech was able to power Marianne's split reality. And it's this duality that needed next gen tech to create the world they wanted for Marianne. In an interview on the Unreal Engine website, lead game designer Wojciech Piejko explained,

> But in my opinion, the most advanced and unique feature of our game is displaying and rendering two worlds at the same time. This feature requires a lot of juice from the hardware, and The Medium would be too challenging to bring to current-gen platforms. Of course, you can downscale any game idea, but it wouldn't be the same game.[12]

This split world informed everything, from cinematic design to level design, even monster design, since the dual world is the focus of *The Medium* and is the locus of Mariana's struggle. In a separate interview, Piejko also cites the need for more advanced technology (such as the memory and rendering power that comes with it) as reason for why *The Medium*, originally slated to be an Xbox 360 game, didn't actually release until the Xbox Series S/X.[13] *The Medium*'s world, filled with da rkness in both realities, couldn't exist without next gen tech to power it.

Procedural Generation of a World: *No Man's Sky's* Planets and *Watch Dogs: Legion's* Population

While I've focused so far on horror games and techniques that have a history in technical limitations, I want to shift gears and talk about how procedural generation (or procgen), as both a programming and a design endeavor, can create opportunities in worldbuilding. So to do that let's talk about procedural generation in two different capacities: generating the diverse terrain in *No Man's Sky* and generating people in *Watch Dogs: Legion*.

First up, let's get into *No Man's Sky* (Hello Games, 2016) and how the game uses procedural generation to create an infinite number of worlds for players to explore. *No Man's Sky* is about interplanetary exploration first and foremost, dotting its vast universe with planets offering different creatures, resources, and vistas. Planets with pink tufts of grass and aquamarine bodies of water co-exist with acrid planets patrolled by robotic sentinels, which co-exist with planets with red grass and lush palm trees. All manner of flora and fauna create distinction to the different planets, ranging from familiar to extreme extraterrestrial. Different planets boast different cave systems or mountain ranges or different flora. All manner of creatures roam these planets, propelling players through crafting loops and missions to chart the stars. Like *Outer Wilds*, each planet in *No Man's Sky* is a world unto itself, crafted for exploration and awe.

In a review of *No Man's Sky*, Christian Harrison writes, "*No Man's Sky* is made up of roughly 255 unique galaxies that can contain three to four billion regions. The regions contain hundreds of star systems and so on. This all goes on to say that if humanity wanted to discover every planet in No Man's Sky for just a second, it would take nearly 500 billion years to set foot on them all".[14] *No Man's Sky* is a game that achieves its goal of vast galaxies with many planets to explore as part of the survival game loop through the ability to procedurally generate these planets. To survive, players must explore planets to find the resources they need. And as an exploration game, the planets must be interesting (both visually and mechanically) for players to play on.

In his 2017 talk "Building Worlds in No Man's Sky Using Math(s)", Hello Games' Sean Murray discusses some of the challenges and opportunities in using procedural generation to create the variety of terrain available on each distinct planet. Specifically in this talk, Murray explores the ways in which they used noise generation[15] to create meaningfully different terrain that still felt believable and was supportive of play in that space. Murray explains different techniques and solutions they employed in trying to create terrain that was both believable and compelling to explore, and notes that while they were able to use noise generation models based on real-world terrain, that sometimes these terrains could actually be quite boring to just walk through.[16] Even if in scale there were geographical distinctions (like mountains and valleys), for a player in these spaces, this distinction is scaled so much to render it one consistent experience. From a distance we see all of the unique and interesting aspects of the terrain, but on a detail level, it can often feel flat or mundane, the difference in perspective akin to seeing geographical features in an airplane and then the way those distinctions become vast and rendered different when on the ground.

So for *No Man's Sky*, terrain generation became about changing the scale to change the feel of being in that place, since exploration is a key part of the game's fantasy. And this atmosphere isn't just about how each planet looks—it is heavily about how it feels to be on the ground there, exploring. This is an excellent example of the concept of believability versus strict realism. *No Man's Sky* needed its terrain to be believable, but still keyed and tuned to maximize its effect for on-ground exploration. Strict realism actually worked against the goals of exploration in the game because it rendered mundane and boring environments. But striving toward believability allowed them to achieve the perfect balance of plausible terrains that were still surprising and fun to explore. A mountain range is enticing to explore when it's an achievable visual contrast to the flatness of the ground players are currently standing on.

But *No Man's Sky* is about exploration and terrain is only one facet of this. Take this incredible ability to infinitely generate new planets with different terrain and interweave aspects like saturated color palettes (art direction), resource direction (gameplay), creature habitats and behaviors (gameplay), collectibles (narrative), and missions (narrative and gameplay) to amplify the effect of what it feels like to be there—and what it is you can do while you are there. The worlds in *No Man's Sky* feel distinct because their generation (and all aspects of it, from the planets themselves to the resources found on those planets) was built to provide that feeling explicitly.

Then there's the flipside of this, which is a world that is more focused on the sociological aspects of its worldbuilding, aka the populations of people who live in this world and how the infrastructure, geography, and systems of the world are understood via the people who exist there. So to take a look at how procgen can be used to generate people that are meant to be representatives of the state of your world, let's look at *Watch Dogs: Legion*.

In a talk for Ubisoft Toronto, team lead programmer Chris Dragert and team lead game designer Liz England discuss their collaboration to make the Play As Anyone system work. For *Watch Dogs: Legion*, the NPCs in the world all have behaviors that are composed of a myriad of different factors, all designed to create both a strong sense of character and a strong sense of place. Like *No Man's Sky* infinite planets, *Watch Dogs: Legion* needed infinite recruitable NPCs, all with their own distinct personalities, gameplay, backstories, and so forth, in order to create a world that felt alive and that had the context for compelling characters to play as.

To begin compiling how to generate a person, England explains her process for curating categories that constitute interesting people, which actually involves typical worldbuilding techniques. She asked questions like: what cultures exist in this place, what are the demographics, what are the subcultures, but also, what are the individual stories of people occupying this place? The generated people needed to be believable, but they also needed to reflect the dystopian version of London being presented. So the questions that guided the creation of the dataset revolved around understanding how certain aspects of people (their jobs, their cultures/subcultures, the various parts of their identity) reflected the dystopian world they lived in.[17] It was essentially a question of: how do you achieve the feel of the world through the people you encounter? So these data sets created the building blocks (the writing prompts) to create interesting tidbits and facts that made the people feel both distinct but also reflective of the world they existed in. These questions manifested in strings of text associated with NPCs, such as "Detained by SIRS for anti-government protesting", which refers to a fascist control of state, and "Sister died in TOAN bombing", which references the game's own history. These bits and pieces of discrete data, when compiled, created characters with their own identities (such as sexuality, income, job, personal interests, hobbies, etc.), as well as how those identities reflect and are informed by the state of the world (whether or not they support the private military corporation, or are they being watched by the surveillance state, how do they feel about DedSec as a resistance group, and so forth).

Noreen Rana spoke about the importance of good UI in making the generated people of *Watch Dogs: Legion* feel good, particularly in the displaying of the text strings mentioned above. Rana explains that

Clear UI and UX alone isn't enough to present that information to the player. It's a collaboration of characters looking interesting and unique to catch the player's eye, it's presenting the NPCs' unique facts and abilities in a way that a user can understand as quickly as possible without having to stop and read a lot of information in a game that is constantly moving.[18]

For Rana, UI and UX were an important part in nailing the feel of the world by making sure players could easily and readily engage with all the information they needed to assess the NPCs available to them.

England also talks about how the sociological aspects of the character generation wasn't something done in isolation between her and Dragert. Art and animation were exploring fashion styles, hairstyles, and animation styles, while narrative was exploring the stories of these people, and sound/audio were exploring the languages, dialects, and accents presented.[19] A variety of accents and dialects created a diverse world, whereas fashion could indicate inclusion in a culture or subculture, and so forth. In *Watch Dogs: Legion*, the people were so much of the world, and each one contained a detail of worldbuilding that when combined together created a tapestry of sociological responses to the state of the world. This generation of the NPCs allowed the game to explore how characters felt about the surveillance state they lived in, how the crime syndicate influenced tensions in a neighborhood, and how much certain tech adoption affected people's lives. The dystopian London of *Watch Dogs: Legion* is filled with specific details of a world on the verge.

CO-AUTHORING WITH A PLAYER IN PROCEDURAL GENERATION

Procgen can be a great tool for co-authoring your game's story and world with your player. This is because procgen relies both on synecdoche and intentional gaps, creating the necessary symbols and space for players to propel the world's details forward with their imagination. This is similar in emergent narratives (stories that are created from the interactions between the game's mechanics/world and player actions[20]) since there needs to be enough space and enough symbolism for new, unplanned situations to occur.

In the chapter titled "Emergent Narrative in *Dwarf Fortress*" in *Procedural Storytelling in Game Design*, Tarn Adams talks about the tools and approach they implemented for allowing emergent narratives to occur. While explicitly looking at how to design systems mechanically to allow for this, Adams's insight shares a lot of common ground with the concept of using synecdoche and intentional gaps in worldbuilding. Adams writes that "*Dwarf Fortress* relies on widely understood fantasy tropes. Because it is your player building the story, you can use what the player brings to the game beforehand".[21] A truth for worldbuilding of any kind, but particularly true for procgen design, is that you don't need to fill in every detail for your player. Using their imagination (and our tendency for apophenia), players will naturally bring their own thoughts to the table, beginning to build connections and make meaning. Co-authoring requires a level of holding back, providing only what is needed, and creating a space for players to have fun making meaning in your world.

These two examples in parallel are a really interesting exploration of the capabilities of something like procgen for contributing to a variety of aspects of worldbuilding. There's the very literal visual worldbuilding that Murray talks about with noise generation that directly determines how a world feels to be in. But there's also the sociological aspect of what a place feels like to exist in, determined by the NPCs players see who fill up this space, who contribute to the soundscape via accents and languages, and who provide a snapshot into the world's dynamics via their fashion and hairstyles, which then gets stitched together with the stories they tell through narrative devices and gameplay. Worlds are composed of many elements, including both terrain and people, and procgen is a design and engineering-driven endeavor that has an intractable effect on how the world feels to players.

CREATING COMPELLING CONFLICT IN A WORLD

In Chapter 2, I talked a bit about pressures, conflict, and how the concept of conflict is far more broad than it initially sounds. If we think of conflict as drama or as pressures, then our opportunities for finding thematically resonant scenarios to put our characters into expands beyond the typical verbs we're likely used to thinking of to center missions around.

Let's talk about the different categories of conflict briefly. When we speak about conflict, there's often three large buckets that conflict is categorized into: person versus person, person versus self, and person versus world.[22] Conflict can be internal (a person struggling with their emotional connections, feeling lost in a world, battling inner demons, etc.), or conflict can be external (disagreements with another person, somebody being a barrier to achieving what somebody else wants, a society preventing a person from following their dreams, etc.). The point here is that conflict is just drama, and it need not be bombastic or violent to be effective. Conflict can be quiet, or it can be violent, but it needs to serve the story, be relevant to the characters, and be a natural product of the type of world you've created.

Creating conflict for missions that are compelling is key to making your worldbuilding feel alive and present. Not every mission needs to be action-packed to be enjoyable—sometimes quieter or quirkier missions, depending on the tone and genre of your game, are far more engaging and compelling. The key I've found here is to find the motivation for characters because missions let players directly interact with the issues of the world. Missions (or quests) are often how we highlight the pressures the world exerts on its people and how we make these playable. Missions directly surface tensions from worldbuilding, so it's important to know what kinds of tensions already exist in your world.

So let's explore how conflict surfaces tensions from the worldbuilding and how these different pressures can materialize in gameplay.

Finding Yourself in a World: *Stonefly's* Ecosystem and *Sable's* Gliding

Let's take a quick look at *Stonefly* (Flight School Studio, 2021), focused on playable character Annika, a young woman on an adventure to recover a stolen family heirloom. In *Stonefly*, humans and bugs co-exist together and so the world revolves around this conceit: Annika flies on the back of crickets, and the mech she inhabits is reminiscent of a spider. And while Annika goes in search of the bug-mech family heirloom that got stolen, she also has to contend with bugs that are more dangerous than others. Even still, *Stonefly* features non-lethal combat, a comment both on Annika as a character and the world she exists in.

In an interview at *Polygon*, creative director Adam Volker explains that "We figured that these societies would have evolved alongside the other critters of the forest. Some of them are dangerous, but killing them would cut short the role they play in the larger forest's ecosystem".[23] The world of *Stonefly* includes combat, but it is focused on stunning and disabling, not killing, because killing in this world would have a direct and disastrous effect on the world's ecosystem. And that's not what Annika's motivation is. She doesn't want to destroy. She's not trying to survive on a hostile planet. She's trying to recover something of value that was taken from her—something that is also the locus of Annika's own attempt at understanding who she is in this world and in her family.

The conflict of this world isn't centered around war, but rather around Annika finding herself and her place in the world. Sometimes that world is hostile, sometimes it's open, but it's a world centered around co-existence and exploration first and foremost, and so the combat being non-lethal reflects that element of the world. Annika's conflict is largely internal (she's figuring out who she is), but there are external elements to her efforts to retrieve the lost heirloom, as well. Just as she's discovering herself, she's discovering the world and realizing that there are frictions that exist in both. It's a really sweet and sometimes challenging game about exploration of both self and the world.

We see a different side of this same concept in *Sable*. *Sable* is an open-ended game where players are tasked with having the titular character explore her world and learn what it is she wants to do to contribute to her community and society. This coming-of-age exploration experience is called a "gliding". In Sable's gliding, she explores her world first and foremost. She learns how to glide (literally) and how to climb, and after getting comfortable with both, she begins to experience the richness that exists in her world via learning new biomes and meeting new people, both of which provide obstacles for her to overcome. The conflict in *Sable* is never violent, nor is it based around opposition. The conflict are obstacles that Sable needs to overcome to learn more about the world so she knows what she wants to be in it. She must collect badges by completing tasks for others because her goal is to learn and to know, not survival or war.

And it works really well in creating this evocative sense of place that doesn't preclude hostility but isn't based on it. In a fireside chat as part of LudoNarraCon, Meghna Jayanth and Kim Belair talk about their work *Sable*. Jayanth did worldbuilding and narrative design for *Sable*, whereas Belair and Sweet Baby Inc. did the writing. The fireside chat is fascinating and worth watching, as Belair and Jayanth get into the interplay between the worldbuilding Jayanth did and the ways in which Belair honored that work by bringing it to life in the characters of the world. At one point in the conversation, Belair notes that the world of Sable wasn't built from the world's worst moments, but rather from ways in which the culture emerged,[24] and this gave room for *Sable* to truly be a different kind of world and story.

And this works because *Sable* is a game that is deeply about the titular character, a young woman, finding herself through the world. *Sable* is about people and it's about how people exist in the world, so the things the players do, the quests they go on in the game, reflect this. Alongside Sable, the player is learning about different people, different jobs, and different ways of existing in and relating to the world, and the conflict of the game isn't about resisting these or righting wrongs, but rather about discovering where they all fit in. It's a soft internal conflict, one where the obstacle is external in so far as it could be a mountain that must be climbed or a task that must be fulfilled. But more holistically, the tension is purely around Sable needing to learn more, to explore more, to know more fully herself and how she sees herself in the world that surrounds her.

Psychonauts 2's Externalizing Internal Conflict

Psychonauts 2 (Double Fine, 2021) follows the prequel's main character, Raz, as he officially enters the telepathic spy agency, the Psychonauts, after the events of the first game. The Psychonauts are a group of telepaths, who complete epic missions by going into the minds of villains (and each other) in order to save the day. It's wild, it's bombastic, and it neatly collapses the idea of external and internal conflict onto each other.

Psychonauts 2 starts with a high-stakes mission in the mind of the villain (Doctor Loboto) from the previous game. This level is built around dentistry, featuring obstacles made from teeth (lots of teeth). Rife with stylized body horror, this intro mission is fully off the rails, and intentionally so. It starts off with Raz and the Psychonauts trying to trick Loboto into giving up the name of his boss and devolves into them trying to survive Loboto's mental landscape of chattering teeth and bad thoughts. And it immediately establishes the boundaries of this world, namely that there really aren't any boundaries. The worldbuilding contains the boundless capabilities of what lurks in one's mind, and the disturbing tutorial mission of Loboto's teeth nightmare does an excellent job of establishing this non-parameter. The conflicts in this world are an intentional mishmash of internal and external conflict, with high stakes for both the world and the people in it.

After players complete Loboto's teeth-nightmare mission, the game immediately switches gears to the mundanity of the Psychonauts headquarters and Raz's fall from grace from an honorary Psychonaut agent to an intern. The contrast of the high stakes, high drama, and high surrealism of Loboto's hall of teeth-horrors with the bureaucratic and hierarchical world of the Psychonauts HQ creates the perfect tension for Raz to contend with in the game: he is qualified to be an agent, but being a Psychonaut is akin to being an FBI agent and Raz needs to follow protocol. It creates a wonderful juxtaposition in terms of both the capabilities of this world (there really are no boundaries when missions involve people's psyches) and the limitations of this world (there are, however, strict limitations when you're just an intern).

But it's more than just the settings that makes *Psychonauts 2's* conflict so compelling. Levels, art, and the narrative are constructed around externalizing internal conflict when trying to solve missions with stakes higher than just one person's thoughts. The game is full of enemies that reference our internal conflicts, such as Doubts, Bad Ideas, and Censors, all which arise in thematically important moments. Censors essentially act as bouncers, trying to rid anything that doesn't belong in a person's psyche. Raz first confronts a Bad Idea when he is in Agent Forsythe's psyche trying to get her to change her mind about letting interns out on field missions. This a nice, humorous moment to explore the tensions of a world where conflict is epic and has world-altering consequences, but one where you're still dealing with humans, who are fraught, who are complicated, and whose minds are a messy place of emotion. The mission that should be about stopping the Delugians (main enemy faction of the game) actually becomes about Raz trying to fix the damage he did by meddling in Forsythe's thoughts. He's not fighting Delugians or saving the world by going toe-to-toe with the enemy; he's doing so by fixing the errors in thinking he caused when he tried to change Forsythe's worldview on risks and what she associates with risk. The repercussions are huge (and exist outside of Forsyth and Raz), but Raz has to confront the internal landscape of Forsythe in order to help the external mission. Since, as Forsythe says, being a Psychonaut is about helping people fight their own demons, after all.

The UI of the game is also adding important textural elements to this deliberate dual worldbuilding. Raz tracks his missions in his intern orientation manual. His abilities are visualized as patches provided by teachers. This diegetic menu system really reinforces the duality of the *Psychonauts 2* world as exemplified in the mission structure: it's a world with limitless possibility because brains are amazing things, but it's still a world with rules and policy.

EXPRESSING THE ENVIRONMENT OF A WORLD

As mentioned in Chapter 2, the environment of a game world is very closely connected to worldbuilding. Environment art is the very literal creation of the objects, flora, and spaces that players will inhabit and potentially interact with. But of course, a world is more than just the natural environment. A world is composed of flora and fauna, yes, but it's also what the civilization looks like there, who the people are, what their clothing and fashion choices say about the world, in addition to the geographical distinctions of the place.

In a private interview, Nate Purkeypile (solo developer at Just Purkeypile Games and former level artist on games such as *Fallout 3* and *Skyrim*) explained to me that "world design is a very holistic thing where art and design have to come together to build a world that not only helps build the fiction/tone of the world, but also plays well".[25] Environment art isn't just an art-centric approach but is done through a collaboration of what requirements other job disciplines have, such as level design, quest design, story moments, audio soundscapes, etc. The environment in a game is just like the environment in our world: it is full of *stuff*. And this stuff is visual, absolutely, but it's also auditory, it's full of people, of moments and movement. Each area is an ecosystem unto itself, with its own rules and interactions, and collaboration is important here for achieving a place that feels full and believable.

When I say the "environment", I mean the literal environment art and visual direction and distinction of the world. But I also mean everything else that comes with an environment, as well, such as level design, narrative devices, and the soundscape. What I really mean when I say environment here is the place that a player inhabits in a game, in consideration of all the senses.[26] Think of *Fallout 3*'s radio stations. *Fallout 3* features a whole host of dead radio stations across the landscape. Players can break into these areas, flip the switch, and let the broadcasts wash across the area. While these radio stations provide some tangible gameplay rewards (loot), they also are helping to stitch together the environment of the world and the sense of place here. Broadcasting something in Morse code or an S.O.S. feeds into the dystopian landscape and adds an auditory texture to the visual details of the world, while also illustrating the ways in which humans can resist and connect in a dystopian wasteland.

A believable environment is the sum of its parts. And audio is an incredibly important part of creating an unforgettable sense of place. Michelle Hwu explains that

> When it comes to designing sounds for a location that doesn't exist in real life, we have to rely on the narrative team and game directors for audio direction. We need to ask questions like 'What

kind of fauna exists there? Why does it exist there?' to help make a cohesive aural landscape. It's important for sound designers to know the lore of the world so they know how to accent certain sounds or not bring attention to them at all.[27]

Understanding the details and goals of the worldbuilding helps audio designers craft a soundscape that feels congruent with the visual landscape they find themselves in, as well as within the tonal mood of the story and the worldbuilding itself.

And as we saw in the "Determining the Feel of your World" deep dive, technical limitations (and capabilities) are also adding to the sense of the place in your world. The fog in *Silent Hill* was kept in later games when rendering power became more robust because it is atmospheric. Fog is needed less and less to cover for draw distance, but it's still an effective tool in building atmosphere and creating a sense of both place and scale, such as in *A Short Hike*, which uses fog and thick lines in the distance to indicate scale and distance as players climb the mountain higher and higher.

And of course, as both Purkeypile and Hwu establish, level design and narrative are also important elements of bringing an environment to life. The design of the space (level/environment art and audio design) and the implicit and explicit stories that are formed in this space (narrative and level design) all need to work together to create unforgettable and believable spaces.

Outer Wilds' Entire Solar System

Each planet and moon of *Outer Wilds* is a world unto itself. There are these incredibly detailed and highly specific places that feel distinct from each other. And that's because its environment is a compilation of every element of worldbuilding working together, such as physics, environment art, level design, environmental storytelling, narrative devices (text logs), HUD (the ship's diegetic solar system map), and specific soundscapes (the sound of dangerous ghost matter or quantum shards), all of which are remixed and combined in specific ways to really highlight the commonalities and differences of each planet. In Chapter 2, I referenced the incredible physics in the game and how this helps create the distinct feel of each planet and moon in *Outer Wilds*, as well as the level design of the Hourglass Twins. I won't retread that ground here, but only because there's so much to discuss when it comes to how *Outer Wilds* builds its distinct and memorable planets.

To begin, let's establish a quick overview of a few of the planets that exist in *Outer Wilds*. Players start on Timber Hearth, the woodsy planet of the protagonist, and its moon, Attlerock. There's the Hourglasss Twins. There's Brittle Hollow and its moon, Hollow's Lantern (both discussed in Chapter 2 when discussing the physics implementation in the game). Then there's Giant's Deep, an oceanic planet with hurricanes, and Dark Bramble, an overgrown planet of roots and weeds housing monstrous horrors. Each space has a distinct visual design. Giant's Deep's oceans and hurricanes are a distinct visual contrast from Timber Hearth's tall trees and green grass to Dark Bramble's foggy, opaque mass of twisting branches and fog. The palettes of each planet are different, as well, with Timber Hearth boasting lush greens and soft browns, compared to the aquamarine and seafoam green of Giant's Deep. Brittle Hollow is a dark, dark blue, interspersed with hot reds and oranges, and Dark Bramble is a foggy gray, broken up by dark masses of branches.

In a Unity Creator Spotlight on the art of *Outer Wilds*, Wesley Martin (art director at Mobius Digital) and Jon Oppenheimer (3D environment and VFX artist at Mobius Digital) detail their process for the individual planets in *Outer Wilds*, talking about all aspects of the art direction, including the technical art behind the game, such as VFX, tools, and shaders. In that spotlight video, Martin describes the art direction as following the catchphrase of "camping in space", which is a hybrid of rustic and natural environments combined with classic NASA aesthetics of the 1960s and 1970s.[28] It's a beautiful layering of tangible aspects of our real world (national parks) with the grandiosity of an entire solar system, which creates the specificity of the feeling of *Outer Wilds'* entire solar system: these feel like familiar landscapes, despite being totally alien worlds.

Timber Heart's flora is deeply reflective of woods, whereas Giant's Deep oceans give root to disparate patches of islands, with limited trees and more rocky formations that can withstand the rise and flow of the oceans. The distinct flora and fauna of each planet is so crucial to establishing its identity. The cacti on the Hourglass Twins create tiny threats, whereas Brittle Hollow is a planet in a constant state of ruin, with traversal taking into account competing needs for gravity. And this distinctive visual appearance is bolstered by each planet having its own puzzle system driven by the unique level design and physics simulation of each planet. Timber Hearth's gravity is affected by its moon. Dark Bramble requires slow and thoughtful movement. Giant's Deep is frenetic and chaotic. Brittle Hollow is falling apart under your feet. Each planet feels different to be on, in addition to looking so distinct.

But these planets are more than just environmental biomes. They are also homes. Timber Heart is a lively camping planet, with wood huts, campfires and marshmallows, museums and buildings established in the name of understanding their place in the universe. Timber Hearth is warm and welcoming, and the architecture there reflects that. It's presented as a little backwoods, a newly evolved group of slightly amphibian-looking bipedal creatures wearing roughly sewn-together clothes, if only to serve as a contrast to the presence of the Nomai felt elsewhere. Whereas the Hearthians are reminiscent of aquatic creatures finding their legs, the Nomai are regal, as technologically savvy as they are intellectually curious. They are covered in fur and wear robes of green and gold. And these distinctions carry over into the homes of each civilization. The Hearthian civilization feels like a campground, reminiscent of a tight-knit community and one that reflects the woodsy planet they were born on. On the other hand, the Nomai ruins are technologically advanced spaces, complete with structures that require the Nomai's use of telekinesis to navigate, as well as replete with adornments that imply an appreciation of beauty.

But in addition to these aspects, the soundscape of each planet is also hugely important. The first tool players are given is the Signalscope, a telescope designed to track sounds. Set it to different frequencies and players can chase anomalies and track characters based purely on the sounds they emit into the universe. The Quantum Fluctuations frequency tracks quantum shards in the universe, all of which emit a sort of mechanical humming sound. The Distress Beacon frequency pinpoints high-pitched signals leading to abandoned pods. And then there's the Outer Wilds Ventures frequency, which is tuned to track the music played by NPCs in the world, who are scattered in a variety of places across the solar system.

It's the Outer Wilds Ventures frequency that for me is deeply evocative of each individual planet. Tracking Gabbro's flute versus Feldspar's harmonica versus Esker's simple whistling provides distinct soundscapes for the places players eventually find these characters in. The Outer Wilds Ventures form a diegetic soundtrack created by the characters spread across the solar system. But what's really cool about these distinct elements is players are able to position themselves and their Signalscope to get all five Outer Wilds Ventures in line at the same time, and when doing so, each individual sound builds together to create the full, robust, and perfectly synced version of the song they are all playing separately. It provides a beautiful melody, but it's also narratively rich: even separated as they are, everyone in the solar system is still connected. The only other time everyone in the universe is united by the same sound is the musical cue of the explosion signaling the end of the current time loop. And well, the Outer Wilds Ventures frequency is a little bit more welcoming and optimistic than that. But in both instances, the soundscape of *Outer Wilds* is doing such an incredible job of adding to the environment art to create a vivid sense of place in the game.

Cloud Gardens' Flora as Protagonist

A key part of any world is the type of flora that lives there, adding depth and distinction to mark biomes as different from each other. *Ark: Survival Evolved* uses flora particularly well to indicate the type of biome players are in and what resources they can find there. Purple flowers indicate silk and are more common in desert biomes where players will need to craft silk clothing to withstand the heat. Redwoods indicate dense forests with tree-climbing predators and reduced light. Flora is rarely ever just dressing. Different types of flora become important gameplay items, even above and beyond being harvestable resources. Flora can be weapons, such as the Fire Flower power up, originating in *Super Mario Bros* (Nintendo, 1985), or as consumables, such as the different herbs in the *Resident Evil* franchise indicating different types of healing (green for health, red for poison, combined green-red for both). Flora can be used just for set-dressing, but it can also be so much more.

To talk a bit more about how flora gets used in clever worldbuilding ways in video games, let's take a brief look at *Cloud Gardens* (Noio, 2020). *Cloud Gardens* is a lovely puzzle game, set in a dystopian version of our world. The core gameplay of *Cloud Gardens* is to plant seeds on wrecks and ruins to help nature reclaim and grow atop of the destroyed vestiges of our world. It's quiet, it's calm, and it's about growing gardens in the ruins of civilization, so cars, highways, street signs, and broken-down sheds all become planters for gorgeous flowers to bloom.

In a review for Kotaku, Renata Price talks about the juxtaposition between *Cloud Gardens* and a game like *Umurangi Generation* (discussed next). Price writes, "Where *Umurangi Generations* is great at telling stories through its environment, *Cloud Gardens* hands those tools to the player, and gently encourages them to tell their own stories".[29] Both are games set in a messy dystopia, but whereas *Umurangi Generation* is concerned with the humans at the center of it, *Cloud Gardens* displaces humanity entirely. *Cloud Gardens* isn't concerned with humanity, but it is concerned with its sense of place and how the environment reclaims space after catastrophe.

The way in which players grow gardens in *Cloud Gardens* is simple. Find a seed (usually as part of the game's progression). Plant that seed somewhere (different plants have different requirements, but seeds can be planted on sign posts, on chairs, on cars, on the asphalt itself, etc.). Then drop items (garbage, really) nearby in order to make those seeds grow. Players throw garbage, like beer bottles and cans, and the act of tossing these items near the seeds is what makes the plants grow strong and tall. *Cloud Gardens* is about where and how flora grows in a world that no longer has human caretakers but still has the remaining vestiges of their presence.

Aside from dirt and seeds, no natural flora exist in the diorama until the player starts growing things. The growth and the look of the dystopian diorama are entirely in the player's control, making the gameplay revolve around gardening decisions. The flora is integral to this world, and it's also integral to the main gameplay. The plants have characteristics that determine where seeds can be planted (such as do they stick to objects or not, and do they grow horizontal or not), in addition to their visual distinctions, which makes knowing and understanding how the flora grows an important part of creating the dioramas that players want.

The ways in which the plants grow was not just an aesthetic decision, either, although the differences in their growth do add to the game's beauty. In an interview with GameDeveloper.com, creators of *Cloud Gardens* Thomas Vandenberg and Elijah Cauley explain that there were both gameplay and technical aspects behind how this operated: gameplay in the sense that they wanted players to have some control in creating the diorama and have this related to gameplay progression, but technical in that while players could choose where to plant seeds and help them grow, they couldn't decide the exact shape and flow of the grown plant. Limiting player controls was a decision made to not overtax their simulation.[30] So players can choose where to plant a seed, but they can't choose how it grows in that environment, a decision that resulted from a combination of gameplay and technical considerations but that creates this really nice sense of co-authoring the world between the player and the game. *Cloud Gardens* is a world that is indifferent to humanity, so it's a nice symmetry that the plants and flowers don't grow entirely according to player design.

It works. It's part of what makes the experience of *Cloud Gardens* both so relaxing and so evocative. It's small and subtle, but as players plant seeds and grow the flora, they are creating the distinctions of this world. Both plant placement and the objects used to grow the plants feed into what this world is about, the possible stories it could contain, and where the world is heading.

Environmental Storytelling as Mechanic in *Umurangi Generation*

As discussed in Chapter 2, environmental storytelling is perhaps one of the most widely recognized concepts associated with video game worldbuilding. Environmental storytelling includes corpses, the objects found in a home, the scattershot of litter in a street, and the names on the spines of books on a bookcase—all of these contribute to creating a sense of place and story in the environment. And while even static environmental storytelling is a really evocative and effective manner of worldbuilding via level art, level design, and narrative, I want to take a moment to look at *Umurangi Generation* (Origame Digital, 2020) in how it uses environmental storytelling as a mechanic, as not just world flavor and detail, but as a main mode of understanding the world. *Umurangi Generation* is a game about the end of the world, and player's role as a photographer in documenting the evolution of this world. The game occurs at a specific moment in its own history and uses the photography mechanic and environmental storytelling to communicate the escalating world state brilliantly.

The game—a low-fi first-person photography game that leans heavily into gaining and using different lenses and editing tools as gameplay variety—has players hunting for objectives to take pictures of in the environment. In the first level, Maua View, players are tasked with objectives such as taking a picture of "the word 'Mix'", "a Union Jack", "7 birds", "a disposable camera", etc. These objectives and the corresponding layout of the level and its environmental storytelling are setting the stage for the specificity of this place. These are the people, these are their lives, and this is where they live.[31] The objectives are a combination of people, the environment, and details in the level, such as graffiti or objects left in particular places, like the boombox and disposable camera.

But as players progress through the game, the environment and the photographs of that environment begin to coalesce into detailing the political systems at play in this world, the ramifications of war, and climate change. The second level, Otumoe Tai, is a military building and asks for more loaded objectives, such as "a Sarcastic 'Property of the UN'", "a skull and knife", and "10 solar panels". The texture of the world is beginning to become coherent through the settings players are moving through and the details put into these settings. The third level, Kati Kati, asks for a "Manala Memorial", "the word 'Cops'", "15 candles", and so forth, continuing the careful layering of the tensions formed in this world that is being realized as dystopian. Players explore Kati Kati, discovering memorials and a world figuring out how to resist political machinations like war. But there's something bigger growing in the environmental details that players *aren't* asked to look at. The world is changing, disaster is impending, and a sense of doom exists just underneath the layer that the player is being told to look at it. It's a nice moment of distraction—if players only focus on their objectives, they'll still glean a pretty clear state of the world and how people are responding to it. But if players spend time with the non-objective details, the graffiti that doesn't contain any gameplay words, the collection of items and images and posters that won't allow them to progress past the level, a fuller, darker, scarier picture begins to form.

This gameplay-driven hyper specificity creates a really interesting tension. It can cause players (like myself) to gloss over important details in the environment, which clearly reference the game's later reveal and the world state. This creates a productive narrative tension. You are playing as a photographer, somebody whose access to and role in these spaces is to document. But hyper focusing on what you are *supposed* to document (aka what you've been asked to deliver photographs of) can cause players to miss the forest for the trees, creating a subtle commentary on the flawed and subjective process of documenting history as it happens, particularly when considering who is asking what to be photographed (and what not to be photographed) and why.

Umurangi Generation gets weird, going deeper and deeper into its dystopian setting, and maintaining a fascinating tension between the events of the world around the player and the intimate mechanics of documenting the events via details of the world. *Umurangi Generation*'s environmental storytelling is so excellent because it's a game that forces players to really examine and understand the relationship between what the environment is showing, what players are being asked to look at (and how that is a limited perspective on the environment), what they are not being asked to look at, and how all of this is reflective of its world. The game handles contrast between revisiting previous levels in different world states, as well, to really highlight this tension and intimacy with the environment. A photography game, *Umurangi Generation* is built around environmental storytelling and expertly weaves in a story of loss, apathy, resistance, satire, horror, and community through the world and the player's documenting of the world.

DOCUMENTING A WORLD'S HISTORY

As noted in Chapter 2's subsection for "Narrative Collectibles", I alluded to the fact that "lore" might be a contentious word. It's certainly a word that gets used a lot, often in different contexts for different effects, and as such it's actually a bit difficult to nail down exactly what we (and others) mean when we say lore. Do we mean any details about the world? Or more details about the story? Or the in-world explanation for gameplay abilities? Or a character's backstory? Or story information delivered in static formats (collectibles, codex entries, etc.)? Do we mean all of the above or none of the above?

Since Chapter 2 was an overview of how many job disciplines contribute to worldbuilding, I didn't spend too long on the concept of "lore" there or how we deliver it. But I don't want to ignore it entirely, either, because whatever meaning of the word we think of, it means something to many, particularly in worldbuilding. So let's keep using the definition I established in Chapter 2, but let's build it out a bit. Earlier I defined lore as "non-essential story/world details", which is also extremely vague, but a definition we can drill down into. My definition is a bit of a clumsy way of saying: these are the elements that contribute to the texture of the world and not just necessarily the plot development of the game. These details further enhance and enrich players' understanding of the place they are in and the characters that inhabit it by providing additional details, story points, or a history (be it a personal history, a history specific to one place, or a capital h history, which is the geopolitical timeline of major events of the place). It might not help players gameplay-wise and it might not solve burning plot questions players have (it can do both, of course), but it builds out the world through synecdoche and specificity.

The device commonly used to house these highly specific, highly symbolic details are collectibles. What is a collectible exactly then? A collectible is a piece of ephemera from the game's world that contains highly specific information. This information can be character background (an audio log of a NPC's activity right before their death), level and mission information (a key card needed for progression, a trinket that needs to be delivered), or it can exist solely as worldbuilding detail (a book that exists in the world, character diaries focused on world and history). Collectibles take whatever form and shape are important to the game's story and the game's world. Furthermore, the power of a collectible, and its ability to deliver fascinating and engaging world details, is not just in what it says, or what it looks like, but it's also in where it's found and the actions players take to find the collectible. The context of the collectible adds weight and meaning and becomes an opportunity to further draw out the significance of the collectible for the world it exists in.

Tell Me Why's Personal History

Now let's get into all of the good stuff about collectibles. Why are they important? What makes a collectible good? How do different job disciplines (such as UI, object art, and level design) make collectibles feel resonant in our world? And to do so, let's examine the collectible system in *Tell Me Why* (DONTNOD, 2020).

Tell Me Why is a story-driven game about two twins (Tyler and Alyson) reuniting in order to clean up and sell their deceased mom's house. It doesn't sound like there would be a lot of speculative worldbuilding here, except *Tell Me Why* is a game about dualities. It's about two twins and their divergent paths reconnecting. It's about two different lives as the result of a singular, traumatic incident. It's about two different versions of the same story colliding to find the truth. And, when it comes to the worldbuilding, it's about two different worlds simultaneously co-existing. *Tell Me Why* is, for the most part, a realistic game set in Alaska. But this realism gets undercut by a deeply recurrent fabulist[32] thread woven into the game's reality. The twins are psychically connected, a telepathy they shared in their youth and consequently thought was gone as adults, a fiction of a fairy tale childhood and a symbol of their once inseparableness.

But even beyond that, *Tell Me Why* has players explore a world with two different layers: the first is the realistic layer of the house the twins grew up in and experienced deeply traumatic events in, and the second is a fairy tale layer consisting of the imaginary goblin world they created as kids. Tyler and Alyson called themselves "goblins" as children, and with their mother, they authored an entire fantasy world around their lives in a small town in Alaska. The house is full of hints of this, of thematic puzzles they left behind as children, of books and toys and figurines that were all composed in service of this secondary world they imagined they inhabited. And as the twins progress through packing up their childhood home and unpacking the deep trauma they've both lived with, the goblin world seeps into the real world in the form of a shadowy monster that has stalked them since childhood: the Mad Hunter.

But let's rewind a bit and return to the collectibles players find scattered throughout the world of *Tell Me Why*. The main collectible in the game comes in the form of these wood figurines, carvings of all the main characters in the stories Tyler and Alyson wove around themselves, stories told and recorded down by their mother in the book of goblins (a gorgeously detailed book available in game, as well, that offers extraneous worldbuilding and character backstory, as well as gameplay hints, in the form of allegorical fairy tales). But the wood figurines are what I want to focus on here. The figurines are beautiful pieces of digital ephemera. These wood carvings are slightly rudimentary in their execution, but painted with love, these figurines represent important figures to the twins and offer a vehicle for unpacking the various entanglements of their lives. The first two figurines players find are the goblins, one in Tyler and Alyson's rooms, respectively. It's the first moment of bleed between the fairy tale world and the real world. But it's the third figurine that I want to focus on, where the two worlds really begin to collide.

Players can find the third figurine under the back porch of the house, as Tyler. This "under the porch" level design takes on the shape of a dungeon: it's dark, it's a slight maze, and it's full of both garbage and memories. The twins are looking for a key and they know they kept it in their "dragon's lair" under the porch. As players explore this area, they can find a lot of discarded childhood ephemera down there: maps, chalk recordings of the twins' games, the dragon's lair, and another wood figurine, this one of the Mad Hunter. Crucially, this is the moment that Tyler and Alyson realize they still have their telepathic link to each other, so Alyson helps Tyler navigate the maze of the porch. The player is discovering the fairy tale collectibles and ephemera while Tyler and Alyson are discovering that their telepathic link wasn't just a childhood fantasy. It's a deliberate moment meant to collapse the two worlds into one, while also resurfacing the threat of the Mad Hunter as antagonist.

Everything about this scene is working to subtly fold the real world into the fairy tale world. The level design and art of this area beneath the porch function like a dungeon (it's a maze and players are looking for a dragon and its treasure, discovering goblins along the way). Alyson and Tyler are finding it together for the first time via a connection they thought they had imagined. And it's all encapsulated in a quiet, calm moment. Neither is under threat; the path forward is easily found. The game wants players to make these discoveries, of both the things the kid-versions of Tyler and Alyson left behind, but also of the Mad Hunter collectible. The Mad Hunter here represents the threat, the should-be foe if this were a real dungeon. But it's not (yet), and so the moment of finding one of their figurines discarded under the porch serves as a point of no return for the twins, an inevitable collapse of fairy tale and real world.

This moment of finding the Mad Hunter figurine is so deeply resonant of the world the game is showing. This is a world where fairy tales can bleed into reality (and not just in the imagination of two kids), but it's also one where dark figures exist, where trauma and harm is real. If *Tell Me Why* shows fairy tales, it's to show that there's a dark side to the fantasy, as well, that escapism requires an escape from something in the first place. The game purposefully teases a potentially fantastical world living underneath the seams of their otherwise mundane reality, and this fabulist overlay becomes the necessary distance the twins need in order to grapple with the trauma of their mother's death and her mistreatment of them as kids. The game is about heavy, difficult things (transphobia, child abuse, mental illness), and the wood carvings become a way of grappling with these elements slowly.

These wooden carvings are tracing the twins' personal history of their lives and their childhood. They represent significant people and significant events, ones which would never get recorded in a history book or a town hall record, but which are significant enough to Tyler and Alyson so as to shape who they are as adults. These collectibles stitch together a personal history for Tyler and Alyson, becoming both clues and relevant touchpoints as they dive together into their past to uncover the truth about who their mother was and why she treated them the way she did. The collectibles aren't creating a timeline of the small town in Alaska they live in. Instead, the collectibles create a personal history for Tyler and Alyson, a history which is the backbone to the entire game.

Prey's History of a Place Stuck in Time

Like non-narrative collectibles, it's not just the "what" of audio and text logs that is important—it's also the where, the how, and the why. An audio or text log is primarily about what information they contain, yes, but where players find it, how they find it, and why they're compelled to look for it, either as a protagonist or a player, is also crucial in determining how effective these types of narrative devices are.

So to talk about audio and text logs, let's look at *Prey* (Arkane Studios, 2017). *Prey* is a world set in an alternate universe, one that takes a different course from our own where John F. Kennedy isn't assassinated, and the United States and Soviet Union work together to contain a hostile alien presence that made contact with them. And because *Prey* allows for players to freely roam the space station (Talos 1) as they see fit, the use of text and audio logs to stitch together the world of Talos 1 and how that connects to the mystery players are trying to solve plays a crucial part. These logs create an important texture to what life used to be like on Talos 1 so the horror of what has happened is even more real in contrast. They are also the main documents Morgan (the playable character) has in unraveling the catastrophe that has occurred there, as well as understanding their own relationship to the catastrophe. While the documents are just the everyday minutiae of a crew working on a space station, they take on the important role of documenting the catastrophe and providing a timeline of events.

In *Prey*, there are two main modes of collecting these logs: TranScribes (audio) and computers (text). TranScribes in *Prey* are a personal recording device, one which houses all different manner of communication, including voice logs and emails. (The TranScribe is also the diegetic menu for *Prey*, as it's the device that lets playable character Morgan access maps, mods, and inventory.) *Prey*'s audio and text logs do an excellent job of depicting the world of Talos 1, a world that experienced an atrocity and is now in stasis, both living and not.[33] Talos 1 is by no means a dead space station—there is life there (some human, some alien, some a mix of both), but even beyond that, the robust text and audio logs players find of the deceased create such a complete sense of space it's easy for Talos 1 to still feel alive. The NPCs of Talos 1 left behind so much ephemera, both gameplay-driven and not, that while players are mostly alone in the course of the game, it's easy to not feel alone. The corpses are chatty, or at least they've left behind enough ephemera to make Talos 1 still feel alive.

First off, there are the emails. There are plenty of emails to find that provide hints or suggestions for exploring and gameplay (places of interest to visit, people in trouble, how to find passwords and gentle chidings about not making your password easily found), as well as plenty of world-building details (the inventory of expected food on Talos 1, complaints about the lack of sparkling wine, the sort of minutiae you expect to find on a space station). These emails provide characterization, important setting information, as well as reference points for where to go and to explore. The emails are also full of bureaucracy, of people forgetting their passwords, of getting reprimanded, and of simply living their life on this station. They create a sense of fullness to the place and also create familiarity: as players are exploring Talos 1, chances are they've already read about certain NPCs or certain facilities, creating a sort of intimacy with the space even if it's their first time playing the game. This familiarity fits with who Morgan, the playable character, is since while Morgan is not an outsider here at Talos 1, they are beginning to uncover the truth of the motives of certain people aboard the space station, and their own implication.

The audio logs serve these same purposes, as well, but heighten the sense of character and place by adding quality voice acting. The audio logs provide world details, gameplay hints, as well as important textures to the world, such as those found in the audio log recordings of psych evaluations of some of the crew members. These psych evals illustrate both the events of Talos 1 and how the characters that live and work there feel about it. In Danielle Sho's audio log of her psych eval, for example, she refers to political cover ups in reference to both what is happening on Talos 1 and to historical details of events on Earth, suggesting a suspicion and resistance to the events happening on Talos 1 long before Morgan ever begins their adventure there.

Because *Prey*'s setting is a single, interconnected space station, tracking down the bodies of the employees stationed there becomes a common theme of the game. This is a workplace, so each employee can be found and tracked via personnel records from security terminals. And most employees do have a name and a backstory. Talos 1 is a world that is brought to life by the ways in which the mundane reality of it was ground to a halt. We understand the world of what Talos 1 used to be and now is because of the way it is frozen in time.

And while all of these elements are so crucial in developing what Talos 1 is like as a place, to both live and work, I want to now talk about the fictional tabletop roleplaying game, Fatal Fortress, that exists in universe. NPC Abigail Foy is a game master on Talos 1 and has recruited a number of other crew members into her game of Fatal Fortress 2. To learn about the game (and the dynamics of the players), players can collect a lot of ephemera from it, including emails communicating details of getting together to play, character sheets for each player, as well as audio logs that display some of the tensions between the people playing, namely the post-break-up awkwardness between Abigail and Danielle.

The game of Fatal Fortress 2 in the world of *Prey* is dripping with so much personality and world details. While discussing the policies around what can and can't be recorded on TranScribes, it covers the minutiae of work to interpersonal dynamics between characters, such as Abigail and Danielle's complicated relationship, to the ultimate disaster aboard Talos 1, as characters are recorded in the final moments of losing their humanity. While not about Fatal Fortress 2, the tense relationship between Danielle and Abigail is also illustrated in text logs found on Talos 1. Players can find hand-written apologies on crumpled pieces of paper—notably found near waste baskets—where Danielle is working out how to apologize to Abby, but ultimately failing to do so. These, combined with the Fatal Fortress 2 ephemera, stitch together the reality of people living on Talos 1, particularly the ruined relationship between the two women.

The Fatal Fortress 2 ephemera begins to coalesce into a mission, as well. Abigail has planned a treasure hunt for her players, and players need to find the maps that belong to each of the players in order to track down a code to open a treasure (a chipset for the player's suit). Finding the hand-drawn maps really creates such an intense sense of space on Talos 1. They are crudely drawn, but effective in guiding the player to where they need to be to solve the long-dead treasure hunt. And players find them in heartbreaking places, on corpses, and other places loaded with meaning. Each location becomes a piece of the puzzle of not just what happened to the Fatal Fortress 2 players, but also what has happened on Talos 1. While not explicitly about the typhoon (the aliens) or the catastrophe, these logs help to create a highly specific history of Talos 1. Yes, these logs depict a world flash frozen at this specific point in its own history. But the history of Talos 1 isn't just the catastrophe—it's the history of the people who lived and worked there and all of the baggage humans bring to a space station.

THE TENSIONS WITH HISTORY

While I've been using the word "history" in this section to refer to the world's history, such as characters and past events and not in the academic sense of history (the study of history or the complete history of a place), it is worth talking about the way in which games present a world's complete history. While the concept of capital h history is grandiose and often an integral part of worldbuilding, it isn't always something that is surfaced directly to the player.

When I say "capital h history", what I mean is the entire history of a place and the sorts of details that would be coalesced into a timeline spanning generations. This differs from the personal history of a game like *Tell Me Why*, which isn't concerned with the history of Alaska or the towns there, but rather with Alyson and Tyler's personal history and accepting their past in order to move on. And this differs from the contained history of a place like Talos 1 in *Prey*, which is a timeline of specific events related to a catastrophe, rather than the history of the world Talos 1 exists in.

So when I say "capital h history", I mean the history of it all, the events and details that constitute the expansive legacy and major events of a place, concerned with sociological aspects as well as geopolitical ones. I want to focus on this meaning of history as distinct because this type of history is fraught, yet important to the understanding of a place and its relationships and its legacy. I say history is fraught because history is necessarily a subjective account, one in which the details that are either included or discarded is the result of a biased and subjective decision-making process. (We get a bit of this in *Prey*, with Danielle's suspicion of cover ups in Talos 1.) We all know the refrain of history is recorded by the victors. History, while presented as sterile and clean, is full of drama. In the chapter "Generating Histories" in *Procedural Storytelling in Game Design*, Jason Grinblat writes about the process they undertook to procedurally generate a history for their game *Caves of Qud* (Freehold Games, LLC, 2015). Grinblat took care, also, to emphasize that given the subjective and sometimes volatile nature of capital h history, "...all games that incorporate history make arguments about it, explicitly or implicitly".[34] Grinblat's point (and a lot of what makes *Caves of Qud* so good) is that history isn't neutral–it is deeply subjective and that subjectivity is the reflection of the people who exist in that world.

Some games directly challenge our relationship with this type of history, as well. Particularly, games like Elizabeth LaPensée's *When Rivers Were Trails* (Elizabeth LaPensée, 2019). *When Rivers Were Trails* is a 2D adventure game that is a subversive take on *The Oregon Trail* (Minnesota Educational Computing Consortium, 1985), particularly in how *The Oregon Trail* is criticized for presenting Indigenous peoples stereotypically,[35] a theme not uncommon in a lot of North American history and the media associated with it. So *When Rivers Were Trails* is an approach to the same historical events as *The Oregon Trail*, but from an Indigenous perspective in order to center Indigenous people, who are so often pushed to the margins even in stories and histories where they are—or should be—main characters. Built from the same point in history, *When Rivers Were Trails* uses similar gameplay mechanics to highlight the effect colonization had on an existing world and the people that lived there, a direct contrast to the pioneer fantasy of *The Oregon Trail*.

And while *When Rivers Were Trails* engages with actual history versus a fictional one, it's still a useful reference for considering how we engage with history in our worldbuilding. Like Grinblat emphasized, an invocation of history is saying something about history. History is not neutral, nor is our allusion to specific histories. Of *Caves of Qud*, Grinblat explains that "the game is about engaging with the artifacts of the past without the context that produced them",[36] drawing focus and attention to how players stitch together the events into a coherent narrative. *Caves of Qud* is about letting players create these narrative strands, co-authoring the story with the system, and by doing so, is directly calling to attention the subjective nature of a history. By presenting historical facts without context, the players are generating that context, in a process that is not scientific or sterile, but rather rife with our own cultural and personal perspectives and history.

CASE STUDY: A WORLD MADE FOR MULTIPLAYER IN *SEA OF THIEVES*

Sea of Thieves is a multiplayer pirate action-adventure game, set in an open world where players complete voyages for trading companies. *Sea of Thieves* is both a cooperative game (on boats of varying capacities, you can play with between one to three other players) and also a competitive game (you never know if other boats you encounter on the high seas are friend or foe). Because it's a pirate fantasy game, the goal of *Sea of Thieves* is to complete voyages for specific trading companies (the gold hoarder, the merchant, the order of souls, the hunter's call, and so forth), which players buy from NPCs and then try to complete before being attacked by other players, Krakens, sharks, skeletons, ghosts, and so forth.

In Chapter 2, I already discussed the superb ways *Sea of Thieves* uses day/night cycles and the skybox to create a reactive sense of place that feels alive. *Sea of Thieves* also blends diegetic and non-diegetic UI in impactful, and multiplayer-driven, ways. The map of the world is a fixed feature in each boat, rather than something accessible via a menu. Players have to scour the map table together to find the islands they want to visit and to chart their paths. And every voyage players can complete gets viewed as scrolls that players can look at or can turn around and show to other players. The Tall Tale quests come in physical books that players have to flip through its pages to discover where to go and what to do. There is so much depth to the worldbuilding of *Sea of Thieves*, particularly as a world designed for multiplayer (both cooperative and competitive), its environmental storytelling, and its update cycle as a live game.

Collaboration and/or competition mechanics stitch this world together, giving the world of *Sea of Thieves* a specific tenor and texture of being a pirate. To turn in found loot, players have to physically carry loot to sell it (and gain both gold and reputation for each trading company). This physical act of carrying builds in the need for collaboration with your shipmates: the more pirates on your ship, the faster—and safer—turning in loot goes. This loop also opens players up for attack from other pirates, though. Other players can intercept the turn in process, either by attacking players or their ship or simply stealing their loot. It's a mechanic that reinforces the main ethos of this world: you are a pirate and you are all some manner of thieves.

In addition to its mechanics creating a specific texture of this world, the game uses detailed and robust environmental storytelling, in combination with its diegetic map, to create a sense of place and history to the world of *Sea of Thieves*. Every aspect of *Sea of Thieves* is constructing a world built by and for pirates. The props on each island are common from trading outposts to untamed islands, illustrating a connective tissue between the NPCs who have established life on outposts and who are forging ahead on new islands. Paintings on rocks and in caves tell stories of past adventures on these islands. Corpses warn of danger, both environmental and from other pirates. Even the level design of the islands themselves tells specific stories of places, such as Thieves' Haven, which houses a wrecked ship and evidence of camp and a life started there. Shipwrecks in the water boast names and warn of the dangers of the sea. *Sea of Thieves* is a game of details, with new vignettes and evolutions of these details being added in live updates.

But even *Sea of Thieves'* traditional environmental storytelling is built in such a way as to support collaborative play while also detailing out a lived-in history of this world. *Sea of Thieves* uses scattered skeletons of

NPC pirates brilliantly, particularly in how it combines its environmental storytelling with a riddle system. Certain voyages are riddles that use environmental features to present clues that lead to the treasure. These riddles will tell you to look for elements such as a "painted tale of a monstrous foe", leading to a painting on a rock of a kraken, or the "angler's camp on the North East beach", leading to a small fishing camp, where human bones are sprawled on top of a rock, with the skull replaced with the spine of a fish. The environmental storytelling in *Sea of Thieves* is pulling its weight in creating a coherent sense of place and history at the same time by leaving all sorts of clues behind of the dangers of this world and vignette-style adventures of long-lost pirates. Enough pirates have met treacherous ends on these islands that their bones have become landmarks for intrepid treasure hunters, which indicates both the danger inherent to, but also the levity of, this world.

But what makes the environmental storytelling work so well in *Sea of Thieves* is the way in which it works best when knowledge can be pooled, a collective resource among the pirates you share your ship with. The environmental storytelling creates a shared mythology of the islands, with players remembering where things are based on experienced and storied knowledge of the island. Players' experiences on specific islands—fighting skeletons, hiding from other players, doing quests, etc.—all create moments of engaging with and understanding the little details of the environment. When riddles tell players to look for a palm tree that doesn't see sunlight, experience can guide them toward a specific cave system. Even clues and details are creating this mythology, because once a player has scoured an island looking for a skeleton next to a broken rowboat that experience forms their knowledge base of the islands. This type of environmental storytelling rewards intimate understanding of the islands, as well as collaboration. The game doesn't necessarily expect players to know every environmental vignette associated with a riddle—but it does expect players to be able to explore or work with others to solve it.

Additionally, what *Sea of Thieves* also does brilliantly is it layers thematically resonant worldbuilding with each of its updates in an act of mythopoeia (discussed in Chapter 1). Each update brings out a coherent evolution of the game's world, providing more details and nuance to a world that is, by design, open and expansive. When the game introduced story-based quests (Tall Tales), these quests built out the history of the world via the adventures of specific NPCs and skeleton enemies. These quests are multi-stepped and introduced quest-specific mechanics to the game, while also building out key elements of the world by exploring what adventures happened on the open seas before players embarked on their journey. This self-referential quality, when combined with the existing emergent narrative and worldbuilding built up from play, is creating a specific texture of myth and legends to the world of *Sea of Thieves*. Every detail contains a legendary quality, an element of a deeply shared and understood mythic history of the world.

And this is felt keenly in the way *Sea of Thieves* handles some of its live events, particularly those focused on the megalodons. The original megalodon live event, The Hungering Deep event in 2018, and the subsequent The Shrouded Deep live event in 2022, both created specific instances of mythopoeia and worldbuilding focused on collaboration and cooperation between separate ships, rather than just competitive play. The Hungering Deep event was the first instance of introducing the monstrous and gigantic megalodons to the game. But in order to summon a meg, at least two separate crews had to agree to work together by playing a specific sea shanty (players received the shanty and instrument from an NPC on an island, and all players had to travel to a specific location on the map, with one player constantly and consistently playing the tune) in order to summon the mythic monster. Not only did this update introduce a host of new mechanics (a drum to play sea shanties with, a megaphone to be able to communicate with other players at longer distances, and, of course, megalodons to fight), but it was also an act of myth-making created by players that fleshed out the game's worldbuilding. Players still share their stories of the original meg-summoning ritual, even though the event is no longer playable nor has it been for years.

Then a related event was launched in 2022, with a similar act of myth-making and mechanic. Rather than summoning an all-new creature to fight, The Shrouded Deep live event was focused on summoning the Shrouded Ghost, an ultra-rare megalodon that, because of its elusiveness and rarity, earned a sort of mythic reputation itself. The play-based urban legends that surround the Shrouded Ghost are vast, communal theories shared on how to get the Shrouded Ghost to spawn, such as maybe it only spawns in fog or that turning your ship lanterns off may help draw it out, and so forth. These theories, these player-driven urban legends, create the mythic quality of both the Shrouded Ghost, but also of *Sea of Thieves'* worldbuilding largely.[37] This is a world that could contain these sorts of tricks, so the urban legend nature of them fits nicely. In The Shrouded

Deep event, players once again had to find another player ship to cooperate with because a key mechanic of summoning the Shrouded Ghost in this event required five players to play a specific sea shanty[38] (and the largest boat can only host up to four pirates). The Shrouded Deep event built on the existing worldbuilding (certain sea shanties can summon megalodons when played at specific locations) and offered players an explicit adventure to fight their own white whale.

So much of *Sea of Thieves* (its mechanics, its diegetic UI elements, its environmental storytelling) is built around constructing a collective pool of knowledge between players. Understanding the islands' distinctive features and how to read the game's sky creates a sort of mythopoeia out of the game, letting emergent player stories create the texture and lived history of the world, which is bolstered by the game's environmental storytelling, cooperative mechanics, and live events. Play sessions in *Sea of Thieves* become self-referential, certain adventures from previous sessions being reified in players' minds and forming the basis for future adventures. It's magical and mythical and expansive, with room for both future updates to further flesh out the worldbuilding and for player experience to help stitch together the mythopoeia of the world.

NOTES

1. I'm saying "people" here but it really means whatever lifeform you are centring your story around.
2. With apologies to every other character, especially Thane.
3. I'm speaking broadly here, but of course there are exceptions to everything. Text-based games might not require character art or voiced dialogue, but there are still other aspects related to creating characters, such as gameplay verbs. The point is that broadly characters are a culmination of a lot of factors, but even in the most scaled down form, characters in video games are still more than just story points.
4. Tran, V. 2019. Why Fashion in (Most) Games Sucks, and Why You Should Care. GDC. https://youtu.be/Pr7rzcwOz_g.
5. Tran, V. 2019. Why Fashion in (Most) Games Sucks, and Why You Should Care. GDC. https://youtu.be/Pr7rzcwOz_g.
6. While not relevant here because of this book's focus on worldbuilding, it is really fascinating now to watch the spread of makeup brands collaborating with video games, like MAC's *The Sims* collab and Xbox's partnership with nail polish brand OPI. Allure has a good article as a starting point for this, if you're interested: https://www.allure.com/story/beauty-brands-video-game-collaborations.

7. Rogers, Paula. 2019. Neo Cab – Anatomy of a Character. Fellow Traveller. https://www.youtube.com/watch?v=jGbB7XWS_qM.

8. *Neo Cab*'s publisher Fellow Traveller put out a diegetic YouTube video that's an ad for both Feelgrid and the game itself. It's the type of worldbuilding marketing that I adore. It's diegetic, it's fun, and it's satiric: https://youtu.be/MKqHTCtr0Bo.

9. Dimoploulos, K. 2020. *Virtual Cities: An Atlas & Exploration of Video Game Cities.* Countryman Press.

10. If you want to read more about this, I highly recommend Bernard Perron's book *Silent Hill: The Terror Engine.* It's an excellent look at how *Silent Hill* uses a lot of different techniques in creating terror throughout the franchise.

11. Craig, J. 2020. The Medium Producer Explains Dual Reality and the Reason Behind Fixed Camera Angles. The Gamer. https://www.thegamer.com/the-medium-dual-reality-fixed-camera-angles/.

12. Crecente, B. 2020. How The Medium Uses Next-Gen Technology To Deliver Dual-Layered Horror. https://www.unrealengine.com/en-US/developer-interviews/how-the-medium-uses-next-gen-technology-to-deliver-dual-layered-horror.

13. Williams, C. 2021. Bloober Team Says The Medium Was Only Possible on Next-Gen Hardware. Gamerant. https://gamerant.com/the-medium-next-gen-bloober-team/.

14. Harrison, C. 2021. No Man's Sky and Minecraft's Map Sizes Are Unfathomable. GameRant. https://gamerant.com/no-mans-sky-minecraft-map-size-limitless-world-design.

15. Noise generation here refers to ways of creating elements, such as terrains, clouds, populations—all the elements of a world.

16. Murray, S. Building Worlds in No Man's Sky Using Math(s). GDC. https://youtu.be/C9RyEiEzMiU.

17. England, L. and C. Dragert. Watch Dogs Legion: The Design and Tech Behind Play As Anyone. Ubisoft Toronto. https://youtu.be/mMFqK7dn5Wo.

18. From a personal interview for this book.

19. England, L. and C. Dragert. Watch Dogs Legion: The Design and Tech Behind Play As Anyone. Ubisoft Toronto. https://youtu.be/mMFqK7dn5Wo.

20. Emergent narratives are not unique just to procgen, as well.

21. Adams, T. Emergent Narrative in Dwarf Fortress. *Procedural Storytelling in Game Design.* ed. Short, T.X., and T. Adams, 154. Publisher Boca Raton: CRC Press/Taylor & Francis.

22. These are reductive and oversimplifications, absolutely, but they provide a useful framework for discussing the variety of ways conflict can manifest in a game.

23. Carpenter, N. 2021. Stonefly, A Chill Mech Game, Respects the Environment and its Creatures. Polygon. https://www.polygon.com/interviews/22523571/stonefly-impressions-interview-flight-school-mech-game.

24. Belair, K. and M. Jayanth. 2022. Fireside Chat with Kem Belair & Meghna Jayanth. LudoNarraCon. https://youtu.be/waoixDVSxY8.

25. From a personal interview for this book.

26. Minus taste, of course.

27. From a personal interview for this book.

28. Martin, W. and J. Oppenheimer. 2021. The Art of Outer Wilds, Unity Creator Spotlight. Unity. https://youtu.be/Ww12q6HsmJA.

29. Price, R. 2021. Cloud Gardens is a Relaxing Game About the End of Our World. Kotaku. https://kotaku.com/cloud-gardens-is-a-relaxing-game-about-the-end-of-our-w-1847630552.

30. Coutoure, J. 2021. Getting Tangled Up in the Beautiful Landscapes of Cloud Gardens. GameDeverloper.com https://www.gamedeveloper.com/design/getting-tangled-up-in-the-beautiful-landscapes-of-cloud-gardens.

31. It's also worth noting that each of the names of the levels are names of specific places in Māori.

32. Fabulism as a literary genre has its roots in fairy tales and folklore and speaks to a sort of allegory that blends reality in folkloric and surreal ways. It transports fantasy into our realistic settings. This might sound like "magic realism" and it's close, but there's an important distinction here between the purposes of fabulism versus magic realism and who tends to use which genre. Magic realism is a politically steeped genre, often used by colonized writers of color and Indigenous creators as a method of decolonizing and resistance, whereas fabulism is not.

33. Schrödinger's space station, if you will.

34. Grinblat, J. Generating Histories. In *Procedural Storytelling in Game Design.* ed. Short, T.X., and T. Adams, 182. Publisher Boca Raton:CRC Press/Taylor & Francis.

35. Landry, A. 2018. 'It's a White Thing': 'The Oregon Trail' Game Doesn't Tell Complete History. Indian Country Today. https://indiancountrytoday.com/archive/white-thing-oregon-trail-game-doesnt-tell-complete-history.

36. If you're interested in learning more about procgen and generating story snippets, I highly recommend reading the entirety of *Procedural Storytelling in Game Design*, edited by Tanya X. Short and Tarn Adams.

37. For example, there are even Reddit posts of players asserting that they don't even think the shrouded ghost is real. Its rarity has made a cryptid in the world of *Sea of Thieves*.

38. A quick note: the use of sea shanties in these events, and in the game at large, is also an important aspect of building out the believable and tangible world of *Sea of Thieves*.

Identity, World Systems, and Responsibility

N OW THAT WE HAVE all this theory and best practices under our belts, I want to shift focus. Worldbuilding is, inherently, a political practice. And worldbuilding is not worldbuilding in a vacuum. Yes, we can create brand new secondary worlds, with new sociopolitical systems, with new interpersonal dynamics, but at the end of the day we are still human and we will be drawing upon our existing framework, whether we want to or not. And because this book is about cross-discipline collaboration as a key part of worldbuilding, I want to focus on our responsibilities as worldbuilders when it comes to the potential for replicating harm we possess; in other words, what is our responsibility to each other when we are building new worlds and how can we navigate worldbuilding conscious of this responsibility? This book is about how we build worlds together, so being conscious of the human elements is important for safe and productive collaboration.

This chapter is asking us, as worldbuilders and game developers, to be considerate of the real ramifications of the media we are creating. Media ripples out toward culture, both positively and negatively, and being intentional in our worldbuilding practice is crucial. I believe that while we can contend with difficult subjects in our creative works (I made horror games about trauma, about abuse, about eating disorders, all which relish in their horror tropes and genre), but I also believe that we need to be responsible in that endeavor. Essentially: Be bold, but don't be a dick.

DOI: 10.1201/9781003345619-6

WORLDBUILDING AND THE REAL WORLD: BEING AWARE OF SYSTEMS OF HARM

Because we are human, we cannot separate our biases and worldviews from how we go about creating new worlds. What systems we replicate or subvert, and the ways in which we imagine our characters interacting with, responding to, and being empowered or oppressed by systems carry weight for our audiences, who exist in the real world and who bring their own perspectives, experiences, and biases to the table. So much of video game worldbuilding is about co-authoring and creating space for our players to participate in the world alongside us as creators, and so approaching our worldbuilding with intentionality is our responsibility as creators.

In the post-conference writeup of one of N.K. Jemisin's talk on inclusive worldbuilding for Wired, Jason Parham says, "World-building does not mean predicting the future—it's about mirroring the present".[1] This is an important aspect of what makes worldbuilding compelling, that is the ways in which worldbuilding mirrors our current concerns, issues, desires, and so forth. Being a mirror to the present doesn't mean to then go and thoughtlessly recreate the harmful systems of oppression at play but is rather a call to be intentional and thoughtful in how we talk about power—who wields it and who is harmed by it, in all its various incarnations and at a variety of intersections for people. This includes interrogating the visual appearance of characters, dialects/accents, fashion, as well as the mechanics and verbs available to specific characters. Almost every aspect of a video game is contributing to worldbuilding, as we saw in Chapters 2 and 4, and so it's important to be intentional in how we are constructing those elements, and to consider what systems, stereotypes, and biases from our real world we are invoking, and to seriously ask ourselves if we are we doing enough to earn[2] the conversations we are having about these systems.

Who Are the Heroes?

Worldbuilding is not storytelling. But that doesn't mean they aren't inextricably related—they are. And that's because worldbuilding creates the foundation to tell stories on (as well as the foundation to build mechanics and systems out of). The world your story takes place in dictates possibilities, conflicts, opportunities, and drama for your story, and, importantly, for your characters. (That's because, as discussed in Chapter 1, worldbuilding is an engine for both stories and gameplay and not just a static background for your story.)

An important way worldbuilding lends to storytelling is creating the parameters for who gets to be the hero. This is because as we're building our world, we're creating the systems and the tensions that give rise to heroes.[3] Heroes aren't just characters and they aren't just story devices—they are representatives of implicit aspects of your world, particularly the values, hopes, and morality of your world. Who gets to be a hero says a lot about your world, intentional or not. So be intentional about it! Consider (and make choices about) who can be the hero(es) of your world and why. What makes them heroic? What systems of injustice are they responding to? What pressures from the world have created the conditions for them to respond in this way? (And so forth.) Answers to these questions don't need to be robust or complicated, but they do need to exist. Because when we don't approach worldbuilding with intentionality, we're more likely to fall back onto our assumed opinions of certain values about a world and biases about who can fulfill those roles in that world.

Important note: I'm using the word "hero" here, even though it's not my favorite word for describing protagonists. The word "hero" comes with a lot of baggage, and often has ingrained connotations that can exist at odds with impulses and desires to dismantle certain systems of oppression. In Western spaces, there's a good chance that the word "hero" is already pre-loaded with a thousand images of different types of white, straight, able-bodied cis men, wielding a fabled weapon and fumbling through their role in the world. But beyond even that, in the keynote for DIGRA India's 2021 conference, Meghna Jayanth talks about how the very concept of heroes and heroism is "a white fantasy, and an imperial one—the fantasy of saving the world is in fact necessary to conquering it, and has provided 'moral cover' for brutal conquests and wars in the real world".[4] The concept of heroism is loaded not just with pre-baked assumptions and biases about who the default hero tends to be, but also with what the concept of a hero means about the world—and a hero's relationship to structures, systems, and people in that world.[5] Having a "hero" in your world positions that character in relation to certain aspects of your world; a hero is a reciprocal relationship, one often fraught with unassumed biases of why certain worlds even need heroes in the first place.

With that in mind, I'm going to switch from "hero" to "protagonist". I wanted to start with the word "hero" here in order to establish a baseline that we can now deviate from. I'm less interested in heroes and more interested in compelling characters who are challenged and grow and who are worlds unto themselves. They can become heroes, but I view being a hero as more of a goal than a personality trait—and not all protagonists need to have that goal to be worth rooting for or to provide a compelling friction point against a variety of world systems.

So when we sit down to think of the worlds for our games, we need to be intentional about how we consider our characters, their identities, and any biases we may be replicating. This is particularly relevant for genres like fantasy, which often (but not exclusively) draw on historical texts as frames of reference (for environment, for fashion, for dialects/accents, and so forth). In an article on *Tor*, SFF writer Tansy Rayner Roberts writes about the erroneous concept of sexism in fantasy being historically accurate by taking to task the presumed authority of historical texts. Roberts writes, "History is actually a long series of centuries of men writing down what they thought was important and interesting, and FORGETTING TO WRITE ABOUT WOMEN".[6] Roberts is calling out the inherent fallibility of history as a text that was written by people with their own biases, versus being an objectively authoritative account.[7] Which is a texture to history that is important for worldbuilders to consider: "authoritative" texts are subjective accounts, full of biases that reflect world systems that favored a certain type of person at the time.

Games like *A Plague Tale: Innocence* (Asobo Studio, 2019) position a young girl, Amicia, at the center of a deeply historical world (*A Plague Tale: Innocence* is set during the Hundred Years' War and follows Amicia and her younger brother as they flee the French Inquisition). Amicia is positioned as the protagonist of this world, equipped with a sling as befitting a child, with a heavy focus on stealth mechanics versus combat. While not a hero, she is the locus of the world's tensions at this point in history: the story could be about her father, a lord and a knight, but it's not. It's about Amicia and her younger brother navigating a world that is bigger than them, that has certain beliefs about them, and that is hostile to them because of those beliefs. The mechanics (stealth, use of a sling) connect nicely with who Amicia is, and the focus on navigating two children through this hostile world creates a compelling experience that exists outside of the typical stories of medieval knights we see.

And of course, the pretense to history as infallible (and the exclusions this creates) is true for groups of people beyond just women, but for anybody who exists at an intersection[8] of marginalized identities, particularly

Black, Indigenous, people of color, queer and trans people, and disabled/neurodivergent people.[9] Who our protagonists have been in history has been subjectively decided by a certain set of repeated, self-reified perspectives. In fantasy based on historical records, there's an erroneous trend in leaning on "historical realism"[10] as the basis for exclusion or stereotypical inclusion of Black, Indigenous, and people of color. In an article for *The Guardian* on the history of racism in role-playing games, Payal Dhar writes that "Although fantasy affords us every freedom to imagine new worlds and cultures, for the last 200-odd years, humans have mostly managed derivative facsimiles of our own. This includes reproducing the scourge of systemic racism".[11] Sometimes referred to as "fantasy racism", this includes both replicating real-world racist systems and structures, as well as transplanting those biases onto fictional races, such as elves. When done unintentionally (and without including people of diverse identities in production and development), recreating these systems of harm not only reduces our world and the experiences of these characters, but it also replicates this harm in our real world and our media.

Moving from fantasy to sci-fi, artistic movements like Afrofuturism (and the subsequent Indigenous Futurism) are motivated by placing Black creators and characters at the center of their sci-fi worlds. "Afrofuturism is the intersection between technology, black cultures, the imagination, and liberation with a heavy dose of mysticism", says Ytasha L. Womack, author of *Afrofuturism: The World of Black Sci-Fi and Fantasy Culture*.[12] And Afrofuturism is finding a home in video games, as well. *We Are the Caretakers* (Heart Shaped Games, 2021) is an Afrofuturist sci-fi squad management RPG about protecting endangered animals and your planet from extinction. *We Are the Caretakers* tasks players with tracking down poachers, detaining them, and does so in such a way as to center the beliefs, culture, and experiences of Black people. In a review of *We Are the Caretakers* on *Wired*, Junae Benne talks about the trend in media to often allegorically talk about issues like racism or queerphobia by swapping in different beings in place, like elves or mutants. Benne writes,

> The more common approach is to swap in a mythological species for the struggles of real humans, or present racism in terms of genocide or warfare, which only encourages viewers or readers to have empathy when lives are at risk: something that doesn't truly include or value those lives. *We Are The Caretakers* doesn't take this approach.[13]

Every aspect of *We Are the Caretakers* is centered around placing Black people as the protagonists, in a multitude of personalities. This includes the soundtrack, as well as the look of the characters (their outfits, body shapes, the varying color of their skin), and the naming—all which were inspired by existing African outfits and languages (such as Twi and Swahili). Conservation is an important theme in *We Are the Caretakers*, and the move set available to the characters reflects this value position in the world. Combat is focused around draining a poacher's stamina or will (versus health), and a combat round ends with a finishing move called "detain". In the section on verbs in Chapter 2, I talked about how changing the verb associated with a common mechanic, like changing the "attack" verb to "connect" in the deck-building game *Signs of the Sojourner*, creates a particular identifier for the values and social contracts of the world. The same here is happening in *We Are the Caretakers*, which uses the same tactical mechanics as other games like *XCOM* but switches the verbs from "kill" to "detain". This is creating a world built on different values that are normally associated with tactical RPGs, re-shifting the focus to have a different conversation. Every element of *We Are the Caretakers* is an intentional reflection of aspects of Black experience that deserve to exist in video games: culture, values, identity, all which exist in every detail of the game.

Inspired by the Afrofuturist movement, there's also Indigenous Futurism. In the introduction to the anthology *Walking the Clouds: An Anthology of Indigenous Science Fiction*, editor Grace L. Dillon writes that "...sf provides an equally valid way to renew, recover, and extend First Nations peoples' voices and traditions".[14] For a genre that is often rife with unexamined reflections of colonialism, sci-fi has become a locus of empowerment for Indigenous storytellers and artists. Embracing sci-fi also positions Indigenous people, culture, and belief as not just historical, but as contemporary and even futuristic as well, re-asserting that Indigenous people don't just exist in the past, but they are modern.

Meagan Byrne, founder of Achimostawinan Games, examines the role of Indigenous Futurism in her own work. Achimostawinan's first game, *Hill Agency: Purity and Decay* (Achimostawinan Games, forthcoming in 2022) is a detective game that tasks players with solving a range of mysteries, from crimes to global conspiracies. *Hill Agency* is set in the far future purposefully. Byrne explains that the setting (and narrative) for *Hill Agency* revolve around the core question of: "What would our world look like on the brink of freedom from colonial oppression?"[15]

The answer the game is providing is a sort of freedom of character expression, where characters can exist in their culture but roam genres and engage in different modes of play than have typically been allowed. The world is no longer built on their oppression, so a world freed from colonial oppression is a multitude of possibilities. *Hill Agency* is pulpy, it's noir, and it sets Indigenous characters and experiences at the center of this futuristic world.

Of course, there is always space to invoke forms of oppression in order to interrogate them or have moments of catharsis (via our protagonist's triumph) but doing so requires a great deal of intentionality in the approach (and being aware of which stories are your own to tell, and which ones might not be). Fantasy author Hadeer Elsbai explains that "it can be empowering to watch characters fight against and ultimately defeat the sorts of injustices we struggle with in real life. It's cathartic".[16] For some worldbuilders and for some audiences, the inclusion of prejudicial systems and power imbalances becomes a way of fighting back—but these systems are replicated in such a way as to provide the space for that, made by people that get to claim that catharsis.

And, of course, as we're considering how to incorporate diversity into our games, it's important to remember that it is a cross-discipline endeavor. The fashion we dress our characters in, the dialects and accents we give them, the animations accompanying their movements, the mechanics and verbs we provide those characters—these all matter in creating the overall effect of our characters and all carry weight when demonstrating who that character is and how they fit into and reflect back the world they are apart of. Mechanically, associating Indigenous characters with the natural world and spiritualism is a stereotypical shorthand, one which reduces the robustness and diversity of the people, their worldviews and capabilities. Pigeon-holing women characters as healers and magic-wielders likewise reduces the complexity and power of women as characters. Consider every facet of what your game is saying about a people or a culture through all of the aspects of a video game, from story to art to audio to gameplay.

Even in works that are gender-equal, don't invoke racist structures or systems, support disability, or are queernorm,[17] intentionality in how other harmful systems of power are replicated in the world matters. And when considering the systems that give rise to our protagonists, it's important to remember how intersectionality informs the way people access and are denied access to power, happiness, fair treatment, and so forth, and how intersectionality operates in response to different structures and systems of power (and lack of power) in worlds. People are more than just one aspect of their identity; they are full of intersections that create their perspective on the world, as well as their lived experience of the world. And so for our purposes as worldbuilders, it's important to think about how characters with different intersections and different privileges in a world are allowed to operate more fully in that world. Intersectionality and privilege are helpful concepts for worldbuilding because they inherently are connected to systems of power.[18]

UNDERSTANDING CULTURAL APPROPRIATION

For our protagonists (and antagonists, discussed next), it's important to understand what types of shorthand we may be unintentionally taking from real-world cultures and the very real ramifications of that.

In their excellent webinar "Cultural Appropriation: What It Is and How To Avoid It" for *Writing the Other*, K. Tempest Bradford and Nisi Shawl talk about what cultural appropriation is and what it isn't. Importantly, Shawl and Bradford note that cultural appropriation isn't the same as "writing the other", which is the concept of writing characters that do not reflect your own intersections. Bradford says,

> The thing that we teach in *Writing The Other* is accurate representation of a character and that character's experience. Whereas Cultural Appropriation is not accurate representation. It is when you as an author are assuming you have the right to use and to depict, or even deliberately revise, someone else's culture.[19]

They note the importance to consider where the power rests when considering cultural appropriation (and importantly, how it differs from concepts like cultural exchange).

Fashion, rituals, beliefs, art, traditions, tattoos, and makeup are all elements that have been culturally appropriated in a variety of forms of media. Even when we think we are recreating aspects of characters and cultures from whole cloth, we are drawing upon our own understanding and worldviews—all which have had the capacity to be influenced both by our lived experiences, as well as the media we consume—which leaves the door open for our own biases and assumptions to infiltrate our worldbuilding. Cultural appropriation reduces a culture into de-contextualized aspects of it and can even have a knock-on effect of making it harder for people from that culture to make their own art about it.

Who Are the Villains?

On the flipside of understanding who our protagonists are, it's important we understand who we are establishing as our villains and what implicit biases we've attached to villainy. Writing advice for creating villains often follows the adage of opposites—in that your villain should, in so many distinct ways, be the opposite of your protagonist. It's the push-pull of this dynamic (two opposite forces standing in each other's way) that is the impetus behind this advice. It's compelling when two people have competing goals and are obstacles to each other. But as we've seen, if heroes in our media have tended to be white, straight, cis, able-bodied men, then it's easy to see how we've created a tapestry of villains who are othered in some way.

Queer (or queer-coded) people, people of color, empowered women, disabled people, fat people have all shared a history of being represented as the villains, the main antagonists to a default assumption of a specific hero/protagonist. In horror in particular, mental illness is often a short-hand for evilness, or if not, then reduced to scare gimmicks and tropes. In her excellent book *Disfigured: On Fairy Tales, Disability, and Making Space*, author Amanda Leduc interrogates the relationship between disability and fairy tales, and in particular, the ways in which disability is associated with either villainy or a deficit. Referencing Scar from *The Lion King*, Quasimodo in *The Hunchback of Notre Dame*, and Ariel in *The Little Mermaid*, Leduc writes, "Why, in all of these stories about someone who wants to be something or someone else, was it always the individual who needed to change, and never the world?"[20] Villainy has been encoded in our society and in our media to present a certain way, and just as it's important to create protagonists who look like the diverse audience we make games for, it's also important to understand the repercussions of how we code villainy and what this means about systems of power and injustice in our worlds.[21]

In a post-mortem on *Don't Wake the Night*, director Santo Aveiro-Ojeda reflects on why the game included an ominous atmosphere, and it's because for a game that revolves around community and conflict resolution in a world without colonialism, the tension in the game comes from characters that understand they are doing something wrong (summoning a spirit) and face internal conflict on how to rectify this. Aveiro-Ojeda writes,

> Since *Don't Wake The Night* takes place in a fictional world free of colonialism, the main obstacle these characters face is a unique one: they don't know what punishment is, and are at a crossroads of deciding whether or not they will have to figure out what 'punishment' is.[22]

This was established as a way of avoiding typical moral binaries of good or bad and positions characters as neither heroes nor villains, but rather creates a space to explore and interrogate how we view restorative justice on a community level, and how we make space for growth from mistakes. Villainy (or performing actions conceived of as wrong or harmful) isn't coded a specific way but is rather a nuanced texture to how believable characters approach understanding they have violated an important law of their world. It allows for complex, messy characters because they are human, and interrogates the situation from that lens.

In *Don't Wake the Night*, the player isn't able to directly converse with the characters. So with the limited camera views and ability to only influence characters rather than make outright decisions, the player is essentially occupying a place of eavesdropping. This isn't a game about guiding players down a moral binary and arriving at a "good" ending or a "bad" ending but it is rather about creating the space necessary to sit, listen, and reflect. Players are neither protagonist nor antagonist, nor do they exist in opposition to the other characters in such a way. *Don't Wake the Night* creates a wonderfully thoughtful interrogation into conflict management in community, one that purposefully exists outside of gamified experiences of moral choices and player agency.

Villains—or even just antagonists—can be such an important part of your story, and how villainy gets included (whether as a moral evil or just as a texture to mundanity) speaks volumes about the values and taboos of your world. Villainy and antagonism exist in response to power systems in the world. Are they responding to an injustice in class, political power, or a personal slight? How do they fit into the world's existing sociopolitical system? What about the world has driven them to this stage of their actions? What elements of the world are even dictating them as heroes (i.e., what values are they violating or what taboos are they inhabiting)? Like heroes and protagonists, antagonists and villains are shaped by and exist in the world. So understand this connection and what it says about your world.

And when considering what pressures in your world drive people to villainous actions—or to become the antagonist to your protagonist—we need to consider carefully who we are filling into this position and what that says about the systems we uphold as good in our world, and who are the markers for this. As Leduc poignantly asks, maybe it's not the characters who are at some fault, but rather it is something else about the world that needs to be updated to accommodate characters who have typically existed in the margins or in positions of villainy.

CHALLENGING FATNESS AS VICE

Fatness and fat characters have a long history of negative associations with them, in both media and our culture at large. Often associated with laziness or slovenliness, fatness stereotypically has been presented as a vice, a moral failing of the character, and therefore is a hallmark of not just villainy but also moral corruption. But fatness isn't a vice, nor is it a moral failing, nor is it even unhealthy, but societal misunderstandings, bias, and beauty norms have coded it as such. So, when thinking about the diversity of protagonists (and who we often stub in as our antagonists), it's important to consider body size, as well. Fat people can be protagonists, they can be heroes. Beauty norms are the result of societal pressures and create oppressive systems for people to try and navigate. While they seem character-centric at first, they are actually deeply ingrained aspects of a world—what that world values and why.

Ellie in *Borderlands 2* is still one of my favorite characters in any video game. She's a mechanic, she's confident, she's unhinged, and, as the daughter of the innuendo-dripping Moxxi, Ellie is sexy. And Ellie knows she's sexy, an intentional decision from the team. In an interview with *PC Gamer*, the Gearbox team explains that, "We also wanted to make sure that, through her dialog and visual design, we never cast her in a light where the player is encouraged to pity, laugh at, or mock her".[23] Ellie exists in a world where everyone sits along some continuum of villainy (or as an anti-hero), but her body is never a factor in this. It's part of who she is, but it does not make her evil or morally corrupt.

In Chapter 2, I discussed how the options in character creators contain inherent values and indicators of the world in which these characters situate themselves. And the same is true for body size, as well. A world without fatness is a choice. A world with fatness, and how fatness is then treated in the game's world, story, art, and mechanics, is also a choice. For example, *Sea of Thieves'* character selection features a wide arrange of body types, and all are treated the same. There are no moral choices associated with any of the body types; they are presented neutrally. Crucially, *Sea of*

Thieves also normalized their hitboxes so mechanically, playing as a thin or fat pirate doesn't offer any strategic advantage in PvP play.[24] There is no inherent value to playing as a certain size, no markers from the world or the mechanics making one a better choice than the other. Fatness just gets to exist, equal to thinness.

Fatness is a politically charged subject because of the ways beauty norms and societal misunderstandings and systems of oppression treat it as such. And as worldbuilders, we can explore avenues toward constructing more open and inclusive beauty norms in our worlds. The LARP *Glitter Pits* by Kat Jones tasks players with either rejecting or queering[25] beauty norms to find less oppressive modes of understanding and celebrating attraction. By engaging in this collective ritual, Jones's game is expanding what beauty means in a world by changing the relationship people have with beauty norms. In an interview in *The Queer Games Avant-Garde*, Jones says, "With the beauty norms that you want to be queer, it's this exercise in deciding how to take a norm that makes certain people feel ugly or excluded and open it up to new ideas of beauty".[26] We can expand what beauty is in our worlds and, by doing so, create opportunities for people to find different relationships to their own bodies.

Dream Daddy: A Dad Dating Simulator (Game Grumps, 2017) is a gay dating sim, and players can choose to make their avatar a variety of aspects, including trans and fat. Beyond just the character creator, the romance options for the game also includes fat characters, such as Brian, a single dad who loves fishing. Including fat characters in *Dream Daddy* constructs a world where fatness is seen as attractive and not an indicator of vice, or any of the other values that have been arbitrarily assigned to fat bodies. Like Jones's *Glitter Pits*, it is presenting a world that doesn't value fat bodies less, but instead acknowledges the value in fat bodies and people and imagines a world where that value is inherent.

RE-IMAGINING WORLDS: QUEERING WORLDBUILDING

As a queer, genderfluid person, queerness informs every aspect of who I am, and importantly, how I relate to and exist in the world. Queerness is about sexuality, but also my gender identity, and how I view community. Queerness influences every part of my life, including how I approach and make art. And to me, in so many ways, queerness is about subverting default systems. It is a politic, it is an identity, and it can also be a practice. So as such, I want to explore what "queering worldbuilding" does and could mean, and how queerness can illuminate different avenues toward compelling worldbuilding, including queernorm worlds but also beyond that into queer story, queer spaces, queer mechanics, and so forth.

In the introduction to their book *Video Games Have Always Been Queer* Dr. Bo Ruberg asserts, "Queerness and video games share a common ethos: the longing to imagine alternative ways of being and to make space within structures of power for resistance through play".[27] For us as world-builders, this creates an interesting impetus for examining the ways in which we are building structures of power in our worlds, and the avenues toward upholding them and resisting dominant ones that have typically upheld oppression and discrimination. Worldbuilding is the fodder for mechanics, for characters, and for facilitating dynamics that can challenge accepted structures through story and play.

Queering as an artistic practice is something that's important to me, not only on a level of character representation (we deserve believable queer characters, who are messy and authentic) and support of real-world creators (as queer creators, we deserve to make the kind of art we want to make, whether it's explicitly queer content or not), but also in every facet of design. The concept of "queering" comes from the practice of queer reading, a way of challenging our media beyond cisheteronormativity, and it's a practice that has necessarily grown to include looking at other systems that perpetuate a default identity as cis, white, straight, male, and able-bodied, since queerness intersects with other identities.

Queering worldbuilding, then, of course includes practices like creating queernorm worlds, worlds where homophobia, transphobia, and biphobia don't exist, where queer characters exist freely. This can also be applied to the types of family structures that are normalized in our worlds. What do family units consist of? Why? Polyamory/non-monogamy and other modes of relationships and family structures are important aspects of our worlds in how they reveal integral values (and taboos) and can even contribute to practical worldbuilding in exploring what homes built for non-monogamy look like. In a short blog post, fantasy author Adesina Brown discusses the potential liberation of queernorm worldbuilding for queer people:

> When offered the vision of an identity-diverse world, we receive much more than pacifications of fortitude and hope; instead, we are gifted the radical imagination of wider liberation and cannot be satiated with incremental changes. We now know what else is possible.[28]

Queer art allows queer people and creators the space to imagine possible worlds and systems where we don't have to settle for just tolerance.

Queer worldbuilding, of course, can also include prejudice and bias against queer characters in order to interrogate it in ways that are meaningful and productive for creators. Queering worldbuilding, either via creating queernorm worlds or worlds that take queerness as a structural ethos in terms of subverting dominant forces and binaries, includes the potential for imagining and accessing more avenues toward change. Queering, as a practice, is subversion, and through subversion, resistance.

I want to talk about *Bugsnax* again. While *Bugsnax* features fuzzy bipeds in place of humans, the game's approach to queerness for their characters aligns and supports a queer worldbuilding ethos really elegantly. In *Bugsnax*, characters are just queer: there are queer relationships (Chandlo and Snorpy), and there are trans characters (Floofty is non-binary). In an interview about queerness in the game, creative director Kevin Zuhn and story editor Sage Coffey say,

> Everyone's normal is different. Being gay is normal, being trans is normal, and I think by not including a cis-explainer[29] scene, we're reinforcing that inclusion in the game. *Bugsnax* is for everyone, and I don't want anyone to feel othered while playing.[30]

While not about queerness explicitly, *Bugsnax* introduces a queernorm world that is steeped in queerness in how the game's world (narrative) and structure (mechanics) involves community, as well as expanding on concepts of bodies and how changing bodies causes us to relate to the world and each other in different ways. Structurally, *Bugsnax* explores concepts of how a world can be reconstructed around community and cooperation, rather than individualism or heroism, and how non-normative bodies play a role in this.

Queering worldbuilding can also be applied to mechanics and how we envision mechanics in relation to the elements of power and systems in our worldbuilding. In an interview for *The Queer Games Avant-Garde*, tabletop roleplay game designer Avery Adler explains that "These days, queerness means an otherness from dominant narratives and from dominant modes of exchanging power—an otherness that relates to desire, the body, and gender".[31] This concept of being structurally queer is applied to Adler's game *Monsterhearts* (Avery Adler, 2012), where sexuality and desire can be fluid based on mechanical rolls of the dice. In *Monsterhearts*,[32] different characters can turn each other on based on a dice roll, which challenges preconceived notions of identity, attraction, and expectations of both based on how players initially understand their monster character in the world. While an analog game, *Monsterhearts* is a great example of queer mechanics informing specific states of the world and challenging accepted systems in the world of who and what types of bodies can be considered desirable (a direct attempt at subverting the ways in which different world-views direct shame and guilt onto certain types of bodies).

"Queer mechanics are more about building connections and breaking down categories," artist Tonia B****** says in an interview in *The Queer Games Avant-Garde*.[33] We see this strongly in *Don't Wake the Night*, where gameplay is not about establishing characters as good or evil, but is rather about exploring what conflict resolution looks like as a community practice. *Don't Wake the Night* features a dissolution of binary morality and instead focuses on connection-building via communal understanding and account-ability. There is a central theme in queering as a practice, in that it is both subversive (breaking down of established systems of harm and exclusion, systems of homophobia, biphobia, transphobia, as well as anti-fatness) as well as a focus on rebuilding new connections in place of these old ones. *Monsterhearts* is about finding new avenues toward understanding attraction, beauty norms, and our own role in these systems on a societal level. *Bugsnax* is about rebuilding community through difference, and through the constant changing of bodies, a re-evaluation of one's relationship with their body and how their body causes them to relate to the world. Queerness in these games extends to the ways the mechanics ask us to challenge certain aspects of our world and ingrained assumptions of default systems.

Queer Heritage, Level Design, and Worldbuilding

Queerness—as do other intersections of identities, particularly race—changes how we relate to spaces. Which spaces are safe, are inclusive, but also what modes of play exist for marginalized people in these spaces. As discussed in the level design section of Chapter 2, cities are a reflection of people and how those people exist within certain world systems, such as privilege and class.

In the real world, the concept of queering spaces is applied to how we can construct queer-friendly public spaces, and I want to take a quick diversion through this ideology in order to then consider how we can apply the concept of queering to level design and worldbuilding in our games. The research paper and proposal *Queering Public Space* is a collaboration between Arup and the University of Westminster, and it offers insight into how queer people use (or aren't allowed to use) certain public spaces. *Queering Public Space* notes that

> Cities grow and morph historically, with the past constantly being repurposed in the present. As a result, we make sense of our cities through the layers of memory that tell the story of the past and the people who shaped it.[34]

For the purposes of queering real-world public spaces and cities, this endeavor exists at the intersection of how people have been allowed to use public space and how they in turn shape the use of public space.

An important aspect of this is memorials. Structures of power in our world (and our worldbuilding) determine who and what gets memorialized, and where. The statues of our world, the names of buildings and parks and streets: all of these stitch together a history of a place, but a history from the perspective of those in positions of power to determine what is important. This leads to obvious tensions when historically those in power have supported slavery; built residential schools; denied Black, Indigenous people, people of color, and women the right to vote; supported violence against queer and trans people in the form of conversion therapy and discriminatory laws; and so forth. Memorials are never neutral—they are full of meaning.

Memorials in our world reflect our societal values—they are not just static representations of the past. It's why in the United States there is a movement to take down Confederate monuments[35]; why one of the universities in Canada renamed itself to avoid memorializing a man instrumental in the creation of residential schools,[36] and so forth. Alongside the decades worth of advocacy work from groups toward these (and other more inclusive city-design goals), the concept of allowing queer groups in city spaces to preserve their own history is so important. *Queering Public Space* asserts that

> Another important means of including LGBTQ+ people in public space is by preserving their heritage. This should include encouragement to interventions by local LGBTQ+ communities to mark their own heritage in public space, enabling new layers of memory and meaning to emerge organically in these locations.[37]

Memorials are manifestations of the past in our public spaces, and the concept of queer heritage here is a call toward understanding that queer people have always existed in public spaces and to recognize that there are important landmarks associated with this heritage, such as historically queer-friendly bookshops and other establishments.

For us as worldbuilders, we can draw from these movements toward inclusive city design in the real world to imagining new city spaces that uphold values inherent to our worlds, be it queernorm or not. Memorials of oppression are common in dystopian settings—busts of oppressive antagonists and villains dot city spaces, either to intimidate or to satirize, like the statues of Handsome Jack in Opportunity in *Borderlands 2*, which feature Jack in grandiose poses and the mission text of "No revolution is complete until you've destroyed a few statues of a fascist dictator". But just as memorials of oppression exist as world texture, so too can memorials of hope, of revolution, of joy, of queerness, and of other identities, as well. *Queering Public Space* goes onto to explore how, currently, queer heritage memorials are temporary and volunteer-created, such as the annual memorials constructed on the Trans Day of Remembrance.[38] In addition, in Canada, pride flags and stickers (and stickers for Black Lives Matter, for Every Child Matters, for non-eviction of transient people in encampments) dot restaurant and shop fronts, declaring the politics of spaces. Even the need to put up these ephemera indicates a system of exclusion and discrimination in the larger city-space, but the lack of them don't necessarily indicate an inclusive, accepting, anti-racist, or queernorm world.

In his thesis "Cruising Game Space: Game Level Design, Gay Cruising, and the Queer Gothic in *The Rawlings*", artist Tommy Ting asserts that spaces change their meaning and purpose through the events happening in them. Spaces are not static sites of meaning, but are rather contextual, that the people and their actions in those spaces alter what those spaces represent and ultimately mean.[39] Spaces gain meaning through their use, and these meanings can be layered and different depending on who is using the space and if they know what to look for. Of cruising spaces specifically, Ting writes, "These are spaces that exist on top of existing spaces and [are] often invisible to the uninitiated, a magic circle that cannot be seen unless you know the secret".[40] The concept of queer spaces existing in conjunction with each other provides a layering of meaning based on who knows how to access these spaces—and why secret, hidden spaces need to exist in the first place.

Furthermore, Ting explores the ways in which spaces aren't static, not just from the ways in which meaning is attributed to spaces, but also in how use changes those spaces. Humans litter, humans rearrange, humans change what a space looks like, and we do this constantly.

In discussing the ways in which the cruising space in Stanley Park in Vancouver changed with each subsequent visit, Ting realized that to recreate a space designed for cruising in his game, he needed to introduce this flux in the level art and level design. Ting writes, "I had to reorder spatial patterns every play or walkthrough, creating gameplay experiences that are site specific but spatially different each time".[41] This feeling of change invites a lived-in sense of space: people are here and people use this space.

In terms of applying these modes of queering spaces to our own worldbuilding, we can already begin to see ways of letting this ethos influence what values are being memorialized (permanently and temporarily); what that means about traditional acknowledgment of power struggles and historical events; who has privilege; who doesn't; and how this can influence environment design, graphic design, level design, soundscapes, and the stories these spaces are telling, as well as have the capacity to tell. The concept of queering spaces, particularly cities and public spaces, encourages us as worldbuilders to imagine the ways in which cities are shaped not just by history, but by the people who inhabit them and how their use of those spaces transforms them into something new, and the new modes of play and the stories available there.

CREATING ENVIRONMENTS IN THE WAKE OF CLIMATE CHANGE

To conclude this chapter on evaluating how to intentionally frame the assumptions and biases we inherit from our own world into our fictional worlds, I want to talk about climate change and the environment. We're at this stage now where we can't avoid talking about climate change, the damage done to our world, and our responsibilities in that—and in how we imagine new futures and paths to sustainable futures as a fallout of this. As a medium, video games are contending with this in a variety of ways, particularly around how this aspect of the world affects elements of the game, particularly in relation to their mechanics and story.

With recent installations like *Frostpunk* (11 Bit Studios, 2018), *Terra Nil* (Free Lives, 2021), and *Block'Hood* (Plethora Project, 2017), city-builder games, notorious for god-like abilities to construct cities, are gaining a reputation for interrogating society's role in climate change and focusing on how to build with sustainability in mind.

In *Terra Nil*, players are tasked with recovering an ecological wasteland. *Frostpunk* similarly explores a dystopian, alternate universe post ecological disaster. Likewise, *Eco* (Strange Loop Games, 2018) is an MMO focused on everyone working together to build a sustainable civilization, with responsibility and accountability baked in as part of the play. City-builder games are reckoning with the tensions they are asking of their players: imagine building cities but imagine building cities with an explicit need to be conscious of the world they exist in and the relationship between civilizations and what is taken from the environment. Whether intentional or not, civilizations are in a give-and-take relationship with the environment–but sometimes what civilizations give back is harmful, instead of supportive.

Block'Hood is a city-builder game with a focus on sustainability in its gameplay. What's particularly interesting about *Block'Hood* is the way in which the game doesn't require an extraction of resources from the ground (there is no mining), but rather strives for building and returning in equal measure. Building too many apartment buildings and convenience stores (which your neighborhood needs as part of its resource production) can result in a lack of green space, and in turn, not having enough trees can drive down your fresh air rating (which throws your neighborhood out of balance). Is the wilderness being cared for at the same time that you are constructing wind turbines for electricity? Are bees in growth or decline? *Block'Hood* is a game about balance, focused on creating neighborhoods and buildings that are in balance with what they are demanding of the environment and giving back to the ecosystem in equal measure.

There are also games that zero in on specific issues of climate change and the ways in which we harm our natural world. *Beyond Blue* (E-Line Media, 2020) has players inhabit Mirai, a deep-sea explorer and scientist, with a focus on ocean ecology and conservation. As Mirai, players perform dives and investigate the ocean life that lives there, with a particular focus on whales, as a way of asking audiences to engage with ocean life and the future of the ocean as an important ecological system. In an interview on *The Verge*, E-Line co-founder Michael Angst explains that "We thought it would be interesting to set the game in the near future, not so much to project [it], but to invite players to be part of imagining what our ocean's future might realistically be".[42] *Beyond Blue* is about using the capabilities of worldbuilding and play to co-author worlds where the ocean ecosystem can be restored.

Even games that don't feel explicitly focused on sustainability can build their world up and from a response to the effects of climate change on our world. Creator of *Umurangi Generation* Nephtali Faulkner explains that the game was born out of his experience with the bushfires in Australia and the ways in which governments fail to respond to environmental disaster.[43] The phrase "umurangi generation" refers to "the last generation that has to watch the world die" in the game itself, and this implication of the end of the world is a strong backdrop to the photography mechanics. *Umurangi Generation* asks: what would it be like to document the end of the world? And even if players are not contending with environmental disaster or other stressors on our world throughout the game, it situates players directly in relation to these events since it is an inseparable facet of the game's world. And this facet of *Umurangi Generation*'s world is built up in its environmental design, its story, and the ways these are put in contrast with each other via the photography mechanic. Players can't save the world. All they can do is bear witness and document.

These games use environmental and climate change as an inseparable facet of their worldbuilding in order to create play experiences that invite players to contend with the current state of our own world. While a game like *Beyond Blue* strives for education, *Umurangi Generation* doesn't necessarily, but both invite this aspect of their worldbuilding to be interrogated and engaged with by players. Neither is ignoring the realities of our world but is instead using its own worldbuilding and the resulting modes of play to engage with it, in some meaningful way.

CASE STUDY: *BOYFRIEND DUNGEON'S* MESSY, FANTASTICAL REAL WORLD

Boyfriend Dungeon (Kitfox Games, 2021) is a dungeon-crawling dating sim, where the playable character is tasked with fighting random, everyday objects in dungeons in a mall, with humans that also transform into weapons. The two genres of this game meld together nicely: in order to get to know the romanceable NPCs in the game, players must go on dates with them in their human forms, while also dungeon crawling with them in their weapon forms (calling wielding).

The world of *Boyfriend Dungeon*, Verona Beach, is an urban fantasy world where the fantastical merges at the seams in the forms of people that can transform into weapons and with monsters that are prowling about. And it's an inclusive world, one designed for players to represent their playable character however they want. The character creator lets players select pronouns from she/her, he/him, or they/them for their protagonist, and it allows any clothes to be put on any body types. The clothing options also include a headscarf and a turban.

This inclusivity extends beyond who players inhabit and toward the romanceable NPCs, as well. The characters of the world include a range of body types, ethnicities, and genders, supporting a worldbuilding where beauty norms are open and accepting. In a world where people can shape-shift into weapons, it makes sense that beauty norms are naturally more fluid, where romanceable characters include non-binary characters, characters of color, and fat characters. And while *Boyfriend Dungeon* is a dating sim through and through, it also presents the option for the protagonist to just meet people for platonic or non-romantic/sexual relationships, as well, creating a space for asexual and aromantic playable characters. In the tutorial of the game, the protagonist's cousin, Jesse, says, "Remember, wielding isn't romantic. Perfectly platonic friends can wield each other, okay?" This is a world built for getting to know other people, and who those other people are is reflective of more than one type of person.

But characters in this world don't just exist for the player. They are given identities, wants, and desires that exist in service of them as characters and not just as romanceable quests for the protagonist. One character, Olivia exists as a character for herself, and no matter what dialogue options the player chooses, she will always reject a date. Olivia as a character in a dating sim who refuses to be dateable creates a nice distinction to the world of Verona Beach: this is a world filled with people, and not all people exist in service of the main character. Like Morris meeting NPCs who don't exist to fulfill or serve his quest-based whims in *I Am Dead*, not all of the characters in *Boyfriend Dungeon* exist to be romanced by the player. It's a believable world, filled with stakes and consequences and with characters who represent real personalities and interactions.

Not everybody in this world can transform into weapons, and those who can't, like the protagonist, are called wielders. Dungeon crawling is introduced as both a fitness fad and a way to meet people (which makes sense, since characters players can meet are weapons). So weapon-people and wielders can bond during dungeon crawls, forming a gameplay-driven loop for building connections and bonds with the romanceable cast of characters. The world of *Boyfriend Dungeon* is deeply rooted in real-world issues and themes that are a natural by-product of the themes of the game. *Boyfriend Dungeon* follows a protagonist who is scared of talking and meeting new people, and so the game revolves around these attempts at building connections with others. The monsters players fight in dungeons (an old phone, a VHS tape, a martini, and so forth) are manifestations of fears (according to combat tutorial character and datable estoc, Isaac, "Here, your own psychology will create monsters to fight"). Dungeons are literally about fighting your fears. The first monster players fight is a phone, and after the encounter, Isaac wonders if it's about a fear of communication, intimacy, or helplessness. Isaac shares that his unresolved feelings of masculinity from his father resulted in manifestations of all kinds of trucks. But the point is: for a game about meeting other characters, possibly romantic and sexual or not, it makes sense to ground that in the protagonist's fears about intimacy and connection.

And because this is a game that is primarily about meeting people, overcoming fears, and building relationships, the main tensions and conflicts in the game also revolve around intimacy, emotional manipulation, and overstepping of personal boundaries, even (and especially) beyond the dungeon-crawling combat. *Boyfriend Dungeon*'s central conflict revolves around stalking and emotional manipulation from a character, a conversation the game endeavors to earn by focusing on the messiness and nuance involved in meeting new people and dating. These real-world issues inform the ways in which players relate to the characters because the game is, fundamentally, about meeting new people and the excitement, messiness, and potential danger inherent to this. This is a world where the pressures that exist in it come from connection-building and come from intimacy, and the game revolves around figuring out both how to meet new people but also the inherent danger and pressures that exist within that. Dating sims as a genre, with their gameplay and themes focused on meeting and building intimate relationships with characters, aren't a stranger to exploring the dangers and fears involved in building connections and starting new relationships. Even a silly dating sim like *Hatoful Boyfriend* (Mediatonic, 2011), where players play as a human character romancing pigeons, includes potential love interests harming the playable character, including portrayals of inappropriate relationships between teachers and students, and murder.

Despite the bright colors of *Boyfriend Dungeon* and the emphasis on depicting characters as relatable, real people with real problems and personality, this is a world that is also dangerous. Not even just from the monsters that inhabit dungeons, but also from the potential love interests themselves. The game includes a content warning for stalking and features a major plot beat focused on this issue, introducing a messiness and difficulty into the game that pulls on existing harm and danger in our real world. The worldbuilding of *Boyfriend Dungeon* creates a world that is queernorm, with polyamorous relationship structures, and that is pushing back against prejudicial beauty norms, while at the same time as creating the space to talk about the fact that worlds like this still contain the possibility for danger. For a world built for connection, intimacy, and relationship building, it also then looks at the ugly parts of dating and building relationships with strangers.

Despite the urban fantasy setting, the big danger isn't fantastical. It isn't a mythical monster or a power-hungry villain. It's a normal person behaving horrifyingly. The pressure this world is exerting is one, inherently, between normal people. This is not a fantasy conflict, but instead an extremely real and personal one, which many real people have experienced. (A fact that Kitfox was aware of with the implementation of a content warning for stalking and emotional manipulation, a content warning that was subsequently updated with more precise language soon after the game's release.)[44]

While using real-world pressures, tensions, and conflict to inform the conflict of *Boyfriend Dungeon*, the team also includes the ability for players to opt out of receiving supportive text messages from the protagonist's mom. Aware that not everybody has a positive relationship with their mother, Kitfox included (at the start of the game) the ability for players to turn off these messages entirely. *Boyfriend Dungeon* is a game about meeting people and relationships, not about navigating parent-child relationships, and so it makes sense that the messages from the mother character aren't an integral part of the game or the worldbuilding and thus could be turned off. It's a conscious and considerate move, one that speaks to an awareness of how teams try to create the proper space for difficult conversations, and, importantly, for a team that knows when it isn't creating that space and therefore creating opt-outs for players for those situations. Stalking is a serious subject matter that makes sense given the themes and central core of the game, and so *Boyfriend Dungeon* includes a content warning about stalking and emotional manipulation because the game isn't about surprising players with difficult subjects but rather about preparing people to engage in both the fun and the scary of building relationships.

But even beyond the central conflict of the game, *Boyfriend Dungeon* is a sweet game, filled with charming and distinct characters. It's a deeply queer game, in both story, character, and mechanics and exists as a realistic reflection of the messiness inherent to dating (either straight or queer), and it isn't an idealized distillation of romance. It eschews stereotypes and tropes and presents a messy, nuanced look into intimacy and dating backed by a world that is built around interrogating and supporting this messiness.

NOTES

1. Parham, J. 2019. For N.K. Jemisin, World-building is a Lesson in Oppression. Wired. https://www.wired.com/story/nk-jemisin-how-to-write-science-fiction-wired25/.
2. This is a bit of a difficult sentiment to nail down, but at its heart, it essentially is asking worldbuilders to make sure that when they are invoking harmful systems in their world, to ensure that they aren't just a gimmick or there without thought or interrogation.
3. And, conversely, who gets to be villains, which we'll talk about next.
4. Jayanth, M. 2021.White Protagonism and Imperial Pleasures in Game Design. Medium. https://medium.com/@betterthemask/white-protagonism-and-imperial-pleasures-in-game-design-digra21-a4bdb-3f5583c.
5. Jayanth's talk (and the transcript she posted, as well) is a critical resource for engaging in video game creation thoughtfully and with an eye toward examining complicitness in re-enabling and re-inscribing systems of harm and oppression and I encourage everyone to read/listen to it in its entirety. https://medium.com/@betterthemask/white-protagonism-and-imperial-pleasures-in-game-design-digra21-a4bdb3f5583c.
6. Roberts, T.R. 2012. Historically Authentic Sexism in Fantasy. Let's Unpack That. Tor.com https://www.tor.com/2012/12/06/historically-authentic-sexism-in-fantasy-lets-unpack-that/.
7. For further reading on the amazing feats women have performed throughout history, check out *Wonder Women: 25 Innovators, Inventors, and Trailblazers Who Changed History* written by Sam Maggs and published by Quirk Books, 2016.
8. Coined by Kimberlé Crenshaw in 1989 in her paper *Demarginalizing the Intersection of Race and Sex: A Black Feminist Critique of Antidiscrimination Doctrine, Feminist Theory and Antiracist Politics*, intersectionality acknowledges that people's identities are a confluence of factors, elements that sit at specific intersections with each other. For further reading, here is a link to Crenshaw's paper: https://chicagounbound.uchicago.edu/cgi/viewcontent.cgi?article=1052&context=uclf.
9. A quick note on identity-first language versus person-first language. In most activism conversations I've been privy to and have had the opportunity to learn from, the concept of person-first language (aka a "person with

disability") tends to ignore the inseparable intersections of disability and identity, and can, despite coming from a place of good intent, further create stigma and perpetuate misunderstandings. Thus, following suit, I've opted to use identity-first language (aka "disabled person") here.

10. For further reading on whitewashing medieval history (https://www.publicmedievalist.com/race-racism-middle-ages-tearing-whites-medieval-world/) and for racism and video games (https://www.gamedeveloper.com/disciplines/can-videogames-teach-us-about-race- , and http://www.firstpersonscholar.com/how-fantasy-games-deal-with-race/).

11. Dhar, P. 2020. It's Time for Fantasy Fiction and Role-Playing Games to Shed Their Racist History. The Guardian. https://www.theguardian.com/games/2020/nov/03/racism-fantasy-fiction-role-playing-games.

12. Minor, J. 2014. Video Games' Afrofuturism Frontier. Media Diversified. https://mediadiversified.org/2014/07/19/video-games-afrofuturism-frontier/.

13. Benne, J. 2021. We Are the Caretakers Puts Afrofuturism Front and Center. Wired.com https://www.wired.com/story/we-are-the-caretakers-afrofuturism-game/#:~:text=Afrofuturism%2C%20if%20you're%20unfamiliar,yet%2C%20making%20them%20central%20themes.

14. Dillon, G. L. 2012. Walking The Clouds: An Anthology of Indigenous Science Fiction, edited by G.L. Dillon. 2, Arizona: University of Arizona Press.

15. Shankar, B. 2022. Ubisoft Indie Series Winner Achimostawinan on the Importance of Indigenous Stories IN Gaming. Mobile Syrup. https://mobilesyrup.com/2022/05/16/achimostawinan-games-meagan-byrne-hill-agency-purity-and-decay-ubisoft-indie-series-interview/.

16. Elsabi, H., E.J. Beaton, K.H. Rao, R. Miller, and S. Hawke. 2021. Women, Worldbuilding, and Fantasy: Guest Post. *The Fantasy Hive*. https://fantasy-hive.co.uk/2021/07/women-worldbuilding-and-fantasy-guest-post/.

17. "Queernorm" is a term used in queer, speculative lit spaces to refer to worlds built around the concept that there is no homophobia or transphobia, and worlds which tend to center queer voices and experiences.

18. For a more robust guide to understanding intersectionality and characters, check out Writing The Other's resources: https://writingtheother.com/intersectionlaity-and-characterization/.

19. Bradford, K.T. and N. Shawl. 2021. Cultural Appropriation: What It Is & How to Avoid It Webinar. Writing The Other.

20. Leduc, A. 2020. *Disfigured: On Fairy Tales, Disability, and Making Space*. Toronto: Coach House Books.

21. Just a quick note that I am not arguing against messiness and complexity in our protagonists and antagonists. As marginalized people, we are messy. Humans are messy. Instead, I am arguing for intentionality in who we are slotting in what roles and for us to examine what possible biases and stereotypes we may be introducing into our worlds.

22. Aveiro-Ojeda, S. 2020. Conflict and Community: A Don't Wake the Night Postmortem. Indigenous Gave Devs. https://www.indigenousgamedevs.com/2020/10/13/conflict-and-community-a-dont-wake-the-night-postmortem/.

23. Wilde, T. 2012. Meet Borderlands 2's Ellie: The "Opposite of How Most Females Tend To Be Represented in Games". PC Gamer. https://www.pcgamer.com/meet-borderlands-2s-ellie-the-opposite-of-how-most-females-tend-to-be-represented-in-games/.

24. Sea of Thieves official Twitter account, 2018. Twitter. https://twitter.com/SeaOfThievesHQ/status/971830196801359875?s=20&t=jS3n5XhV4ieL4vD movMapQ.

25. Discussed more in-depth in the following section on queering worldbuilding, a quick and reductive explanation of the concept of "queering" involves subverting default systems of understanding of love, bodies, and so forth, a way of countering binaries and oppressive categories.

26. Jones, K. 2020. Bisexuality, Latina Identity, and the Power of Physical Presence. *The Queer Games Avant-Garde*. ed. B. Ruberg, 199. Durham: Duke University Press.

27. Ruberg, B. 2019. *Video Games Have Always Been Queer*, 1. New York: New York University Press.

28. Brown, A. 2021. The Liberating Politics of Queernorm Fiction: A Guest Post By Where The Rain Cannot Reach Author Adesina Brown. LGBTQ Reads. https://lgbtqreads.com/2021/11/03/the-liberating-politics-of-queernorm-fiction-a-guest-post-by-where-the-rain-cannot-reach-author-adesina-brown/.

29. A scene that directly explains that a character is queer, trans, or non-binary, thereby implying the audience is for a cisgender audience and not for a queer one.

30. King, M. 2021. How Bugsnax Became a Source of Wholesome Queer Representation. Rock Paper Shotgun. https://www.rockpapershotgun.com/how-bugsnax-became-a-source-of-wholesome-queer-representation.

31. Adler, A. 2020. Queer Storytelling and the Mechanics of Desire. *The Queer Games Avant-Garde*. ed. B. Ruberg, 91. Durham: Duke University Press.

32. Partly a response of my experience as a horror writer, editor, and game-maker, but there's a trend I've noticed in queer art that finds acceptance in monsters and monstrosity. While it's true villains have often been queer-coded, there's been a growing use of embracing monstrosity as a signifier against heteronormativity and the structures of order and law that uphold heteronormativity and force queerness into the margins (and the ways in which violence is enacted on queer people because they are different). For some queer creators, monsters are this locus of difference, of finding meaning and power in difference, and are a mode of resistance against established, cisheteronormative structures of meaning and power.

33. B, T. 2020. Making Games About Queer Women of Color by Queer Women of Color. *The Queer Games Avant-Garde*. ed. B. Ruberg, 159. Durham: Duke University Press.

34. Azzouz, A. and P. Catterall. 2021. Queering Public Space. Arup.

35. Southern Poverty Law Center. 2019. Whose Heritage? Public Symbols of the Confederacy. Southern Poverty Law Center. https://www.splcenter.org/20190201/whose-heritage-public-symbols-confederacy.

36. Rancic, M. 2022. Ryerson University Officially Changes Its Name To Toronto Metropolitan University. University Affairs. https://www.universityaffairs.ca/news/news-article/ryerson-university-officially-changes-its-name-to-toronto-metropolitan-university/.

37. Azzouz, A. and P. Catterall. 2021. Queering Public Space. Arup.

38. Azzouz, A. and P. Catterall. 2021. Queering Public Space. Arup.

39. Ting, T. 2019. Cruising Game Space: Game Level Design, Gay Cruising, and the Queer Gothic in The Rawlings. OCAD University Open Research Report, 53. http://openresearch.ocadu.ca/id/eprint/2563/.

40. Ting, T. 2019. Cruising Game Space: Game Level Design, Gay Cruising, and the Queer Gothic in The Rawlings. OCAD University Open Research Report, 66. http://openresearch.ocadu.ca/id/eprint/2563/.

41. Ting, T. 2019. Cruising Game Space: Game Level Design, Gay Cruising, and the Queer Gothic in The Rawlings. OCAD University Open Research Report, 61. http://openresearch.ocadu.ca/id/eprint/2563/.

42. Maher, C. 2020. A New Wave of Indies Are Using Games To Explore Climate Change. The Verge. https://www.theverge.com/2020/2/13/21135321/video-games-climate-change-beyond-blue-bee-simulator-temtem-endling.

43. Sims, D. 2020. Talking Climate Change and Maōri Culture With Umurangi Generation. Indie Game Website. https://www.indiegamewebsite.com/2020/06/05/talking-climate-change-and-maori-culture-with-umurangi-generation/.

44. Shepard, K. 2022. What Did Indies Learn from the Boyfriend Dungeon Content Warning Discourse? Fanbyte. https://www.fanbyte.com/games/features/boyfriend-dungeon-validate-i-was-a-teenage-exocolonist-content-warnings.

CHAPTER 6

Conclusion

It's in the Details

WORLDBUILDING IS THIS MAGICAL thing, and this craft at times feels too conceptual, too unwieldy, yet too integral not to be done with care. Worldbuilding isn't just concept; it's the details. And this book, as a walkthrough of my process and approach for worldbuilding, is hopefully a testament to the fact that all of the details in every domain has the potential to add something important to our fictional worlds. Because for me, and as argued in this book, worldbuilding matters for more than just story, and good worldbuilding provides the ground for every aspect of games to grow from. Worldbuilding is not just a world bible. It is a skeleton, sometimes seen and known, other times not, but important for structure and function nonetheless.

And, to be honest, I hope you chewed on parts of this book. I hope you marked it up or got inspired by examples or developed counterexamples or even disagreed with parts of this book. While I strove for clarity and specificity in my definitions and examples, video game development is a craft with different processes and paths through it, so I expect others to have different perspectives, practices, and opinions. We learn well through discussion and identifying what works for us and what doesn't. Which is why I keep using the word "lens" when referring to this book. I didn't write this book to be the definitive word on worldbuilding for video games—I wrote it to be a perspective into my own process and craft so that others could further hone their own process and craft. Because even as I was writing this, I was learning, giving language to instincts and finding new tools to add to my own existing arsenal. I wrote it based on my experiences, which include over a decade of experience, solo learning, much collaboration, trial and error, fiction editing experience, media analysis and criticism, and a dragon's hoard of canceled games, so everything in this book is a culmination of where I was at the moment I was writing it.

So as I've said a few times throughout this book, I hope this book was a useful lens to those making video games who want to use worldbuilding holistically to create coherent and resonant games. This book wasn't written to be exhaustive but was rather written from my perspective in order to foster an approach to worldbuilding for video games that is intentional, respectful, and collaborative. So if nothing else, then I hope at least reading this book encourages respect and care toward each other's skills and craft. Respect domain expertise, listen to each other. That's where the magic comes from.

Index

Note: **Bold** page numbers refer to tables.

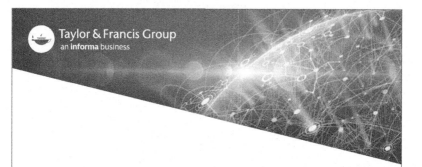